Hot Flashes, Hormones & Your Health

Also from McGraw-Hill and Harvard Medical School

The Harvard Medical School Guide to a Good Night's Sleep, by Lawrence Epstein, M.D., and Steven Mardon

The Harvard Medical School Guide to Lowering Your Blood Pressure, by Aggie Casey, R.N., M.S., and Herbert Benson, M.D., with Brian O'Neill

The Harvard Medical School Guide to Lowering Your Cholesterol, by Mason Freeman, M.D., with Christine Junge

The Harvard Medical School Guide to Overcoming Thyroid Problems, by Jeffrey R. Garber, M.D., with Sandra Sardella White

Living Through Breast Cancer, by Carolyn M. Kaelin, M.D., M.P.H., with Francesca Coltrera

The Harvard Medical School Guide to Healing Your Sinuses, by Ralph B. Metson, M.D., with Steven Mardon

Beating Diabetes, by David M. Nathan, M.D., and Linda M. Delahanty, M.S., RD

The Harvard Medical School Guide to Achieving Optimal Memory, by Aaron P. Nelson, M.D., Ph.D., with Susan Gilbert

Raising an Emotionally Healthy Child When a Parent Is Sick, by Paula Rauch, M.D., and Anna C. Muriel, M.D., M.P.H.

The No Sweat Exercise Plan, by Harvey B. Simon, M.D.

Eat, Play, and Be Healthy, by W. Allan Walker, M.D., with Courtney Humphries

Healthy Eating During Pregnancy, by W. Allan Walker, M.D., with Courtney Humphries

The Breast Cancer Survivor's Fitness Plan, by Carolyn Kaelin, M.D., M.P.H., Francesca Coltrera, Joy Prouty, and Josie Gardiner

Hot Flashes, Hormones & Your Health

JoANN E. MANSON, M.D.,
with SHARI S. BASSUK, Sc.D.

New York Chicago San Francisco Lisbon London Madrid Mexico City
Milan New Delhi San Juan Seoul Singapore Sydney Toronto

The McGraw·Hill Companies

Library of Congress Cataloging-in-Publication Data

Manson, JoAnn E.
    Hot flashes, hormones, and your health / by JoAnn Manson and Shari Bassuk.
        p.   cm.
    Includes index.
    ISBN 0-07-146862-5
       1. Menopause—Hormone therapy.   2. Middle-aged women—Health and hygiene.
  I. Bassuk, Shari.   II. Title.

    RG186.M296   2007
    618.1'75—dc22   2006021409

1 2 3 4 5 6 7 8 9 10 11 12 13 14 15 16 17 18 19 20 21 22   DOC/DOC   0 9 8 7 6

ISBN-13: 978-0-07-146862-6
ISBN-10:   0-07-146862-5

McGraw-Hill books are available at special quantity discounts to use as premiums and sales promotions, or for use in corporate training programs. For more information, please write to the Director of Special Sales, Professional Publishing, McGraw-Hill, Two Penn Plaza, New York, NY 10121-2298. Or contact your local bookstore.

The information contained in this book is intended to provide helpful and informative material on the subject addressed. It is not intended to serve as a replacement for personalized professional medical advice. Any use of the information in this book is at the reader's discretion. The author, publisher, and the President and Fellows of Harvard College specifically disclaim any and all liability arising directly or indirectly from the use or application of any information contained in this book. A healthcare professional should be consulted regarding your specific situation.

This book is printed on acid-free paper.

◉

To my husband, Christopher Ames, and our children, Jennifer, Jeffrey, and Joshua,
for their boundless love, support, and forbearance. And to the memory of my mother,
Theresa Palay Manson, who first inspired me to devote my life to women's health.
—JEM

To my husband, Paul Markowitz, and to the memory of my grandmother, Ann
Ostrofsky, for their unwavering love and encouragement.
—SSB

◉

CONTENTS

◉

PREFACE

◉

EVERY YEAR, MILLIONS of women worldwide enter menopause, a universal female experience. Although some women sail through the transition with few problems, three of every four experience symptoms due to the wide fluctuations of the female hormones estrogen and progesterone during this time, and one in four experiences major symptoms. The most common symptoms include bothersome hot flashes, drenching night sweats, disturbed sleep, mood swings, vaginal dryness, concerns about sexuality, and worries about memory slippage—all of which may affect a woman's most important relationships and her ability to function effectively at home and/or at work.

Although these symptoms can be quite troubling in the short term, the good news is that most symptoms will eventually subside over time as the hormonal tempest calms and one's body adjusts to its new steady state of lower estrogen levels. In the meantime, however, women are faced with one of the most complex healthcare decisions that many have ever had to make: to take or not to take hormone therapy. Many women (and their doctors) feel that they are in great need of guideposts in making informed and rational choices about this treatment.

There is little debate that hormone therapy offers highly effective relief from hot flashes and some (though not all) of the other menopause symptoms mentioned—it clearly does! Where the complexity arises is with regard to hormone therapy's safety and whether benefits will outweigh risks. Only a short time ago, hormone therapy was considered fairly safe for most women. But a seismic shift in attitudes toward hormone therapy has occurred in recent years because of apparent discrepancies among results of different types of studies. Dozens of observational studies, which examine large numbers of people over long periods of time and record their health-related characteristics and behavior in relation to their health outcomes, have suggested major health benefits of hormone therapy, including reductions in heart disease, hip fractures, and colon cancer, as well as major risks, such as breast cancer, stroke, and blood clots in the legs or lungs. More recent findings from randomized clinical trials, which use a figurative flip of the coin to assign either an active treatment or an inactive placebo to participants, have not only appeared to refute the idea that hormone therapy protects the heart but also suggest it may actually increase the risk of heart disease.

The largest of these clinical trials, which my colleagues and I carried out as part of a huge study called the Women's Health Initiative, assigned more than 27,000 women to a five- to seven-year course of hormone therapy or placebo to determine the impact of such treatment on a myriad of health outcomes. The heart disease findings became major news and convinced many women and their healthcare providers that the potential risks of hormone therapy outweighed the potential benefits. Women began to abandon hormone therapy in droves, feeling betrayed by the earlier assurances of its benefits.

While the pendulum has swung from the view that hormone therapy is good for all women to the view that it's harmful for all women, both positions are oversimplifications that have confused and alarmed women, not to mention their doctors. In my opinion, the answer is much more subtle and individual. A "one-size-fits-all" approach is inappropriate, yet very few physicians can provide women with truly satisfactory answers to their questions about hormone therapy—that is, answers tailored to a patient's particular situation and health profile. (Along with doctors, nurse practitioners and other health professionals are on the front line of giving advice and providing care to women as they navigate the menopausal transition. Although for brevity's sake I tend to use the words *doctor* or *physician* throughout this book, in most instances what I am saying also applies to other healthcare providers.)

After initially giving up hormone therapy, many women are now finding that their untreated menopausal symptoms are eroding their quality of life. In 2004, the American College of Obstetricians and Gynecologists stated that 25 percent of U.S. women who had stopped taking hormone therapy had restarted it—a mere two years after the Women's Health Initiative trial reported that such therapy increased the risk of cardiovascular disease. They apparently found the symptoms simply unbearable.

But how did it happen that decades of research suggested heart protection from hormone therapy only to have clinical trials, when finally undertaken, seem to show the opposite? What are the reasons for such discrepancies between earlier and later research? And why am I now saying that the new conclusion that hormone therapy is "bad" for all women is an inaccurate oversimplification?

Only in the past year have we come to a "unifying theory" that can explain the apparent discrepancies in the research and that can help women and their doctors make appropriate use of hormone therapy. I have had the privilege of being a lead investigator on two of the largest and most comprehensive research studies on the health of U.S. women undertaken to date—the Nurses' Health Study, which has observationally followed more than 121,000 female nurses for three decades and is still going strong, and the Women's Health Initiative, mentioned previously. My colleagues and I developed the unifying theory based on detailed analyses of data from these and other observational studies and randomized clinical trials. Some of the results have been recently published, and others will appear in the medical literature in the coming months. I have also had the opportunity to become involved with a new randomized clinical trial testing low-dose hormone therapy in recently menopausal women. This trial, the Kronos Early Estrogen Prevention Study (KEEPS), is assessing the effects of oral versus patch estrogen on the development of atherosclerosis as well as on quality of life and memory and thinking ability.

The key concept of the unifying theory is that hormone therapy tends to be *beneficial when started early after menopause* (as was done in the observational studies that seemed to show favorable results) and *harmful when started late after menopause* when women already have less-than-healthy blood vessels (as was the case with most women in the randomized clinical trials, which showed the negative results). In other words, a woman who starts taking hormone therapy when she already has advanced atherosclerosis is particularly susceptible to having a heart attack or stroke while on treatment, while a woman just entering menopause who has healthy blood vessels may even receive heart protection. A similar pattern may apply to the effect of hormone therapy on memory and cognition: hormone use may help preserve thinking ability when initiated in newly menopausal women but hasten the progression of preexisting memory problems when started later in life.

There are several biological reasons for these differences in outcomes, which I'll explain in detail in these pages. But let me clarify—although the evidence is mounting, it is not yet conclusive, and no woman should begin taking hormones for the express purpose of preventing cardiovascular disease or cognitive decline. However, the findings to date can be reassuring to women who have recently entered menopause and are considering hormone therapy for treatment of moderate-to-severe menopausal symptoms. (At the very least, such women generally have an extremely low underlying risk of heart attack, stroke, and other complications.) This book is the first to present the unified theory in a way that I hope will be accessible to any woman who is struggling with the decision of whether or not to take hormones.

And I know that there are many of you out there. Besides having had the extraordinary opportunity to investigate the relation between hormone therapy and women's health in not just one but two landmark research studies, I've also been fortunate enough to have had nearly 20 years' experience as an internist and endocrinologist in a clinical practice largely devoted to women's health. In that role, I've been called upon by innumerable patients for advice on how to best navigate the menopausal transition. Some of my patients requested a prescription for hormone therapy for relief of their symptoms with nary a thought about the potential health consequences, while others wouldn't hear of taking hormones under any circumstances, even though their hot flashes and night sweats were making them miserable. Yet by far the most common situation I've encountered is that of the perplexed patient who sought a clear explanation of the benefits and risks of menopause hormones so that, with my input, she could ultimately make the choice with which she was most at ease. When I began practicing medicine, providing satisfactory answers to these women was hard to do, because I was acutely aware of how little information about the health outcomes of women on hormone therapy was actually out there. But now that such data have begun to accumulate, it's possible to give evidence-based answers to those questions. So that's why I wrote this book.

I'm often asked if there was a particular event that inspired my interest in women's health and my commitment to helping women get the health information they need. When I started medical school, I was curious about endocrinology and the effects of hormones on health, but I didn't know that medical research would become my mission. But early in my medical training, my mother died of ovarian cancer at a relatively young age, an event that raised my awareness—in a profoundly painful and personal way—of the relative inattention paid by the medical establishment to women's health issues in comparison to men's. Once I realized how little research had actually been done on health issues unique to women, including the effects of hormones on health, I decided to pursue my interest in endocrinology and plan a dual career in both research and patient care. But let's return to the present.

Several health concerns should figure prominently when you weigh the potential benefits against the risks of hormone therapy, and heart disease is only one of many that should be factored into your choice. This book provides a step-by-step personalized framework for making the most informed hormone-therapy decision for your own symptoms and health profile. The following issues are addressed:

- Which women are now considered good candidates for hormone therapy and who should avoid hormone therapy at all costs?

- How can you calculate your personal risk for common conditions likely to be affected by hormone therapy—namely heart disease, stroke, blood clots in the legs and lungs, breast cancer, and hip fracture? How should these calculations guide your decision making about hormone therapy?

- For women who are good candidates, what is the best formulation and dose of estrogen to take, the preferred progestogen, and the optimal duration of treatment?

- For women who can't—or prefer not to—take hormone therapy, what are the best options for symptom relief and general health?

- What is the appropriate role for soy, black cohosh, and other alternative remedies in relieving menopausal symptoms?

- How can you work effectively with your healthcare provider to manage the transition to menopause?

In short, this book is my attempt to clear the confusion regarding the latest scientific data on hormone therapy—to make sense of the seeming chaos, so to speak—and present the facts you need to help you decide if hormone therapy is right for you. We are still in the thick of the learning process, but the evidence is now sufficiently firm that you can make an informed choice about using hormones for relieving symptoms of menopause with the reasonable expectation of keeping healthy and active for many years to come.

Disclaimer: The Women's Health Initiative (WHI) study and Nurses' Health Study (NHS) are supported by the National Institutes of Health (NIH) and conducted in collaboration with study investigators. This book does not necessarily reflect the opinions or views of the NIH or of study coinvestigators. Guidelines in this book are not intended to replace advice and medical care provided by your personal physician or other healthcare provider.

ACKNOWLEDGMENTS

◉

THE INFORMATION AND guidance offered in this book owe much to the research of my colleagues in the Nurses' Health Study, Women's Health Initiative, and the Kronos Early Estrogen Prevention Study, as well as faculty and staff in the Division of Preventive Medicine at Brigham and Women's Hospital, Harvard Medical School, and the Harvard School of Public Health. In particular, I'd like to thank Drs. Walter Willett, Francine Grodstein, Kathryn Rexrode, Meir Stampfer, Frank Hu, Graham Colditz, Frank Speizer, Jacques Rossouw, Ross Prentice, Marcia Stefanick, Robert Langer, Matthew Allison, Larry Phillips, Elizabeth Barrett-Connor, Margery Gass, Isaac Schiff, and Mitchell Harman for many stimulating and spirited discussions of menopausal hormone therapy and health.

Our understanding of the benefits and risks of hormone therapy has been made possible not only by talented scientists but also by the dedicated women who participate in research studies. Advances in medical knowledge depend on these volunteers' commitment and altruism. In particular, I thank the participants in the Nurses' Health Study and the Women's Health Initiative, and add to this my appreciation for the hundreds of thousands of participants in other research studies throughout the United States and worldwide. I have also learned a great deal from the patients in my care during nearly 20 years of clinical practice and have strived to earn the trust that they have placed in me.

I would like to acknowledge Dr. Anthony Komaroff, editor-in-chief at Harvard Health Publications, for recognizing the need for this book and providing the opportunity to turn the concept into a reality. Associate editor Raquel Schott worked tirelessly to ensure that the illustrations were completed on time and in optimal form. Ed Wiederer and Scott Leighton did a magnificent job in creating these illustrations. I am also grateful to editors Judith McCarthy and Deborah Brody at McGraw-Hill for championing the book's cause, helping to shape the book's message, and overseeing its successful completion. And project editor Nancy Hall expertly shepherded the manuscript from copyedit to final pages.

I also thank my coauthor, Dr. Shari Bassuk, whose extraordinary talent and commitment helped make this book possible. An experienced science writer, Shari was able to transform an enormous mass of complex medical research into highly lucid and accessible information. Sharing a commitment to the book's mission to help clear the confusion about hormone therapy and provide guidance to women in their decision making, Shari selflessly embraced each and every demand of this project. Her diligence, rare ability to combine attention to detail with "big picture" thinking, keen intelligence, and unusually lucid writing style are evident throughout this book. It has been an honor and privilege to have worked with Shari on this important project.

Finally, I thank my husband, Christopher Ames, and our children, Jennifer, Jeffrey, and Joshua, who have sustained me by their love, support, encouragement, and patience.

1

Explaining Perimenopause and Menopause

◉

Menopause is the beginning of a new, and often liberating and empowering, phase of life for women. Although it marks the end of cyclic functioning of the ovaries and thus of menstrual periods, it is a natural transition to a phase of life that can last 30 to 40 years, or even longer! After roughly four decades of nurturing and releasing an egg each month (pregnancy excepted), your ovaries call it quits on the reproductive front. Given that the average age of U.S. women at menopause is 51 years, most of us will spend more than one-third of our lives in the postmenopause. Symptoms of the underlying hormonal shifts that lead up to this event may manifest themselves for up to 10 years beforehand.

Perimenopause (the prefix *peri-* is Greek for "around" or "near") refers to the interval before menopause when fertility wanes and menstrual cycles become irregular, through the first year after the final menstrual period. Perimenopause varies greatly from one woman to the next. On average, it lasts three to four years, although it can be compressed into just a few months before the final menstrual period or extend as long as a decade. Some women feel buffeted by hot flashes or mood swings and wiped out by heavy periods or insomnia, while others have no bothersome symptoms. Menstrual periods may cease rather abruptly or continue erratically for years.

For someone planning a pregnancy, confronting her declining fertility can be a major issue. Even for those who do not wish to become pregnant, harbingers of menopause such as hot flashes and fluctuating periods that occur well before the actual event can be bewildering. To demystify what is happening to you, let's take a look at the midlife hormonal changes that underlie your symptoms.

What's Happening to My Body? Understanding Hormonal Changes

Hormones are chemicals that are produced and released into the bloodstream by a variety of specialized endocrine glands and by a region of the brain called the hypothalamus. (Listed in order from head to toe, these glands are the pineal and pituitary glands near the brain, the thyroid gland in the neck, the adrenal gland and the pancreas in the midsection, and, further down, the ovary [in women] and testes [in men]. Other select cells throughout the body, such as those in the fat tissue, also have the ability to make hormones.)

The word *hormone*, derived from the Greek word for "messenger," is a fitting name. Hormones travel to cells and tissues throughout the body, exerting a powerful influence on our health, feelings, and behaviors. During the menopausal transition, the starring hormone is the estrogen produced—or, as we will see, *not* reliably produced—by the ovaries. To understand estrogen's importance, we first need to back up and examine its role in reproduction—and health—earlier in life.

Menstrual Cycles: A Carefully Orchestrated Hormonal Dance

Women are born with a large reserve of eggs—one to two million of them—in their ovaries. Each egg is enclosed in a tiny, fluid-filled sac called a follicle. Although the ovary makes estrogen and other hormones throughout the life span, the egg-containing follicles are dormant in childhood. But as we enter puberty, the follicles become active, which greatly boosts the ovaries' production of estrogen.

During our peak reproductive years, the amount of estrogen in circulation rises and falls fairly predictably throughout the menstrual cycle as part of a finely tuned hormonal messaging system that operates between your brain, pituitary gland, and ovaries each month (see Figure 1.1).

The process is kicked off (on day one of the menstrual cycle) with a hormone called gonadotropin-releasing hormone (GnRH) secreted by the brain's hypothalamus. When the GnRH reaches the pituitary, it tells that gland to start producing follicle-stimulating hormone (FSH). This hormone then signals the ovaries to rouse some of the long-dormant egg-containing follicles, stimulating them to grow and to produce large quantities of estrogen. About a week later (on day seven of the

Figure 1.1 Hormonal Control of the Menstrual Cycle

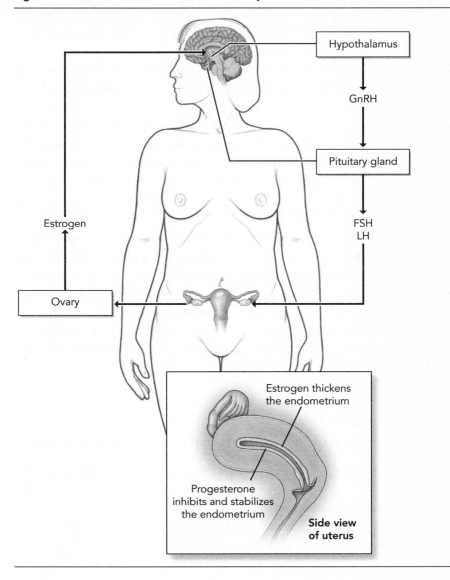

cycle), one of the group of growing follicles becomes significantly larger than the others; the others eventually die off and are reabsorbed by the ovary.

When the estrogen—along with more recently discovered hormones called inhibins—secreted by the follicles reaches a certain level, the hypothalamus directs the pituitary to turn off the FSH and to release luteinizing hormone (LH). This hormone prompts the dominant follicle to rupture and release its egg (usually around day 14 of the cycle), an event known as ovulation. The egg bursts through the ovary wall and enters the nearby fallopian tube, where it may or may not meet up with sperm from a male partner and be fertilized. Meanwhile, the empty follicle left behind in the ovary is transformed into a gland-like structure known as the corpus luteum that secretes large amounts of estrogen and a hormone called progesterone (see Figure 1.2).

This torrent of activity in the ovaries leads to changes in the lining of the uterus—the endometrium. It thickens in response to the estrogen produced by the developing follicles and is further stabilized by the progesterone produced by the corpus luteum. These changes prepare the endometrium for a possible pregnancy and increase the chance that a fertilized egg will successfully implant itself in the uterine lining.

If fertilization does not happen, the corpus luteum starts to degenerate, leading to a precipitous drop in progesterone and estrogen levels (around day 24 of the cycle). The fall in progesterone triggers the constriction of blood vessels and the contraction of muscle tissue in the uterus. Deprived of its oxygen and nutrient supply, the uterine lining rapidly disintegrates (around day 28 of the cycle) and is sloughed off as menstrual blood beginning on day 1 of the next cycle. And the low estrogen levels prompt the hypothalamus to secrete GnRH, thus starting the hormonal dance all over again.

PERIMENOPAUSE: A MIDLIFE TRANSITION AND A TIME OF FLUCTUATING HORMONES

As nature would have it, the body wasn't meant to have babies indefinitely. Your ovaries have peak reproductive function throughout your twenties and into your early thirties. Researchers aren't exactly sure what triggers the loss of fertility but surmise that it has to do in part with a dwindling supply of eggs and in part with a breakdown in the delicate hormonal communication system between the ovaries and the brain.

An average 40-year-old woman has only 5,000 to 10,000 eggs left in her ovaries, and the number falls off sharply after that. Moreover, the follicles that do remain often respond poorly to the FSH signal sent by the pituitary. For example, although

Figure 1.2 Changes During the Menstrual Cycle

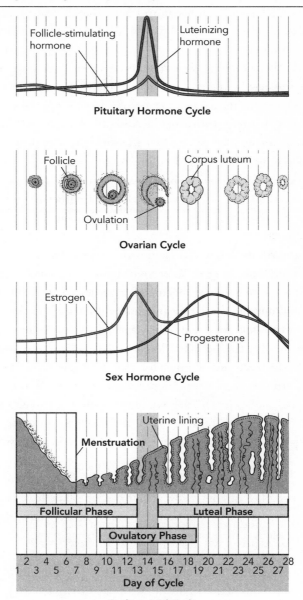

Day 1 is the first day of menstrual bleeding.

Source: Merck Manuals Online Medical Library: Home Edition. *(with permission)*

the developing follicles may produce enough estrogen to thicken the uterine lining, the amount may no longer be sufficient to trigger the LH surge that prompts the dominant follicle to release its egg. Therefore, ovulation will not reliably occur in every cycle.

If there is no ovulation, there is no corpus luteum to make progesterone. And if there is no progesterone, there is no way to stabilize the uterine lining for pregnancy. Moreover, because there is no progesterone drop to trigger endometrial shedding, there may be irregular menstrual bleeding. That is, the uterine lining may either disintegrate prematurely or continue to proliferate over time, shedding only when it grows too thick for its blood supply. Alternatively, even if ovulation does take place, the levels of estrogen and progesterone produced may not be enough to keep the hormonal dance in sync, so your cycle may lengthen or shorten, and your menstrual flow may become heavier or lighter. Eventually, your periods will stop altogether.

Unlike menopause, which is associated with consistently lower—but not completely absent—levels of estrogen, perimenopause is actually a time of wild swings in estrogen levels. As the follicles become less responsive to FSH, the pituitary responds by cranking out ever larger amounts of this hormone in an attempt to prod the ovary to create a dominant follicle and achieve ovulation.

During some cycles, the high FSH levels will trigger a very powerful response from the ovary, which activates multiple follicles and sends estrogen levels spiking. In other cycles, the ovary will not produce follicles in response to the increasingly urgent FSH signal, and estrogen levels will remain low. It is this erratic fluctuation of estrogen that is believed to cause many of the symptoms of perimenopause, including hot flashes, night sweats, insomnia, headaches, and mood swings (see Figures 1.3 and 1.4).

Because these symptoms occur in an unpredictable fashion, some women may feel a disconcerting loss of control over their bodies. Some have compared perimenopause to the ups and downs of puberty. And, from a scientific standpoint, the hormonal fluctuations during puberty and those during menopause are actually quite similar.

Indeed, one hypothesis that neatly explains both the triggering of puberty and of menopause is that our brain begins to lose its sensitivity to estrogen at an early age.[1] In childhood, the hypothalamus is acutely able to sense the small amount of estrogen produced by our ovaries and remains content with that amount. But as we enter puberty, the hypothalamus isn't quite as able to detect that small amount of estrogen, so it kicks into high gear, sending out GnRH to jump-start the cascade

Figure 1.3 Average Blood Levels of Ovarian and Pituitary Hormones During the Menopausal Transition

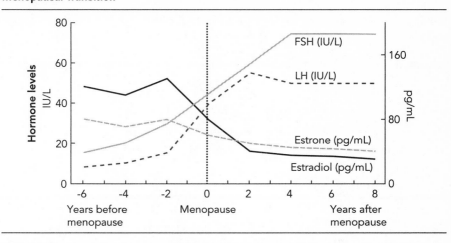

FSH: follicle-stimulating hormone; LH: luteinizing hormone; IU/L: international units per liter; pg/mL: picograms per milliliter.

Adapted from Shifren, J. L., and I. Schiff. Journal of Women's Health and Gender-Based Medicine *9 (2000): S3–7. (with permission)*

of pituitary and ovarian hormones that fuel the menstrual cycle. After a few uncomfortable teenage years during which kinks in the hormonal communication system are ironed out and our bodies adjust to higher estrogen levels, everything runs smoothly for decades. As we enter middle age, the hypothalamus, which continues to become more and more unable to sense the presence of estrogen, makes increasing demands on the poor ovaries to produce more of it. But the ovaries, now largely depleted of their follicles, can't reliably rise to the challenge. After trying for awhile, eventually the ovaries decide that enough is enough; they will continue producing estrogen, but on their own terms, thank you very much. The brain and pituitary never give up, though, as evidenced by the high FSH levels that are released by the pituitary throughout the remainder of a woman's life.

Although we tend to think of estrogen as a single entity, the ovaries actually make three forms of it—estradiol, estrone, and estriol. Estradiol is the most abundant estrogen before menopause, while estrone dominates after menopause. Estriol levels peak during pregnancy. Knowing about these different forms of estrogen is important because different estrogen medicines use different types of estrogen, and they may have somewhat different effects on a woman's body.

Figure 1.4 One Perimenopausal Woman's Hormones

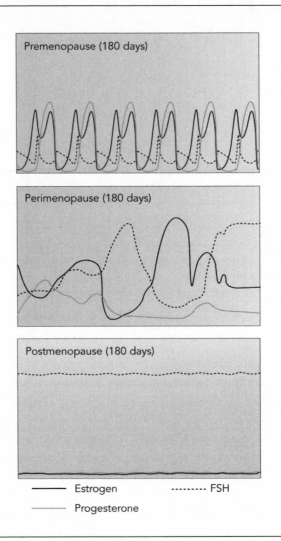

By comparison with the regularity of hormone levels before perimenopause (top graph), the course of one perimenopausal woman's hormones over a six-month period (middle graph) looks like Mr. Toad's Wild Ride. Not all women's hormones are so adventurous.

Adapted from Santoro, N., et al. Journal of Clinical Endocrinology and Metabolism *81 (1996): 1495–1501.*

Menopause: A New Steady State

Not all women feel at the mercy of their hormones during perimenopause. However, for those who do, there is good news. As women move further past menopause, the hormonal highs and lows begin to disappear, and estrogen levels stabilize, albeit at a lower level. This often relieves many symptoms of perimenopause, and women tend to regain a sense of control over their bodies. However, some symptoms, such as hot flashes, may persist for several years, and symptoms related to low (rather than fluctuating) estrogen, such as vaginal dryness, may worsen.

There is no denying that menopause is an unmistakable sign of aging and may, for some women, be hard to face in our youth-obsessed society. On balance, however, the leveling off of hormones makes menopause a bit of a relief for most women. Freedom from menstrual cycles can make life easier, and, with contraception no longer a worry, many women enjoy a newfound sexual freedom. Psychologically, the years after menopause can be a time of profound growth, challenges, and opportunities. In a 1998 poll conducted by the North American Menopause Society of 752 women between ages 50 and 65, the respondents were asked, "In which period of your life did you feel the most content or were you the happiest?" Fifty-one percent reported being most content after age 50. Only 16 percent chose their 40s, 17 percent their 30s, and 10 percent their 20s as the period in which they were most content and happy.

Sex Hormones Are Not Just for Baby-Making

The preceding discussion notwithstanding, the ovary is more than just a storehouse for eggs. The hormones that it produces ensure that our bodies will function properly throughout our lives, not just during our reproductive years.

I mentioned earlier that hormones travel in the bloodstream to cells and tissues throughout the body, powerfully affecting our health. But once hormones reach their intended destinations, you may wonder, how do they actually exert their effects? Cells that depend on hormones to function properly have protein molecules called hormone receptors that act like tiny ignition starters. And the hormones, logically enough, act like tiny keys. When a hormone—say estrogen—encounters a cell that has a receptor for estrogen, it's like when you put your key into your car's ignition and turn it on to start the engine. When estrogen binds to and turns on the estrogen receptor, it stimulates the cell to produce a cascade of proteins that influence its behavior.

Estrogen receptors are found not only in the cells of reproductive organs, such as the uterus and breast, but also in the cells of the liver, digestive system, urinary tract, heart, blood vessels, bone, skin, and the brain (see Figure 1.5).

The exact effect of estrogen depends on the type of cell that it encounters. For example, in the uterus and breast, estrogen's main effect is to cause the cells that line the uterus and the milk ducts to grow and divide in preparation for pregnancy. In the liver, estrogen acts to control the production of cholesterol in ways that influence the buildup of harmful fatty deposits in the arteries. In the skeleton, estrogen preserves bone strength by helping to maintain the proper balance between bone buildup and bone breakdown. And in other parts of the body, estrogen appears to play a role in the regulation of body temperature, the ability to recall information from memory, and the elasticity of arteries and skin. This is only a partial list of estrogen's effects.

When estrogen levels drop, the rate of bone loss accelerates rapidly. Indeed, the average woman loses 2 to 3 percent of bone mass a year for the first three years after menopause. As a result, osteoporosis is much more common in the decades after menopause. A woman's risk of heart disease also increases sharply after menopause, but estrogen's role in this process is still under study.

Two types of estrogen receptors—*alpha* and *beta*—have been identified. Scientists have known about the alpha receptor since the 1950s, but the beta receptor was identified only in 1996. In general, there are more alpha receptors in the reproductive organs (e.g., uterus and breast) and the liver, while beta receptors are more abundant in other tissues, such as bone and blood vessels. Estradiol appears to bind equally well to both types of receptors, while estrone binds preferentially to the alpha receptor and estriol to the beta receptor. We do not fully understand the role of the two types of estrogen receptors, their exact functions, or how they relate to the benefits and risks of our natural estrogen or the estrogen in traditional hormone therapies for menopause.

Nevertheless, recognition of differences in receptors has allowed pharmaceutical companies to manufacture a new class of medicines called selective estrogen

Figure 1.5 Selected Estrogen Receptor Sites

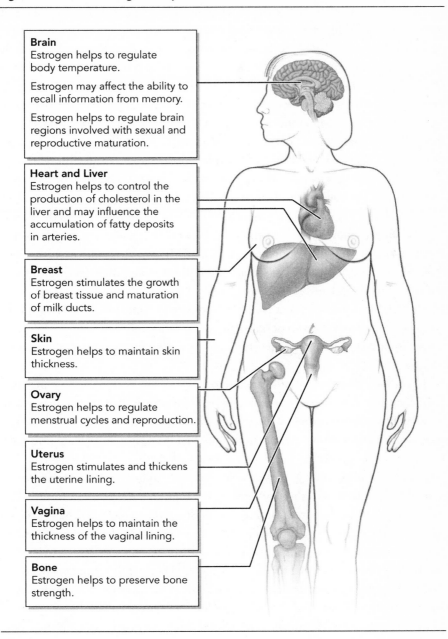

Brain
Estrogen helps to regulate body temperature.

Estrogen may affect the ability to recall information from memory.

Estrogen helps to regulate brain regions involved with sexual and reproductive maturation.

Heart and Liver
Estrogen helps to control the production of cholesterol in the liver and may influence the accumulation of fatty deposits in arteries.

Breast
Estrogen stimulates the growth of breast tissue and maturation of milk ducts.

Skin
Estrogen helps to maintain skin thickness.

Ovary
Estrogen helps to regulate menstrual cycles and reproduction.

Uterus
Estrogen stimulates and thickens the uterine lining.

Vagina
Estrogen helps to maintain the thickness of the vaginal lining.

Bone
Estrogen helps to preserve bone strength.

receptor modulators (SERMs)—or, to use the more glamorous name, "designer hormones"—that act on one or the other of these receptors to selectively block or stimulate estrogen-like action in various tissues.

One of the first SERMs to be developed was tamoxifen. Known by its trade name Nolvadex and also available as a generic, tamoxifen is prescribed to treat breast cancer and prevent its recurrence in women with a history of the disease and to prevent its development in women at high risk. In the breast, tamoxifen acts as an antiestrogen by binding to the alpha receptor, thus preventing estrogen from accessing it. In other parts of the body, however, tamoxifen acts like estrogen. Another SERM, raloxifene, known by its trade name Evista, is approved for prevention of bone thinning in women after menopause and is being studied as a way to prevent breast cancer. In a recent "head-to-head" trial, raloxifene and tamoxifen provided similar protection against breast cancer but raloxifene had fewer risks. Both of these SERMs increase hot flashes and the risk of blood clots, however. In the future, watch for additional developments with SERMs, which could eventually be designed to ease symptoms of menopause and protect bone and heart health without adding to the risk of breast cancer.

As with estrogen, receptors for progesterone also come in at least two forms. However, even less is known about their precise roles and functions, or how this information could be used to develop safer or more effective forms of hormone therapy.

In addition to estrogen and progesterone, generally known as the female sex hormones, the ovaries, along with the adrenal glands, produce small amounts of male sex hormones known as androgens, including testosterone. Testosterone levels in women are only one-tenth as high as in men. Androgens are thought to work in concert with estrogen to maintain a woman's sex drive, bone and muscle health, energy level, and psychological well-being. Indeed, androgen receptors are found in many of the same cells that have estrogen receptors.

Interestingly, a large proportion of the androgens produced by the ovary and adrenal gland are converted to estrogen by an enzyme called aromatase found in fat and muscle. (Other organs that contain aromatase include the brain, hair, skin, and bone marrow.) After menopause, this conversion actually represents the main source of estrogen in women. Because aromatase is found in fat cells, women who are overweight or obese tend to have higher levels of estrogen than thinner women. At the same time, because muscle cells are also rich in aromatase, women with more muscle mass are more likely to have higher estrogen levels than their scrawnier counterparts. This is thought to be why heavier women, and women who keep their muscles active with physical activity, may be less likely to suffer from certain symptoms of menopause.

In recent years, medicines called aromatase inhibitors—anastrozole (Arimidex) and letrozole (Femara)—have been approved to treat women with early-stage breast cancer. These medicines work by blocking the aromatase enzyme, thus preventing the conversion of androgens to estrogen in fat, muscle, and other tissues. Together with tamoxifen, aromatase inhibitors form a powerful new arsenal to fight breast cancer. (Not all breast cancer cells have estrogen receptors, though. These medicines stifle the growth of breast cancer cells that have estrogen receptors but do not affect the growth of breast cancers that lack estrogen receptors.)

AT WHAT AGE DO PERIMENOPAUSE AND MENOPAUSE OCCUR?

On average, women in Western nations can expect to enter perimenopause at age 47 and to have their last menstrual period at age 51. But it varies widely. Some women report irregular periods and hot flashes in their late 30s and stop menstruating when they are still in their 40s; others have no obvious symptoms and menstruate through their late 50s. Induced menopause—due to surgical removal of the ovaries or damage to the ovaries from chemotherapy or radiation therapy—can happen at any age. Premature menopause—whether natural or induced—is defined as menopause that occurs before the age of 40. About 1 percent of women will have a natural premature menopause.

Research has shown that about 80 percent of the time, a woman will experience menopause at roughly the same age as her mother and sisters, which suggests a genetic link. Although many studies support this link, a genetic basis is not considered conclusive, because family members also share a common environment.

One behavioral factor has been conclusively proven to affect a woman's age at menopause—smoking. Smokers reach menopause about two years earlier than nonsmokers. (If your mother smoked—and you don't—add two years to her age at menopause to get a rough idea at what age you might expect to have your last period. But your ovaries are highly susceptible to toxins in cigarette smoke, so secondhand smoke—including the smoke to which you were exposed while still *in utero* and during childhood—are also thought to lower the age you go through menopause.)

Other factors that may be associated with menopause occurring earlier than average include never having delivered a baby, never having used birth control pills, having a low body weight, having a history of heart disease, and treatment of childhood cancer with pelvic radiation or some types of chemotherapy. The age at which you got your first period does not predict the age at which you will go through menopause.

The Study of Women's Health Across the Nation (SWAN), which surveyed 15,000 ethnically diverse U.S. women aged 40 to 55 in 1996, has provided the first systematic look at the relationship between race and age at menopause in this country.[2] After factoring out the effects of smoking and the other behavioral variables noted previously, Hispanic women were found to experience menopause about six months earlier than white women, while Japanese women had a later menopause by approximately three months. Black and Chinese women experienced menopause at the same age as their white counterparts. SWAN is now studying a subgroup of these women over time to see how they move through the menopausal transition, including the hormonal and behavioral factors that shape their experience.

INDUCED MENOPAUSE

Induced menopause occurs when the ovaries are surgically removed or are damaged by chemotherapy or radiation therapy. Oophorectomy, the surgical removal of the ovaries, may be done together with or separately from hysterectomy, the surgical removal of the uterus.

A hysterectomy alone usually does not cause an immediate menopause in the hormonal sense because the ovaries are left in place and continue to produce estrogen, progesterone, and androgen. However, without a uterus, menstrual bleeding stops and the woman can no longer bear children. Even if the ovaries are not removed, a hysterectomy causes the hormonal changes of menopause to occur about two to three years earlier than they otherwise would have, probably by disturbing the blood supply to the ovaries. Women who have a hysterectomy still go through perimenopause as their ovaries gradually secrete less estrogen. But without a uterus, a woman will no longer menstruate, so she will not have the most reliable indicator of the beginning of perimenopause—irregular periods.

When a woman has her ovaries removed, she will experience menopause immediately. Induced menopause is generally much tougher for women than natural menopause. Levels of all ovarian hormones—estrogen, progesterone, and androgen—plummet instantly. This dramatic and abrupt drop is likely to result in more intense symptoms from estrogen loss (such as hot flashes) and from androgen loss (such as low sex drive) than what would occur in a natural menopause.

Women with induced menopause, especially when it occurs well before the typical age at menopause, as well as those with a premature natural menopause have special longer-term health concerns. Because they live more of their lives with lower-than-expected levels of these hormones, they are at increased risk for various aging-related diseases, such as osteoporosis and heart disease. Therefore, these women are among the most likely to derive benefit from traditional hormone therapy (see Chapter 7).

How Do You Know It's Perimenopause and Menopause?

There is no reliable test for perimenopause. Some clinicians recommend blood tests to look for high levels of FSH or low levels of estradiol in women who are still menstruating. But these tests are not reliable because FSH and estradiol levels can fluctuate unpredictably during the menopause transition. Seemingly normal results can be misleading and be misinterpreted to mean that a woman's symptoms are not linked to menopause. This can leave many women feeling like "it's all in their heads."

If your doctor does recommend an FSH test, be sure to have your blood drawn on the third day of the menstrual cycle. Of course, if your bleeding is erratic, it may be hard to figure out when the third day is. High FSH levels on the third day of the cycle have been shown to correlate with reduced fertility, which is an early indicator of perimenopause. Generally speaking, FSH levels of less than 10, 10 to 20, and 30 or more international units per liter (IU/L) have been shown to indicate a good, fair, and poor likelihood of a woman's ability to become pregnant.

Although there isn't any clear-cut test for perimenopause, you can track important changes that you notice. Is your cycle noticeably different from a few years ago? For example, is your cycle shorter or your flow heavier? Keep a calendar to record these changes, as well as hot flashes and other symptoms (see Chapter 2). The more accurately you can describe any irregularities, the easier it will be to pinpoint changes related to perimenopause.

A definitive "diagnosis" of menopause can be made only after the fact—when you've gone one full year without a menstrual period. By then, your hormone levels will have stabilized, so blood tests become a more reliable indicator of menopause. Your FSH level will consistently be above 30 IU/L and your estradiol will be below 30 picograms per milliliter (pg/mL). But at that point, unless you have been taking medications that have temporarily altered or stopped your periods (such as birth control pills), you will not need blood tests to know for sure that you are past menopause.

2

THE SYMPTOMS OF PERIMENOPAUSE AND MENOPAUSE . . . AND HOW TO TREAT THEM

◉

It can sometimes be difficult to disentangle the symptoms that result directly from the hormonal changes of menopause and symptoms that occur with general aging or in response to common midlife stressors, such as children leaving home, changes in primary relationships or careers, or illness or death of parents. A 2005 report from the National Institutes of Health and the Agency for Healthcare Research and Quality concluded that hot flashes, night sweats, and vaginal dryness have been unequivocally linked to menopause in research studies, and that menopausal hormone therapy effectively treats these "core" symptoms.[1]

Other symptoms commonly attributed to menopause, including sleep disturbance, mood swings, memory and concentration problems, low sex drive, and urinary complaints, may also be related to fluctuating or low estrogen levels, but, with the possible exception of sleep, existing studies have not established a definitive causal tie. Moreover, whether or not hormone therapy is helpful for some of these "secondary" symptoms is controversial. However, the core symptoms of menopause often have cascading effects. Frequent, severe hot flashes may disrupt sleep and contribute to fatigue, anxiety, irritability, and scattered thinking. Vaginal dryness may make sexual intercourse painful and ultimately dampen a woman's desire for sex. Therefore, to the extent that hormone therapy relieves the core symptoms of menopause, it may also help with some of the secondary symptoms as well.

This chapter will help you recognize signs of the menopausal transition and suggest ways to cope with the physical and mental changes that may arise in the five- to ten-year period before and after menopause. In addition to discussing nonhormonal strategies, I'll also tell you whether hormone therapy appears to be benefi-

cial—or not—in relieving the various symptoms that can crop up during the perimenopausal and menopausal years.

HOT FLASHES AND NIGHT SWEATS

Hot flashes are the most commonly reported symptom of perimenopause among
women in Western countries. Although estimates vary, studies indicate that up to
80 percent of women in the United States experience hot flashes at some point during the menopausal transition. Hot flashes, which generally last no more than four
to five years, tend to peak in severity during the two years after a woman's final
menstrual period before gradually tapering off. However, about 10 percent of
women will continue to have hot flashes indefinitely, perhaps even for the rest of
their lives. Women whose ovaries have been surgically removed or damaged by
medical conditions or treatments that decrease the ability of the ovaries to produce
hormones are particularly prone to hot flashes.

Hot flashes come on rapidly and typically last from one to five minutes, although
one-hour episodes are not unheard of. Women feel as if a heat wave is spreading
over their face, neck, and chest. A mild hot flash might be likened to a fleeting sense
of warmth, whereas a major hot flash gives the feeling of being consumed by fire
from the inside out, as if one is burning up. The more severe hot flashes induce
flushing (reddening) of the skin and profuse sweating, often followed by chills and
clamminess. Heart palpitations and feelings of lightheadedness, confusion, anxiety, tension, or a vague sense of dread are not uncommon.

Some women become agitated right before they start flashing. Others report a
pins-and-needles tingling in their hands or fingers, or itchy sensations, as if insects
were crawling in or on their skin. The scientific name for this crawly skin sensation is formication, after the Latin word for "ant." (Sometimes heart palpitations
or formication occur in the absence of hot flashes.) Needless to say, flashing at an
inconvenient time—such as during a speech, job interview, or romantic tryst, or
while driving—can be quite disconcerting.

The frequency of hot flashes varies widely. The average flash frequency is 3 to
4 per day, but some women have only 3 or 4 per week, while others may experience 10 or more each day, plus some at night. Hot flashes that strike in the wee
hours are called night sweats, for good reason. You may jerk awake to find yourself

in sweat-soaked pajamas and sheets. If your heart is pounding, it can be hard to calm down and fall back to sleep. This sleep deprivation can make you anxious and prone to mood swings.

In the United States, the prevalence of hot flashes differs among racial and ethnic groups. In the SWAN study, black and Hispanic women were more likely to report hot flashes than white women, while Chinese and Japanese women were less likely to do so.[2] Studies of women in other countries also suggest the phenomenon is not universal. For example, in Mexico's Yucatan peninsula, Mayan women do not report hot flashes at all. Researchers have speculated as to whether these variations are the result of differences in diet, exercise, perceptions of hot flashes, or other cultural factors. However, answers remain elusive.

What Causes Hot Flashes?

Perhaps the biggest mystery about hot flashes is the physiologic mechanism that causes them. Estrogen is involved—if it weren't, estrogen therapy wouldn't relieve hot flashes as effectively as it does—but it's not the whole story. Before puberty, girls have low estrogen but no hot flashes. Conversely, women in the late stages of pregnancy may have hot flashes at a time when their estrogen levels are high. And in perimenopause the level of estrogen in a woman's blood is not a reliable predictor of whether or not she will have hot flashes. Researchers have speculated that it is the irregular fluctuation in estrogen—or, alternatively, complex interactions between estrogen and other hormones or substances in the body—that trigger hot flashes.

An intriguing theory of hot flashes has been proposed by Dr. Robert Freedman of Wayne State University School of Medicine, who has studied the phenomenon for 25 years. He and his colleagues have measured skin temperature, blood flow, and skin conductance (an electrical measure of sweating) in menopausal women before, during, and after a flashing episode. They've asked their research subjects to wear monitors to record hot flash data, swallow radiotelemetry pills to measure core (innermost) body temperatures, and spend nights in a sleep laboratory to have their hot flashes tracked.

Freedman's research shows that, compared to their counterparts who don't have hot flashes, women who do have them have a markedly reduced tolerance for small increases in the body's core temperature.[3] The body tries to maintain its core temperature within a comfortable "thermoneutral" zone. When our core temperature rises above the zone's upper limit, we rid ourselves of excess body heat by sweating and flushing. The reddening of our skin is caused by dilation of our outermost blood vessels so that heat can more easily dissipate through the thin layer of skin that covers them. When our core temperature drops below the lower limit, we generate body heat by shivering. In women who don't have hot flashes, the width of the thermoneutral zone is quite wide—about several tenths of a degree centigrade. But in women who do have hot flashes, the thermoneutral zone is so narrow that it's virtually nonexistent (see Figure 2.1). As a result, tiny shifts in core body temperature—as little as one-tenth of a degree centigrade—that don't bother some women trigger hot flashes and chills in others.

Why the thermoneutral zone contracts in some women at menopause is not clear. Some evidence suggests that estrogen has the effect of widening the zone, so loss of estrogen at menopause may trigger a narrowing of the zone.

Treating Hot Flashes and Night Sweats

There are several approaches, including lifestyle changes, nonprescription remedies, and prescription medications, to keep cool.

Lifestyle Changes

Depending on their severity and how much they interfere with your day-to-day activities, hot flashes may be lessened by adopting commonsense changes in lifestyle. Possible triggers of hot flashes include warm air temperatures, hot beverages, spicy food, emotional stress, smoking, alcohol, caffeine, and some medica-

Figure 2.1 Hot Flashes and the Thermoneutral Zone

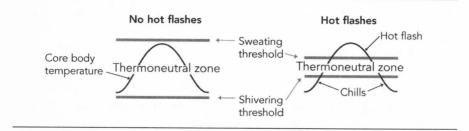

Adapted from Freedman, R. R., Seminars in Reproductive Medicine 23 (2005): 117–25.

tions. If you can identify and avoid your particular triggers, you may be able to head off some hot flashes. Keep a diary to note which of these or other triggers were present before each hot flash occurred. Review it each week to pinpoint the most common triggers.

Dress in layers so that you can remove garments as needed. If possible, regulate the heat and air-conditioning in your environment to accommodate your temperature changes. If you tend to wake up overheated at night, sleep in a cool room. Bedside fans can also be helpful, as can the use of small portable fans during daytime hours. At bedtime, consider taking a tepid (lukewarm) or cool shower. Place a frozen cold pack under your pillow, and flip the pillow at regular intervals so that your head is always resting on a cool surface. Keep a thermos of ice water and a drinking glass by your bed to avoid traipsing to the kitchen in the middle of the night. Have a freshly laundered set of pajamas on hand so that you don't have to rummage through your drawers looking for a change of clothing should you wake up drenched. Keep the bed in the guest room (if you have this luxury) made up so that you can readily decamp to a dry haven on particularly bad nights.

Some women may find deep-breathing exercises helpful. To perform the breathing technique known as paced respiration, take slow, deep, full breaths—expanding and contracting the abdomen gently while inhaling through your nose and exhaling through your mouth—at a rate of about six to eight breaths per minute. One of the best ways to learn paced respiration is by taking a yoga class. Practice this technique twice a day for 15 minutes. You can also use paced respiration whenever you feel a hot flash coming on. Other stress-relief techniques such as meditation, biofeedback, and massage may also be of some benefit.

Physical activity is one stress buster that is often overlooked by women trying to keep cool. Research has shown that women who are physically active on a daily basis are less likely to suffer from hot flashes than their couch-potato counterparts. Aim for 30 minutes per day of moderate-intensity physical activity—brisk walking, for example—on most days of the week. If you have led a sedentary lifestyle until now, plan on easing into an exercise routine. It's true that physical activity, especially if strenuous, may initially trigger hot flashes in women who are unaccustomed to exercising, but it should help in the longer term, after your muscles become conditioned to their new level of activity. Indeed, habitual moderate exercise may reduce hot flashes not only by ameliorating stress but by promoting the conversion of testosterone to estrogen in the muscles. And think of all the other health benefits you'll reap from being physically active (see Chapter 6)!

The role of body weight in hot flashes is controversial. One line of reasoning suggests that because heavier women tend to produce more estrogen than their thinner counterparts after menopause, they may be less likely to suffer hot flashes. On the other hand, their extra layer of fat acts as insulation, making it harder for the body to rid itself of excess heat and keep its core temperature within the target thermoneutral zone. Thus, it is not clear whether losing those extra pounds will exacerbate or improve hot flashes. Nonetheless, there are a myriad of other health reasons to maintain a healthy body weight.

Soy and Other Phytoestrogens

No doubt you've heard the buzz surrounding soy as a treatment for hot flashes. Soybeans are rich in compounds called phytoestrogens, literally "plant estrogens." There are three main types of phytoestrogens: isoflavones, lignans, and coumestans. Isoflavones are found in soy and garbanzo beans and other legumes; lignin is primarily found in flaxseed; and high concentrations of coumestans are found in red clover, sunflower seeds, and bean sprouts. In the plants that make them, phytoestrogens act as growth-regulating hormones. In the human body, phytoestrogens act like weak estrogens. They appear to work by binding to estrogen receptors. In some tissues, phytoestrogens may mimic the action of estrogen, while in other tissues, they may block it.

The estrogen-mimicking activity of phytoestrogens might, in theory, reduce hot flashes. Proponents of soy point out that women living in countries with a high intake of soy, such as Japan and certain parts of China, are less likely to have hot flashes than women living in countries with lower soy intakes. However, results of clinical trials—studies in which half the women received soy or red clover extracts and half received inactive placebos—are less consistent.[4] In a few studies, women who consumed phytoestrogen-rich supplements initially experienced greater relief from hot flashes than those consuming an inactive placebo. But the benefits largely faded after six weeks, and in many studies, women taking a placebo fared just as well as those receiving a phytoestrogen product. That is, hot flashes declined over time in *both* the treatment and placebo groups, with only small differences between them.

Dietary trials of soy foods rather than soy extracts have been similarly disappointing. Still, eating foods rich in phytoestrogens may provide greater benefits than dietary supplement pills. Low-fat varieties of tofu (28 milligrams of isoflavones per serving), tempeh (43 milligrams), or soymilk (10 milligrams), or roasted soybeans are good choices. If you suffer from hot flashes and want to try soy, aim for one to two servings—or 40 to 80 milligrams of isoflavones—per day. Don't overdo it, as the health effects of excessive soy consumption in the long run are uncertain.

(Soy's relationship to breast cancer and heart disease is discussed in Chapter 6.) If soy fails to curb your hot flashes—give it a six- to eight-week try—and if your diet before menopause did not normally include soy foods, it may be prudent to limit yourself to a few servings of soy per week.

Black Cohosh and Other Botanicals

The study of other botanicals as treatments for menopause symptoms is in its infancy. Of alternative botanical therapies that have been touted for relief of hot flashes and other menopausal symptoms, including dong quai, evening primrose oil, ginseng, licorice root, and black cohosh, it is the latter that has shown the most promise in preliminary research, nearly all of which was conducted in Germany.

For example, in the most recent—and the largest—of the German studies, 304 healthy women, whose average age was 53 and who were past menopause, were assigned to take black cohosh extract (40 milligrams per day) or an inactive placebo for 12 weeks.[5] Black cohosh was found to reduce hot flashes significantly more than the placebo, particularly among the women who were the closest to menopause, although an easy-to-interpret numerical estimate of the benefit was not provided by the investigators. On the other hand, in a recent Swiss study that assigned 122 peri- and early menopausal women aged 45 to 60 who reported at least three hot flashes per day to either black cohosh extract (the average dose was 42 milligrams per day) or placebo, there was little difference in hot flash reduction between the two groups overall.[6] But in the subgroup of 53 women whose initial symptoms were of at least moderate intensity, black cohosh was associated with a decrease of 53 percent in hot flashes, compared to only 25 percent for the placebo—a large difference. Other studies have yielded less impressive results.

Although it is used widely in Europe, black cohosh is viewed by U.S. medical authorities with more skepticism. The American College of Obstetricians and Gynecologists and the North American Menopause Society have stated that black cohosh (common over-the-counter supplements include Remifemin and, in combination with soy, Estroven) may be helpful for women with hot flashes, sleep disturbances, or mood symptoms but warn that its putative benefits—and, equally important, its potential risks—have not been rigorously evaluated in long-term studies. The U.S. government is currently funding such trials to determine whether black cohosh indeed lives up to the claims made by its European proponents and is safe for long-term use. While awaiting study results, the aforementioned organizations recommend—and I agree—that women wishing to try black cohosh limit their use of this herb to six months or less and take no more than two 20-milligram pills per day.

Data are inconclusive as to whether black cohosh and the other herbs listed here have any estrogen-mimicking properties; thus, caution dictates that their use not be presumed safe for women with breast cancer.

Documented side effects of black cohosh include mild stomach upset, skin rash, and—in high doses—headaches, vomiting, and dizziness. I should also note that a few cases of liver damage associated with black cohosh have popped up in the medical literature in recent years. In 2002, Australian researchers reported the case of a woman who developed hepatitis and liver failure requiring a transplant after taking black cohosh for only a week for menopausal symptoms. Her physicians say they found no other reason for her liver problems. In 2003, University of Chicago physicians told a meeting of gastroenterologists about a 57-year-old woman who developed a progressive inflammation of the liver after taking black cohosh for three weeks. Her symptoms cleared up in about two months once she stopped the herb and received steroid treatment. Most recently, liver failure was reported in a woman who used an herb mixture containing black cohosh.

It's unclear exactly what caused the liver toxicity in these cases. There are many black cohosh preparations and little manufacturing oversight of these (and other herbal) supplements, so it's possible that contamination was a factor. Also, underlying health conditions or additional medication use may have contributed. Nevertheless, such reports underscore the need for additional scientific study of herbal remedies and more information on possible drug interactions. In any event, be sure to tell your healthcare provider if you decide to try black cohosh, as he or she may want to monitor your liver function while you are taking this herb.

Vitamin E

Some women report that vitamin E reduces the intensity of their hot flashes and eases the sleep disturbances that result from the flashes, although studies do not clearly support these effects. Doctors have traditionally recommended daily doses of 400 to 800 IU. However, data from a few recent clinical trials of vitamin E (taken for reasons other than menopausal symptom relief) have suggested that doses of 400 IU or higher for extended periods of time may carry some risks, including an increased risk of heart failure and even a slight increase in death rates. If you decide to try vitamin E, it may be prudent to take a lower dose—200 or 300 IU per day, especially if you plan to take it for several years or more. In the Women's

Health Study, a large clinical trial of nearly 40,000 women, my colleagues and I have shown that such doses are safe in healthy middle-aged and older women when taken for up to a decade.[7] It may take two to six weeks before you experience symptom relief, if any. (By the way, vitamin E supplements have been largely discredited as a preventive measure for cardiovascular disease and cancer.)

Menopausal Hormone Therapy

Despite the lack of compelling evidence for most of the previously mentioned strategies, they might be worth a try, especially if your symptoms are mild and not too disabling. However, the most effective treatment for moderate-to-severe hot flashes and night sweats is menopausal estrogen therapy. Unless you've had a hysterectomy, you'll also need to take a progestogen—that is, either progesterone or a synthetic form of progesterone known as a progestin—to reduce the risk of endometrial (uterine) cancer associated with the use of estrogen alone.

Research studies, including dozens of randomized clinical trials, have consistently demonstrated that supplemental estrogen, taken with or without a progestogen, reduces the frequency and severity of hot flashes and night sweats by 80 percent or more in most women who use it and often eliminates these symptoms completely. Estrogen preparations taken by mouth (oral estrogens) and by skin patch (transdermal estrogens) are equally effective at providing symptom relief. Clinical trials conducted within the past five years or so show that many women obtain significant relief from hot flashes and night sweats using lower oral or transdermal estrogen doses than have traditionally been prescribed.[8]

In addition to reducing hot flashes and night sweats, oral and transdermal estrogens are also extremely effective at treating vaginal dryness. However, if you're suffering *only* from vaginal dryness and are not also bothered by hot flashes or night sweats, you should opt for a vaginal estrogen—that is, an estrogen preparation that is applied directly to the vagina—instead of an oral or transdermal one. This will minimize any unnecessary exposure to supplemental estrogen. Vaginal estrogens are designed specifically to treat vaginal dryness and are *not* effective for hot flashes or night sweats.

We'll take a close look at the pros and cons of the various hormone preparations—and there are quite a number of preparations to choose from!—in later chapters.

You should know that most doctors will not prescribe hormone therapies designed for use after menopause unless it is clear that a woman has indeed reached menopause—that is 12 months have passed since she last had a period, or, alternatively, at least 6 months have passed *and* her FSH level is above 30 IU/L. Why? In women who are still menstruating, menopause estrogen prescriptions can magnify fluctuations in hormone levels and cause heavy bleeding to worsen. Also, such prescriptions don't provide contraception, and some women can still become pregnant even shortly before reaching menopause (see the following section).

Birth Control Pills

An alternative hormonal strategy to control hot flashes and night sweats until you reach menopause is to take low-dose birth control pills, which contain estrogen and progestogen formulations that are appropriate for women who are still menstruating. Birth control pills will regulate your periods and suppress the hormonal swings of perimenopause. Some women report feeling more on an even keel while taking them. For women who are sexually active, birth control pills have the added advantage of providing contraception. (Believe it or not, the unintended pregnancy rate among women in their 40s, many of whom mistakenly believe they are no longer fertile, rivals that of teenagers.)

Birth control pills are not totally benign. They can increase the risk of heart attack, stroke, and blood clots and greatly increase these risks in women who smoke. Some studies suggest that long duration of use may increase breast cancer risk, but this remains controversial. (On the other hand, if taken for at least five years, birth control pills may reduce your risk of ovarian cancer, uterine cancer, and possibly colon cancer.) And some women suffer side effects like nausea and vomiting. However, unlike menopausal hormone therapy, which is designed to supplement—not supplant—the body's own estrogen, birth control pills essentially shut down your ovaries' production of estrogen and substitute the hormones contained in the pills. Thus, they are far less likely to lead to a potentially dangerous estrogen overload in otherwise healthy, nonsmoking women who have not yet reached menopause.

Nonhormonal Prescription Medications

If you can't or don't want to take hormones, you may find that antidepressant medications known as selective serotonin reuptake inhibitors (SSRIs) such as venlafaxine (Effexor, 25 to 150 milligrams per day), fluoxetine (Prozac, 20 milligrams per day), or paroxetine (Paxil, 10 to 20 milligrams per day) or the antiseizure medication gabapentin (Neurontin, 300 to 900 milligrams per day) alleviate your hot flashes.

Short-term clinical trials lasting 4 to 12 weeks—some of which were conducted in women with a history of breast cancer, a group for whom estrogen therapy is not an option—consistently find that, compared to an inactive placebo, these medications offer measurable relief against hot flashes, although they are not as universally effective as estrogen therapy. In general, women assigned to an SSRI experienced a 60 to 65 percent reduction in the frequency or severity of their hot flashes, compared with a 25 to 35 percent reduction among their counterparts assigned to a placebo.[9]

Although there are few head-to-head comparisons, Effexor seems to be somewhat better at controlling hot flashes than other SSRIs. Scientists aren't sure why but speculate that it has to do with the fact that Effexor increases norepinephrine as well as serotonin levels in the brain, whereas Prozac, Zoloft, and Paxil increase serotonin only. Both of these brain chemicals are believed to play a role in regulating the aforementioned thermoneutral zone. Whether SSRIs effectively control hot flashes for more than a few months has not been rigorously evaluated, although observational follow-up of participants in clinical trials suggests that this may be the case. In any event, unlike the situation for black cohosh, SSRIs are generally considered to be safe for longer-term use on the basis of extensive clinical experience among patients who take these drugs to treat mood disorders. However, extended-release venlafaxine (Effexor XR) has recently been linked to sustained high blood pressure, so blood pressure should be checked regularly while one is taking this medication.

Neurontin has also been shown in clinical trials to reduce hot flashes in women with and without breast cancer. In the largest study to date, an eight-week trial conducted among 360 breast cancer survivors, a 46 percent reduction in hot flash frequency and severity was reported for patients receiving 300 milligrams of Neurontin three times per day, compared with a 30 percent reduction for 100 milligrams three times per day and an 18 percent reduction with placebo.[10]

Low doses of the blood pressure medication clonidine (Catapres, 0.05 to 0.4 milligrams per day) also appear to reduce hot flashes. In one trial among 194 breast cancer patients, hot flashes decreased about 37 percent in the Catapres group versus 20 percent in the placebo group after four weeks.[11] Other blood pressure medications that may be helpful include methyldopa (Aldomet, 250 to 1,000 milligrams per day) or propranolol (Inderal, 40 to 80 milligrams per day).

Talk with your healthcare provider about which of these nonhormonal alternatives may be right for you. Like virtually all drugs, these medications have side effects, especially at higher doses. Antidepressants can cause dry mouth, nausea, diarrhea or constipation, nervousness, insomnia or sleepiness, dizziness, hand tremors, weight gain, sweating, decreased libido, and inability to have an orgasm—paradoxically, some of the symptoms that you may be trying to treat. The most common side effects associated with Neurontin are dizziness, insomnia or sleepiness, nausea, and swelling in the ankles and legs. Blood pressure medications can cause fatigue, headaches, and lightheadedness related to drops in blood pressure.

Above all, keep in mind that as you move further past menopause, hot flashes will most likely eventually dissipate on their own. Sometimes it's easier to cope with something that you know will be a time-limited phenomenon.

Vaginal Changes

Decreasing estrogen levels can cause the tissues of the vulva (external female genitals) and the vagina to become thin and dry and to lose elasticity. Vaginal secretions diminish, resulting in decreased lubrication. The vagina itself also becomes shorter and narrower. These changes can make sexual intercourse unpleasant. The loss of estrogen also leads to a rise in vaginal pH, changing the vaginal environment from an acidic one that fosters the growth of helpful bacteria that fight infection to an alkaline one in which harmful bacteria flourish and promote infection.

In some women, the vaginal tissues can become inflamed—a condition called atrophic vaginitis. Fragile vaginal tissues are prone to injury, tearing, or bleeding and can make intercourse or pelvic exams painful at best and impossible at worst.

Treating Vaginal Changes

Estrogen preparations taken by mouth or via a skin patch are very effective at treating vaginal dryness, as are low doses of estrogen applied directly to the vagina in the form of creams, rings, or tablets. If you are bothered by vaginal dryness but *not* also by hot flashes or night sweats, and you wish to try estrogen, you should opt for a vaginal preparation rather than an oral or transdermal preparation (see Chapter 5).

Hormonal treatment is not the only approach, however. Water-based vaginal lubricants intended for use during sexual activity, such as K-Y Jelly, Astroglide, and K-Y Silk-E, can make intercourse less uncomfortable. Avoid products not specifically designed for vaginal use. Hand lotions often contain ingredients such as alcohol and perfume that can irritate vaginal tissue. Oil-based products such as petroleum jelly and baby oil can also cause irritation, damage diaphragms and condoms, and cling to vaginal tissue, providing a habitat for infection. One exception may be vitamin E oil, which has been reported to provide lubrication and relief from itching and irritation without adverse effects and may be applied up to twice weekly.

A vaginal moisturizer such as Replens or K-Y Long Lasting Vaginal Moisturizer, also applied twice weekly, may be helpful for women who have symptoms of irritation and burning that occur even in the absence of sexual activity. Because these moisturizers help maintain an acidic vaginal environment, they may also help prevent vaginal infections. Vinegar douches or vaginally applied cultures of lactobacilli or yogurt are not effective moisturizers.

Drinking plenty of water—the standard rule of thumb is eight glasses per day but six may be adequate—can help your whole body, including your vagina, stay hydrated, while coffee and alcohol will dehydrate you. Antihistamine medications taken for allergies have a drying effect on all mucous membranes, including those in the vaginal walls, so use them sparingly. Avoid using soap on your genital area; it can further tip the pH of the vagina toward alkalinity. A daily warm-water wash should suffice. Choose toilet paper, sanitary pads, tampons, and laundry detergents that do not contain deodorants, fragrances, or dyes, and forgo the use of fabric softeners altogether. Instead of the traditional bubble bath, soak in lukewarm (not hot) bathwater with four to five tablespoons of baking soda to help soothe vulvar itching and burning. Keep your genital area well ventilated and dry: wear white, all-cotton underwear; avoid tight clothing, especially synthetics; substitute thigh-high nylons for waist-high pantyhose; and remove wet swimsuits and exercise clothes as soon as possible.

Sexual activity of all types, including self-stimulation, can help keep the tissues of the vulva and vagina well lubricated. Sexual intercourse can also help prevent vaginal shrinkage. (As the saying goes, "Use it or lose it.") Women who have not had intercourse for long periods of time—whether because of physical discomfort or lack of opportunity—and wish to resume doing so may find that vaginal dilators are helpful in reacclimating their bodies to the experience. These devices are plastic or rubber cylinders sold by medical supply stores in sets of graduated sizes; the narrowest dilators are the width of a finger. You put them into the vagina along with a lubricant such as K-Y Jelly for a couple of minutes per day, gradually increasing the size of the dilator over a period of several weeks.

Menstrual Cycle Changes

A pear-shaped organ about the size of a fist, your uterus is made mostly of muscle. As you move through perimenopause, your uterus shrinks slightly, and the inner layer of tissue, or endometrium, no longer builds up and sheds on a predictable monthly cycle. Changes in the menstrual cycle are a hallmark of perimenopause. Only 10 percent of women stop having periods with no irregularity in their cycles.

In the early stages of perimenopause, the interval between your periods may shorten or lengthen by a day or two. If you don't normally track your periods on a calendar, or if you've always been a bit irregular, you may not even notice the shift. Bleeding also may become lighter or heavier. These changes will become more pronounced over time, and you may start skipping periods altogether. Going for three months without a period suggests menopause is rapidly approaching, although more than 20 percent of women do menstruate again after such a break.

During perimenopause, one in five women will experience excessive menstrual bleeding, defined as a loss of more than 5.4 tablespoons of blood each cycle, compared with 2 or 3 on average. It's not only a nuisance for many women but also a medical issue, as blood loss can cause anemia and fatigue. Some women experience pain and severe cramping.

Treating Troublesome Periods

For women suffering from heavy and irregular periods caused by the hormonal fluctuations of perimenopause, doctors often prescribe birth control pills or progestins (synthetic versions of progesterone, the hormone that causes the uterine lining to slough), which can reduce blood flow and regularize cycles. The Mirena intrauterine device (IUD), which releases the progestin levonorgestrel directly into the uterine lining, has become an increasingly popular option in recent years. Nonsteroidal anti-inflammatory drugs, such as mefenamic acid, have also been shown to reduce menstrual pain and blood flow. Iron supplements may be prescribed to treat anemia resulting from menstrual blood loss.

If medications don't work, surgical procedures may be appropriate in some cases. Options include dilation and curettage (D&C), in which the uterine lining is scraped away with a small spatula, or endometrial ablation, in which the lining is

Insomnia also can be a problem for women who don't have hot flashes or night ~~s~~eats. Some women may have difficulty falling asleep when they go to bed, but a ~~mo~~re common pattern is to sleep for a few hours, awaken too early, and not be able ~~to n~~od off again. Whether sleep disruptions that occur in the absence of noticeable ~~hot~~ flashes are due primarily to the hormonal changes of menopause is not known. ~~Ho~~wever, recent findings from the SWAN study indicate that a woman's ~~meno~~pausal status is a much stronger predictor than her age of how likely she is to ~~repo~~rt sleep problems, with the prevalence of such problems rising steadily from ~~pre~~menopause to late perimenopause but remaining more or less stable after ~~meno~~pause regardless of the age at which the menopause transition took place.[13] ~~Mo~~reover, when researchers collected daily urine samples from the pre- and early ~~peri~~menopausal participants to assess hormonal changes over the course of a men-~~stru~~al cycle, they found that the women's sleeping difficulties waxed and waned as ~~thei~~r FSH levels rose and fell, respectively. Women had the most trouble sleeping ~~at t~~he beginning and end of their menstrual cycles, when FSH levels were at their ~~high~~est.[14] This suggests that the hormonal changes of menopause may be at least ~~par~~tly responsible for the sleep problems of midlife women.

However, aging-related declines in other hormones such as melatonin may also ~~adv~~ersely affect sleep. Produced by the pineal gland, melatonin seems to be impor-~~tan~~t in setting your circadian clock, the internal timepiece that controls your sleep-~~wak~~e cycle. When everything's working properly, your pineal gland produces ~~mel~~atonin when the light dims in the evening, signaling you to sleep. And it cuts ~~bac~~k on production when daylight resumes, so melatonin levels nose-dive at dawn, ~~rou~~sing you awake.

~~R~~egardless of its origin, insomnia is a troublesome problem that can render its ~~vict~~ims fatigued, tense, irritable, and moody. Moreover, chronic sleep deprivation ~~has~~ been associated with impaired memory and problem-solving abilities, reduced ~~imm~~une function, weight gain, high blood pressure, and coronary heart disease. In ~~the~~ Nurses' Health Study, for example, my colleagues and I found that women who ~~hab~~itually slept less than five hours (or more than nine hours) per night were much ~~mor~~e likely to develop coronary heart disease than those who slept seven to eight ~~hou~~rs.[15]

~~Tr~~eating Insomnia

~~As~~ a first line of attack, take some practical steps to improve your chances of get-~~ting~~ a good night's sleep:

Uterine Bleeding: What's Normal, What's Not?

Normal changes in menstrual cycles attributable to shifting hormones may be exacerbated by other gynecologic problems that are common in midlife, including benign uterine growths such as fibroids, polyps, or a thickened endometrial lining. More rarely, bleeding is due to cancers of the uterus, cervix (the lower part of uterus), or vagina. It is often difficult, if not impossible, for a woman to know whether changes in her cycle are a normal sign of peri-menopause or a symptom of a more serious problem. Therefore, you should notify your healthcare provider of any changes in your bleeding pattern, especially if:

- You have a few periods that last three or more days longer than usual.
- You have a few menstrual cycles that are shorter than 21 days.
- You have heavy monthly bleeding (you soak a sanitary pad or tampon every hour for more than a day).
- You have spotting or bleeding between periods.
- You bleed after intercourse.
- You are taking menopausal hormone therapy and you have bleeding that deviates from the typical bleeding pattern associated with such therapy.

To pinpoint the cause of your bleeding, your doctor may recommend a vaginal ultrasound. This painless procedure uses a small, tampon-sized transducer (probe) inserted in the vagina to generate ultrasound images of the uterus and its lining. If the lining is thicker than expected, or any worrisome uterine growths are seen, the doctor may perform an endome-trial biopsy or hysteroscopy. In an endometrial biopsy, a thin tube is inserted through the vagina and into the uterus to remove a small sample of the endometrium with a suction device. The tissue is then analyzed under a microscope to rule out cancer or a precancerous condition. In a hysteroscopy, the doctor uses a thin fiber-optic tube, or hysteroscope, to get a direct look at the uterus. After numbing the cervical area with a local anesthetic, he or she inserts the tube through the vagina and cervix and introduces a liquid or gas to expand the uterus so its lining can be seen clearly through the scope. During hysteroscopy, the doctor can take tissue samples or can remove polyps or fibroids growing along the inner surface of the uterus; these are common causes of uterine bleeding.

destroyed either by radiofrequency waves, heat, or freezing. Although anesthesia is required, these two procedures are performed on an outpatient basis and don't involve any incisions because the devices involved are inserted into the uterus through the vagina. A more drastic option is hysterectomy—surgical removal of the uterus. Talk with your healthcare provider about your symptoms to determine the best approach.

What About Hysterectomy?

Hysterectomy is less common than it used to be, although it remains the most frequently performed nonobstetric surgery in the United States. More than 600,000 hysterectomies are performed in this country each year, at a cost of $5 billion annually. One in three women in the United States has a hysterectomy by age 60.

Reasons for Hysterectomy

About 10 percent of hysterectomies are done to treat cancer of the uterine lining, ovaries, or cervix. The rest are performed to treat uncontrollable uterine bleeding, fibroids, endometriosis (in which tissue from the uterine lining escapes from the uterus and grows in other parts of the body), chronic pelvic pain, uterine prolapse (in which the uterus drops from its normal position into the vagina), and some precancerous conditions. No universally accepted criteria exist for when a hysterectomy is warranted. Unless your condition is potentially life threatening, talk to your physician about whether a hysterectomy is really necessary. It's always a good idea to get a second opinion. The fact that hysterectomy rates are far higher in the southern United States compared with the northeastern states and other countries such as the United Kingdom suggests that factors unrelated to medical necessity may be at work.

Types of Hysterectomy

In an abdominal hysterectomy, the surgeon makes an incision several inches long in the abdominal wall, just above the pubic bone, and removes the uterus through the incision. In a vaginal hysterectomy, the uterus is removed through the vagina, via an incision made in the vaginal wall. In some cases, the surgeon may use a laparoscopic technique, which involves several small incisions in the abdomen and the insertion of a thin, flexible tube called a laparoscope to view the pelvic organs. The uterus is removed through one of the small inci-

INSOMNIA

Disrupted sleep is a common complaint during perimenopause. The ehot flashes and night sweats cause sleep disruption is not complete women report that they perspire so profusely that they soak the bed li up, while others sleep right through their hot flashes.

sions or through the vagina. Because of the smaller incisions, recovery tim scars are smaller. Hospitalization can be as short as one day.

The Hysterectomy Procedure

To prepare for the surgery, you will usually have general anesthesia. Your ai open with a small tube, and a catheter will be placed in your bladder. You'll an antibiotic to reduce the risk of infection. During the surgery, tissues that to the pelvic wall are cut, and the uterus is separated from the top of the va

In the United States, 55 percent of all women who have a hysterectomy- of those whose hysterectomy is performed between the ages of 45 and 54- ovaries surgically removed at the same time, a procedure known as *bilater* The ovaries are routinely removed in women with ovarian cancer or sus tumors. Women with a strong family history of, or genes for, certain types c ian cancer sometimes elect to have their ovaries removed to reduce their car with severe endometriosis also often have oophorectomy, both because es ovaries can promote the growth of any stray endometrial tissue and becaus the ovaries can spread to other organs. But in many other situations, there rationale for removing the ovaries. Oophorectomy can worsen menopausa increase a woman's susceptibility to osteoporosis and heart disease. For mo risks overshadow the benefit of reducing the risk of ovarian cancer, a relative

After the Surgery

You will no longer have menstrual periods, and you won't be able to becor you recuperate, give yourself time to heal physically and emotionally. Stud level of satisfaction among women who choose hysterectomy. But it is a pe and one that should be made after considering all the alternatives.

- Go to bed and get up at about the same time every day, even on weekends.

- Avoid heavy meals in the evening.

- Avoid alcohol in the evening and caffeine after noon.

- Exercise regularly, preferably in the morning or early afternoon. Habitual physical activity promotes sleep but can be stimulating if performed too close to bedtime.

- Don't overeat close to bedtime or go to bed hungry.

- Stop smoking.

- If hot flashes are a problem for you, don't take hot showers or baths before bed.

- Put aside the work of the day at least a half-hour before you want to sleep.

- Retire for the night only when you are sleepy. If it takes more than 10 to 15 minutes to fall asleep, get out of bed; then read in another room, and try again later.

- Use the bed only for sleep or sex.

- Keep the bedroom quiet, cool, and dark during your sleeping hours.

- Relieve stress and anxiety with exercise or relaxation techniques. Serious mood disorders, such as clinical depression, can powerfully disrupt sleep and may require treatment with psychotherapy or antidepressant medications.

- Seek treatment for other medical conditions that can disturb sleep, such as thyroid disorders, arthritis, sleep-disordered breathing (apnea), or restless legs syndrome. A sleep evaluation study may be needed to diagnose the latter two conditions.

Prescription medications are available for temporary treatment of insomnia but should generally not be taken for more than two to three weeks in a row. A trio of sleeping pills informally referred to as the Z drugs—zolpidem (Ambien), zaleplon (Sonata), and eszopiclone (Lunesta)—has risen rapidly in popularity, overtaking older medications known as benzodiazepines, including diazepam (Valium), lorazepam (Ativan), and temazepam (Restoril). Some benzodiazepines are also used to treat anxiety.

One of the problems with benzodiazepines is that people develop tolerance if the pills are taken for longer than 10 days. If you take them regularly, you may need to keep raising the dose to get the same effect. Benzodiazepines can also cause rebound insomnia (a recurrence of sleep problems after stopping the drug) and other withdrawal symptoms (for example, nightmares resulting from the drugs' interference with REM sleep, the time when we dream most vividly). The newer Z drugs bind more selectively to sleep-regulating receptors in the brain and disappear more quickly from the body, producing fewer side effects. In particular, they are less likely to cause tolerance, withdrawal symptoms, or rebound insomnia—although these and other side effects can crop up with long-term use. Ambien and Sonata should be taken for only one month at a stretch, but Lunesta has been approved by the U.S. Food and Drug Administration (FDA) for up to six months of nightly use. For most adults, the standard Lunesta dose is 2 to 3 milligrams at bedtime, although older women may do better with only 1 milligram. Its most common side effects are headache and a bitter taste in the mouth.

Melatonin supplements and valerian, an herbal therapy, have each been touted as more healthful ways to promote sleep, but rigorous long-term research on these products is lacking.

Does Menopausal Hormone Therapy Help?

If hot flashes and night sweats are keeping you from falling asleep or are awakening you during the night, treatment for these symptoms—including estrogen therapy—may improve your sleep. Among participants in the Heart and Estrogen/progestin Replacement Study (HERS) who reported trouble sleeping before treatment, a slightly higher proportion on hormone therapy (39 percent) than on placebo (33 percent) reported better sleep after one year.[16] (More findings from this seminal clinical trial are reviewed in later chapters.) Hormone therapy was also associated with a reduction in sleep problems among Women's Health Initiative participants aged 50 to 54 who were suffering from moderate-to-severe hot flashes at the start of the trial.[17]

MOOD SWINGS

Studies indicate that moodiness or mood swings—feeling calm and content one minute but anxious, irritable, depressed, or discouraged the next—seem to be more common in early perimenopause, when hormonal fluctuations are most erratic, than in the years following menopause, when ovarian hormones stabilize at a low level. However, these emotional changes do not usually meet the criteria for a formal diagnosis of major depression, a far more profound and disabling state. Although women who have suffered from episodes of major depression earlier in life may be more vulnerable to recurrences during perimenopause, women without such a history are no more likely to develop major depression during these years than at other times of life.

Stressful life circumstances, rather than hormonal changes, seem to be the major drivers of mood symptoms during the menopausal transition. Although most of us have had to deal with various curveballs that life throws at us at earlier ages, we may nevertheless feel ill equipped to face the multiple challenges that can arise at midlife, such as chronic illness in oneself or a family member; a floundering marriage, divorce, or widowhood; shifting relationships with adolescent or adult children; concerns about aging parents and increased caregiver responsibilities; career stress; financial pressures and setting aside money for retirement; and coming to grips with the realization that life is not infinite.

Treating Mood Swings

Many women choose to make lifestyle changes before turning to medications. Seek a better balance between self-nurturing activities and the demands of family and work. Participating in enjoyable activities, getting more sleep, exercising regularly, and practicing stress-reduction techniques can all help even out your mood. Herbal approaches such as the use of Saint-John's-wort or ginseng may also have mood-stabilizing effects. However, these and other herbs are not without risks. Kava, for example, had been used to treat stress and mood changes but has recently been linked to liver damage and has now fallen out of favor. Prescription antidepressants, including the SSRIs, do largely work as advertised, but they are not effective for everyone. Increasingly, doctors are also prescribing antiseizure drugs (such as Neurontin) alone or in combination with SSRIs to treat patients with anxiety disorders.

Does Menopausal Hormone Therapy Help?

Although observational studies have suggested that menopausal hormone therapy can lift or calm one's mood, results of clinical trials provide only limited support for this notion. For example, hormone therapy did not reduce depressive symptoms or improve general mental health among the women participating in the HERS[16] or WHI[17,18] trials. Even when researchers focused only on those participants who reported hot flashes or night sweats at the start of the study, hormone therapy appeared to help only in HERS but not in the WHI.

MEMORY AND CONCENTRATION PROBLEMS

During perimenopause, women often complain of short-term memory problems and difficulty with concentration. Some of these complaints may be caused by age, not fluctuating hormone levels. However, some aspects of perimenopause—stress over heavy bleeding, constant severe hot flashes, loss of sleep, or mood swings—can certainly contribute to scattered thinking, as can excessive worry about memory itself. Relax, you're not the first person to walk into a room or dial a phone number only to forget for what or whom you were looking. It happens to a lot of us. In most cases, slight aging-related declines in memory do not mean that you are destined for more serious cognitive difficulties such as Alzheimer's disease.

Treating Memory and Concentration Problems

Just as physical activity keeps your body strong, mental activity keeps your mind sharp and agile. If you take on new and interesting cognitive challenges, your brain will continue to grow—literally. Regardless of age, an active brain produces new dendrites—connections between nerve cells that allow the cells to communicate with one another. This helps the brain store and retrieve information more easily, no matter how old you are. Play Scrabble, bridge, or chess, or do crossword or Sudoku puzzles. Learn a new musical instrument, sport, or language, or learn how to use the computer or a new software program. Read more books. Stay informed about what's going on in the world. Maintain an active social connection to family and friends, or expand your network by volunteering in your community. The idea is to challenge your mind in new ways.

If you're worried about your memory, you may also be interested to learn of an emerging theme in medical research that can be succinctly summarized as "what's good for the heart is, in most cases, also good for the brain." I will return to this theme in later chapters, but accumulating research, much of it conducted within the past 15 years, show that strategies long known to keep heart disease at bay, such as remaining physically active; maintaining a healthy body weight; eating a nutritionally balanced diet; avoiding smoking; and controlling cholesterol, blood pressure, and blood sugar levels, may also help ward off the onset of memory and other cognitive problems.

You may also find it helpful to deal with the information overload of everyday life that we all experience by using the following memory triggers:

- Write things down. Keep a diary, use calendars, make lists—and refer to them often.

- Establish daily routines. Store easy-to-lose items, such as keys, in the same place.

- Set up cues. When boiling water, use a whistling instead of a silent tea kettle. When cooking or baking, wear a timer that clips onto your clothes. The number of times these simple steps have prevented house fires is probably higher than you might suspect.

- Practice repetition. To help remember a person's name, work it into the conversation several times after being introduced.

Various herbal therapies, most notably ginseng, have been advocated by naturopaths for improving mental acuity, but research to support these claims is lacking.

Does Menopausal Hormone Therapy Help?

Whether or not hormone therapy helps with memory and concentration problems is controversial and may depend on when therapy is started; I review the evidence in Chapter 4.

LOW SEXUAL DESIRE

Sex drive may decline at midlife for a variety of reasons. Diminished estrogen or age-related changes in circulation may reduce blood flow to the genitals and cause a decrease in sensation. As discussed previously, vaginal dryness or thinning can make intercourse painful. And women who have sleep problems may feel too fatigued to be interested in sex. Urinary incontinence may cause embarrassment that diminishes the appeal of sex. Concern about changes in physical appearance and body image can also reduce sex drive.

Sex drive may be more closely associated with testosterone than with estrogen, and it's long been assumed that low blood testosterone levels lead to low sexual desire in both men and women. However, studies published within the past year cast doubt on that assumption. The SWAN study found only a weak link between blood androgen levels and sexual function in U.S. women aged 42 to 52,[19] and a survey of more than 1,000 Australian women ranging in age from 18 to 75 found no link at all.[20] Our understanding of female sexuality remains incomplete. One fact is incontrovertible, though—many women continue to have fulfilling sex lives for decades after menopause.

Treating Low Sexual Desire

It's important to realize that libido isn't driven by hormones alone. Lifelong perceptions of sex and the quality of her current relationship also have a profound impact on a woman's sexual function at midlife. Some women may lack a partner. Some have partners who are emotionally distant or who are themselves suffering from sexual dysfunction; these factors may play a role in a woman's declining interest in sex. Talking with your partner about each of your needs and expectations can go a long way toward solving this problem. Counseling with a trained sex therapist can help open the lines of communication.

Does Menopausal Hormone Therapy Help?

There is little evidence to suggest that reduced sex drive in and of itself is improved by menopausal estrogen therapy. In fact estrogen, at least when taken in pill form, can even lead to a reduction in the amount of testosterone that is available to the body because of its effect on a binding protein. Testosterone therapy is a potential option for boosting sex drive; however, the FDA to date has refused to endorse an experimental testosterone patch for women, citing a lack of long-term safety data. The patch and other drugs designed to enhance desire, sensation, or both are still under study. (See Chapter 5 for information on combined estrogen-testosterone hormone therapy.)

WEIGHT GAIN

Although weight gain at midlife is a significant issue for a lot of women, there's no clear evidence that it's a direct result of hormone changes or even a slowdown in metabolism as we age. In the SWAN study, there was no link between menopausal status per se and weight gain or an expanding waistline.[21] Instead, the classic middle-age spread seemed to stem from a variety of factors, including the fact that older women are simply less physically active than their younger counterparts. Indeed, one clinical trial has demonstrated that weight gain during the menopausal transition is not inevitable and can be prevented by diet and exercise.[22] In that trial, pre- and perimenopausal women aged 44 to 50 were randomly assigned to a lifestyle intervention of reduced calories and saturated fat plus increased physical activity or to assessment only. After five years, during which time many of the women became menopausal, 55 percent of those in the lifestyle intervention group were at or below the weight at which they started the trial, compared with only 26 percent of the women in the control group.

Treating Overweight

To prevent weight gain at midlife, the best strategy is to eat sensibly and exercise regularly. Weigh yourself at least once per week, measure your waistline once per month, and make small adjustments in your diet or exercise routine to nip any increases in weight or waist size in the bud. Consider using a pedometer to guide and monitor your activity program. Losing excess weight that you've been carrying around for years—and keeping it off—presents more of a challenge, but it can be done, especially if you set yourself modest goals. If you're overweight, even a 5- to 10-pound weight loss will almost certainly translate into measurable health improvements—a greatly improved cardiovascular risk profile, for example (see Chapter 6). From a health perspective, there is no question that it's better to strive for and maintain a small weight loss than to aim for a more lofty—and perhaps unrealistic—goal.

Does Menopausal Hormone Therapy Help?

The best available data suggest that menopausal hormone therapy has little effect on weight—that is, it neither prevents nor promotes weight loss. A review of 22 small clinical trials found no consistent effect of menopausal hormone therapy on body weight.[23] In the three-year Postmenopausal Estrogen/Progestin Interventions (PEPI) trial, the weights and waist sizes of women assigned to estrogen with or without progestin crept up slightly less, on average, than those of women assigned to placebo.[24] (Other findings from this important study are discussed in later chapters.) And during the first year of the WHI, women assigned to estrogen plus progestin,[25] though not estrogen alone,[26] were slightly more likely to lose weight and inches around their waist compared to women assigned to placebo. But the differences between the hormone and placebo groups were quite small—on the order of two pounds of body weight and a half inch of waist size over three years in PEPI, for example.

URINARY INCONTINENCE

Between 30 and 40 percent of women aged 50 to 64 suffer from urinary incontinence, compared with, at most, 5 percent of similarly aged men. The disproportionate impact on women is from the effects of vaginal childbirth on pelvic tissues and basic anatomical differences between the two genders.

Decreased estrogen may cause or contribute to thinning in the lining of the urethra, the tube that empties urine from the bladder. With age, the surrounding pelvic muscles may also weaken. Problems may include a more frequent need to urinate; a sudden urge to urinate even though your bladder is not full; the inability to hold your urine in time to get to a toilet; urine leakage when sneezing, coughing, or laughing; or pain during urination. Painful urination is often a result of a urinary tract infection.

Treating Incontinence

Bladder training may be useful for urge incontinence. This entails holding urine for five minutes after feeling the urge to void and increasing the holding period by five minutes each week. Pelvic floor exercises, also known as Kegel exercises, are also effective. They involve repeatedly contracting and releasing the pelvic floor muscles used ordinarily to halt urination. Eliminating diuretic beverages such as coffee, tea, and alcohol, as well as citrus juice and other bladder irritants, may also help. Talk with your healthcare provider about other treatment options, including medications and surgery. If necessary, request a referral to a urogynecologist, a specialist in the incontinence issues facing women.

Does Menopausal Hormone Therapy Help?

Clinical trials show that estrogen therapy may prevent recurring urinary tract infections in women with a history of them. However, hormone therapy did not prevent urinary tract infections in HERS women without prior urinary tract infections.[27]

Although estrogen therapy was previously believed to help incontinence, the latest research suggests that this isn't the case—and that the opposite might be true, at least for conventional doses of oral estrogen. In the Nurses' Health Study, current use of estrogen with or without progestin was strongly predictive of an increased risk of urinary incontinence.[28] After the hormones were stopped, the risk dropped rapidly, and after 10 years it was similar to that of women who had never taken hormone therapy. In the WHI[29] and HERS[30, 31] trials, estrogen therapy with or without a progestin rapidly increased the risk of developing urinary incontinence and worsened the symptoms of women who were already incontinent. However, a trial of low-dose transdermal estrogen taken for two years found that it did not affect the onset or frequency of urinary incontinence.[32]

SKIN CHANGES AND WRINKLES

Many women develop dry, wrinkly, or sagging skin at midlife. While some research suggests that a decline in estrogen may contribute to these problems, it is unlikely to be the primary culprit. Skin aging is largely determined by your genes and is hastened by years of overexposure to the sun and by cigarette smoke.

Preventing and Treating Skin Problems

Protect your skin from the sun with sunscreen, hats, and clothing. Quit smoking. Use moisturizers, especially in the dry winter months. Buying a moisturizer is one case in which the old adage "you get what you pay for" doesn't hold true. Inexpensive moisturizers are often equal or superior to high-end products. Some evidence suggests that loss of facial bone structure contributes to wrinkle and sags, so following guidelines to optimize the health of your bones (see Chapter 6) may also help your skin.

Does Menopausal Hormone Therapy Help?

Small trials suggest that menopausal hormone therapy increases the thickness of the skin and its collagen and water content,[33] and larger trials have also shown that hormone therapy prevents bone loss at the hip and spine, although its effect on facial bones hasn't been examined. Whether these physiologic changes translate into a noticeable reduction in skin wrinkling or sagging—or produce other cosmetic improvements—is unclear, however. One national U.S. survey in which 3,400 menopausal women were examined by dermatologists did find that skin dryness and wrinkling were less common in those taking estrogen than in those who were not, even after factoring out the effects of age, obesity, sun exposure, and smoking.[34] More data are needed to confirm these results.

HEADACHES

Hormonal changes have been linked with headaches. It's not uncommon to hear younger women complain of "menstrual migraines" around the time of their periods, and some women who get migraine headaches say their migraines improve during pregnancy. Experts believe that changes in estrogen levels in the blood, rather than a consistently low level, may trigger migraines. The erratic hormonal fluctuations that precede menopause can make some perimenopausal women especially susceptible to migraines.

Headaches of all kinds can be triggered by a number of factors, including smoke and pollen, alcohol, sleep deprivation, certain foods such as chocolate and aged cheeses, or stress. These triggers may be more likely to induce a headache when hormone levels are fluctuating. Women who have had frequent menstrual headaches may find that the problem worsens during perimenopause. However, some women say their headaches get better or even stop after menopause.

Treating Headaches

Treatment depends on the cause and type of headache. Identifying headache triggers and taking steps to avoid them is a good first step. Talk with your healthcare provider about which kind of medication may be best to treat your kind of headache. Some women find other techniques such as biofeedback or acupuncture to be helpful.

Does Menopausal Hormone Therapy Help?

Hormone therapy sometimes alleviates the problem and sometimes makes it worse. Women's responses to hormone therapy in relation to headache tend to vary greatly. Little research has been done on this subject and more is needed.

3

THE RISE AND FALL AND (CAUTIOUS) RETURN OF HORMONE THERAPY

◉

Once prescribed primarily to cool the hot flashes and dry the night sweats of menopause—two things that it is very effective at doing—hormone therapy (formerly called hormone replacement therapy, or HRT) has for several decades also been promoted as a strategy to forestall many diseases that we associate with aging and that tend to accelerate after menopause, including heart disease, memory disorders, and osteoporosis. Indeed, more than two of five menopausal women in the United States were taking hormone therapy in 2001.[1] In addition, it was becoming increasingly common for doctors to begin prescribing hormone therapy for women in their 60s and 70s and even for women with a diagnosis of angina (chest pain) or previous heart attack. So strong was the belief that estrogen protected the heart and that women of all ages could benefit, many women were being started on hormone therapy 20 to 30 years after the onset of menopause. This widespread use was unwarranted, especially among older women, given the lack of conclusive data on the long-term health consequences of such therapy.

Recent results from the Women's Health Initiative (WHI), a major national clinical trial of hormone therapy in healthy women who were on average more than a decade past menopause, not only appear to refute the idea that supplemental estrogen keeps the heart healthy in older women but also suggest that, when taken in combination with a progestogen (as it normally is to protect against endometrial cancer), it may actually *increase* the risk of heart disease. Moreover, the WHI findings indicate that supplemental estrogen offers no protection against chronic disease overall, and that the health risks associated with estrogen-plus-progestin therapy may outweigh the benefits. However, very few women in the WHI were newly menopausal (within five years of menopause), so the study could not conclusively address the benefits and risks of hormone therapy in that group.

When the first of these unexpected results was announced in July 2002, physicians and other healthcare providers across the country were deluged with calls from frantic patients asking, "What went wrong? I thought hormones were supposed to be good for me—not just relieve my symptoms but keep me healthy!" and, even more urgently, "What do I do about hormone therapy now?" And many doctors found themselves unprepared to provide satisfactory answers to these questions.

It's important not to judge these physicians too harshly. Yes, some were unprepared simply because they had not critically examined the earlier scientific data underlying the belief that hormones were "healthy" for women of all ages and risk-factor status. But others were unprepared because balancing the benefits and risks of hormone therapy for any particular patient can challenge even the most knowledgeable of healthcare providers, including those with a nuanced understanding of the strengths and weaknesses of the existing research.

In this chapter, I'll review how medical research works and how medical thinking regarding menopause hormones has evolved over time—or, as billed in the title, the rise and fall and (cautious) return of hormone therapy. The material covered here is a useful prelude to the detailed look at what we know today about the health benefits and risks of supplemental estrogen that is presented in the next chapter.

What Different Kinds of Studies Tell Us

A brief explanation of the types of studies that contribute to the advance of medical knowledge will help you understand how we reached the crisis of confidence about hormone therapy, after years of widespread belief that it was beneficial for most women.

Laboratory studies, also known as *basic* or *experimental research*, investigate the effects of a given intervention on animals, body cells from animals, or body cells from humans. Such studies allow for far greater control than studies of human beings, but results from animals or cells in tightly regulated environments may not always apply directly to actual people living in the real world. Nevertheless, laboratory studies often provide important insights into whether and how a purported medical treatment might work in humans.

Studies of people living in the real world are known as *epidemiologic studies*. The two main types of epidemiologic studies are observational studies and randomized clinical trials.

In an *observational study*, researchers observe study participants and record their characteristics, behaviors, use of medications, and health outcomes but do not otherwise intervene in the participants' lives. This type of study uncovers possible relationships between various "exposures" and diseases, but it cannot prove a cause-and-effect link. Two common subtypes of observational studies are case-control studies and cohort studies.

Case-control studies gather histories from a group of people who have developed a particular disease (the cases) and a similar group of people who are free of that disease (the controls) and compare the two groups to look for factors that might have contributed to the development of disease. The information is obtained by questioning the subjects or their family members about their history or by reviewing medical, employment, or other archival records. Case-control studies are an efficient way to study connections between exposures and chronic diseases, which usually take many years to develop. However, having a disease may color the participants' recall of their behaviors and use of medications, which can distort results.

Cohort studies assemble a group of people who typically have some characteristic in common, such as occupation, place of residence, or menopausal status. Unlike a case-control study, none of the participants in a cohort study has the disease of interest at the start of the study. The group is then followed over time via periodic checkups or mailed questionnaires, or by monitoring death certificates, to see who develops the disease. Once enough time has elapsed, researchers can examine the information to test a variety of hypotheses concerning the development of disease. By gathering exposure information from participants before the disease has occurred, cohort studies avoid the problems of faulty recall that can sometimes affect case-control studies.

Both cohort and case-control studies have suggested major health benefits of hormone therapy, including reductions in heart disease and hip fractures, but have also suggested major risks, such as an increased chance of breast cancer and stroke. It's because of these results that most healthcare providers have for many years cautioned women who were already at higher-than-average risk for breast cancer or stroke not to choose hormone therapy.

However, observational studies are open to the criticism that the apparent benefits seen in these studies may simply reflect the fact that women who choose to use hormone therapy tend to be healthier, have greater access to medical care, and embrace health-promoting habits, such as eating a nutritious diet and exercising regularly, more readily than women who do not choose to use hormones. In short, the argument goes, it's not that taking estrogen promotes health, it's that being healthy promotes the taking of estrogen. To address this concern, researchers typically use statistical techniques to factor out the effect of variables, such as age, diet, physical activity, smoking, and so forth, that may vary between hormone users and nonusers. This strategy is effective, though not perfect, because it's impossible to anticipate, measure, and account for all the factors that could conceivably distort, or confound, the relationship between an exposure and disease. So there's always some possibility that the results are at least partially due to external factors (so-called "confounders") rather than the exposure of interest.

Enter the *randomized clinical trial*, which is less susceptible to this so-called "healthy-user" bias than observational studies. In a clinical trial, whose purpose is often to test a particular medical treatment, researchers actively intervene in participants' lives by assigning them to the therapy under investigation or to a control group. The most rigorous type of trial—the "gold standard" by which all other studies are usually judged—is the randomized, placebo-controlled, double-blinded clinical trial. In these carefully controlled studies, half of a group of volunteers is assigned at random—via a figurative flip of the coin—to an active treatment (a drug, for example), and the other half is assigned to something that looks like the drug but is in fact an inactive placebo (often called a dummy or sugar pill). Neither the doctors conducting the trial nor the participants knows who is getting the medication and who is getting the placebo—hence the term "double-blinded." The double-blinding ensures that the doctors do not treat the participants differently, and that the patients themselves do not behave differently, based on knowledge of their treatment status.

After a predetermined amount of time, the number of people in the treatment group who have developed the outcome ("endpoint") being studied—for example, death, heart attack, hip fracture, or, as we saw in the last chapter, hot flashes and other symptoms—is compared with the number in the placebo group who have developed the same outcome. If the trial is large enough, the randomization process ensures that the people in the treatment group are virtually identical to those in the placebo group in terms of age, lifestyle, general health, menopausal status, and other possibly important factors. Because the only characteristic that differs between the two groups is the treatment under investigation, it is extremely likely that any difference in health outcomes found in the two groups is attributable to that treatment. This is the main advantage of a randomized clinical trial over an observational study.

Understanding the basic distinction between observational studies and clinical trials will take you a long way in interpreting epidemiologic data. But many other issues must be considered when evaluating scientific research. Indeed, a well-designed observational study can be better than a poorly designed clinical trial for arriving at a sound scientific conclusion. Although this list is not exhaustive, the elements of a good study, whether an observational study or clinical trial, include the following factors.

• **A representative study population:** A study of a particular therapy may be of limited value if the study participants are not typical of the general public who use that therapy. As an extreme example, the first clinical trial of supplemental estrogen to reduce heart disease was actually conducted in men, not women. Because sex hormones differ dramatically between men and women, it's unlikely that the results of such a study in one gender will apply to the other. (The trial showed clearly that estrogen didn't help men, but the story is more complex in women.)

• **Use of actual disease outcomes:** Because it often takes many years for chronic diseases to develop, many studies look at intermediate changes, such as changes in blood levels of cholesterol, changes in bone density, or proliferation of the uterine lining, as proxies for the actual disease of interest, such as a heart attack, osteoporotic bone fractures, or endometrial cancer. However, these changes do not inevitably reflect or lead to changes in the actual disease outcome. Research looking at concrete disease outcomes such as heart attacks is more convincing and reliable.

• **Large number of participants (size matters!):** The larger the study, the smaller the possibility that its findings—whether positive, negative, or neutral—might have resulted by chance alone. The play of chance is such an important issue that scientists routinely employ sophisticated numerical methods to assess whether a study finding is "statistically significant"—that is, unlikely to have occurred simply by chance.

• **Consistency of the evidence:** Consistency is actually not a characteristic of one particular study, but rather of the whole body of research on any given topic. Perhaps the most convincing evidence that an effect may be real is consistent results from a number of researchers at different times, using different study designs, and involving different groups of people. An example would be the connection between cigarette smoking and lung cancer that's been seen in so many different studies. But keep in mind that scientific research progresses in fits and starts, and there is rarely a straight-line path to the right answer or a complete absence of conflicting findings. Indeed, the progress of medical knowledge has been compared to the stock market—sometimes it goes up, sometimes down, but in the long run, the trend is (hopefully) in the right direction.

In the case of hormone therapy, a roller-coaster analogy, at first glance, might seem more appropriate because the ride ends up right back where it started. In a narrow sense, as we will see, this is true: the original reason for taking menopausal hormones—for relief of menopausal symptoms—is, for most women, still the only compelling reason for taking them today. In a larger sense, however, the roller-coaster analogy falls short, because researchers have made great strides, especially in the last decade, in understanding the impact of hormone therapy on many aspects of women's health beyond the relief of symptoms.

Incidentally, keeping these research principles in mind will help you be an educated consumer of the health news reported by the media, which tends to magnify the importance and implications of new studies, especially those that contradict common conceptions, while sometimes glossing over their limitations or failing to provide a context for the research.

A Brief History of Hormone Therapy

In the 1920s, scientists identified the chemical structure of the major female sex hormones estrogen and progesterone. Within a decade, supplemental estrogen became commercially available, and, in 1942, the U.S. Food and Drug Administration (FDA) approved Premarin, a type of estrogen extracted from the urine of pregnant mares, to treat hot flashes and other symptoms of menopause. (Technically known as *conjugated equine estrogen*, or CEE for short, Premarin remains the most widely prescribed menopause hormone even today.) In 1960, birth control pills, which use synthetic sex hormones to block ovulation and prevent pregnancy, came on the market and were quickly embraced by women as a convenient form of contraception, thus habituating many women to the idea of taking supplemental hormones.

The 1966 publication of Dr. Robert Wilson's *Feminine Forever* also did much to popularize hormone therapy for menopausal women. The cover of this bestselling book, written for a general audience of women, proclaimed it to be "a fully documented discussion of one of medicine's most revolutionary breakthroughs—the discovery that menopause is a *hormone deficiency disease, curable and totally preventable.*" Relying heavily on anecdotal evidence, Wilson promoted estrogen therapy not simply for the relief of hot flashes and other symptoms of the menopause transition, but also as a way of retaining the bloom, vitality, and optimism of youth. Menopausal women who chose not to use estrogen risked becoming asexual and unattractive—in Wilson's words, "prematurely aging castrates," not to mention neurotic and a blight to society: "The transformation, within a few years, of a formerly pleasant, energetic woman into a dull-minded but sharp-tongued caricature of her former self is one of the saddest of human spectacles. The suffering is not hers alone—it involves her entire family, her business associates, her neighborhood storekeepers, and all others with whom she comes in contact. Multiplied by millions, she is a focus of bitterness and discontent in our whole fabric of civilization."

Although Wilson's focus was primarily on sexual, psychological, and cosmetic concerns, he also addressed chronic diseases, asserting that, without supplemental estrogen, women will invariably develop osteoporosis and dismissing nascent concerns that estrogen use might cause cancer. Although it is not clear how widely the views of this 71-year-old gynecologist were shared by others in the medical community, the book struck a chord with his target audience of menopausal women, and Wyeth-Ayerst, the manufacturer of Premarin, seized upon the book—and its message that to be feminine forever, one must take estrogen forever—as a great marketing opportunity, handing it out to physicians at medical conferences and funding Wilson's lectures to women's groups. More than 100,000 copies were sold within a few months of its release. As a result, sales of Premarin increased dramatically.

In 1975, observational studies revealed a clear association between estrogen use and endometrial cancer (cancer of the uterine lining), undercutting Wilson's claim that hormones were safe. Estrogen sales promptly plummeted, although the hormone was still routinely prescribed for women who had had a hysterectomy.

In the early 1980s, to counteract the carcinogenic effect of estrogen in women with a uterus, doctors began adding synthetic forms of progesterone, known as progestins, to hormone regimens. A commonly used progestin was Provera (medroxyprogesterone acetate). To replicate the natural hormonal cycling during women's reproductive years, estrogen was originally prescribed throughout the month while progestin was taken only for the last 10 to 14 days, but this cyclic dosing led to bleeding that mimicked menstrual periods, which many menopausal women found annoying. To eliminate this side effect (at least in part—many women still had slight bleeding or spotting), doctors began recommending that women take both estrogen and progestin continuously throughout the month. In the mid-1990s, Wyeth-Ayerst introduced Prempro, a combination pill containing both conjugated equine estrogen and medroxyprogesterone acetate, into the marketplace. Taking a progestin along with the estrogen largely eliminated the excess risk of endometrial cancer associated with estrogen use.

Despite the endometrial cancer setback, hormone therapy quickly regained steam when research suggested it could help prevent chronic diseases associated with aging. Doctors began prescribing it not only for menopausal symptoms but for disease prevention as well. With life expectancy climbing, bone health emerged as a major public health issue, as research revealed that the complications following hip fracture were often deadly among older women. Observational studies found that hormone therapy, if taken over the long term, might postpone the onset of thinning and weakened bones. At the same time, there was a growing realization that women were at risk for heart disease (long considered a primarily male affliction), and observational studies also suggested that hormone therapy might lower that risk by about 35 to 50 percent.

The connection made biological sense. As women and men age, the gender gap in heart attack narrows, a phenomenon traditionally attributed to women's declining estrogen levels (see Figure 3.1). Women have low heart attack rates before menopause but much higher rates afterward, and several studies suggested that women whose ovaries have been surgically removed at a young age have a heightened risk for heart disease. In addition to the observational studies, laboratory studies dating back to the 1950s suggested estrogen could prevent atherosclerosis and improve blood circulation in animals fed a high-fat diet. And small clinical trials in women had found that administration of oral estrogen led to favorable changes in cholesterol and other components in the blood known to affect risk of heart disease.

Thus, the totality of the evidence, albeit indirect, that estrogen therapy might prevent heart disease in women seemed compelling. However, when Wyeth-Ayerst, the pharmaceutical company that manufactures Premarin, petitioned the FDA to allow the drug to be marketed for the prevention of heart disease in women, the agency refused to grant permission, citing the lack of data from well-designed randomized clinical trials to support that claim. And, even though rosy data about heart and bone effects were mounting, observational studies had also begun to suggest that women who took supplemental estrogen for long periods of time faced an increased risk for breast cancer. Together, these events (see Figure 3.2) provided the impetus for the launch of the Women's Health Initiative in the early 1990s, perhaps the largest and most ambitious study of its kind.

Figure 3.1 Annual Number of Heart Attacks, by Age and Sex, in the United States

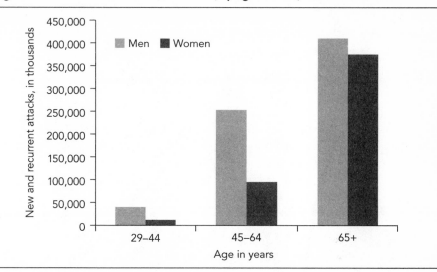

From American Heart Association, Heart Disease and Stroke Statistics—2005 Update. *Dallas: American Heart Association, 2005. (with permission)*

LANDMARK STUDIES OF HORMONE THERAPY

The 1990s marked not only the initiation of the WHI but also the emergence of other groundbreaking research on hormone therapy that rigorously tested various hypotheses that had been percolating in earlier decades. Throughout the rest of the book, I will discuss these influential studies in terms of how they might shape your decision about whether to use hormone therapy. These studies, listed here, were conducted in the United States under the auspices of the National Institutes of Health, a government agency responsible for promoting medical research.

Nurses' Health Study

Information from the Nurses' Health Study and other cohort studies formed the basis of much medical thinking about hormones before the results of major clinical trials became available, and these studies continue to generate invaluable data on the topic even today. The observational Nurses' Health Study began in 1976 when

Figure 3.2 Hormone Therapy History: Timeline of Key Events

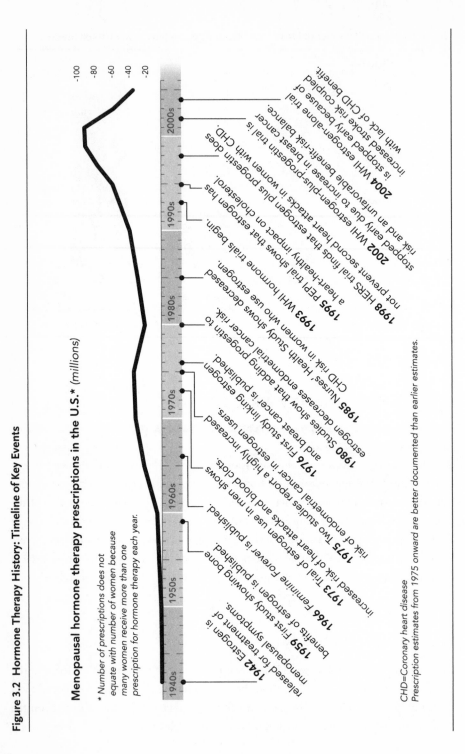

Menopausal hormone therapy prescriptions in the U.S.* (millions)

*Number of prescriptions does not equate with number of women because many women receive more than one prescription for hormone therapy each year.

1942 Estrogen is released for treatment of menopausal symptoms.

1959 First study showing bone benefits of estrogen is published.

1966 Feminine Forever is published.

1973 Trial of estrogen showing increased risk of heart attacks and blood clots.

1975 Two studies report a highly increased risk of endometrial cancer in estrogen users.

1976 First study linking estrogen and breast cancer is published.

1980 Studies show that adding progestin to estrogen decreases endometrial cancer risk.

1985 Nurses' Health Study shows decreased CHD risk in women who use estrogen.

1993 WHI hormone trials begin.

1995 PEPI trial shows that estrogen has a heart-healthy impact on cholesterol.

1998 HERS trial finds that estrogen plus progestin does not prevent second heart attacks in women with CHD.

2002 WHI estrogen-plus-progestin trial is stopped early due to increase in breast cancer risk and an unfavorable benefit-risk balance.

2004 WHI estrogen-alone trial is stopped early because of increased stroke risk coupled with lack of CHD benefit.

CHD=Coronary heart disease

Prescription estimates from 1975 onward are better documented than earlier estimates.

121,700 U.S. female registered nurses between the ages of 30 and 55 returned completed questionnaires about risk factors for cardiovascular disease and cancer. For the past three decades, the participants have completed follow-up questionnaires every two years to update information on their health; diet, exercise, and other daily habits; smoking; use of oral contraceptives; and, as the study population grew older, use of menopausal hormones. Because the participants are medically savvy, they likely report exposures and health outcomes with a high degree of accuracy.

In this cohort, more than 80 percent of the women who chose to take hormone therapy did so within four years of menopause. Among the approximately 70,000 menopausal nurses who were healthy at the start of follow-up, current users of hormone therapy were about 40 percent less likely than those who had never used menopause hormones to develop heart disease, after statistically factoring out the effects of important cardiac risk factors that differed between the groups such as age, body mass index, diabetes, high blood pressure, high cholesterol, age at menopause, smoking, and parental history of premature heart disease.[2]

Postmenopausal Estrogen/Progestin Interventions (PEPI) Trial

Conducted at seven centers in the United States, the Postmenopausal Estrogen/ Progestin Interventions (PEPI) trial assigned 875 healthy menopausal women aged 45 to 64 (their average age was 56) to a three-year course of conjugated equine estrogen—with or without one of three types of progestogen—or to a placebo, to test the effect of these hormones on variables that influence the risk for heart disease and bone mass. In early 1995, the PEPI trial reported that estrogen improved some risk factors for heart disease—most notably, raising HDL cholesterol and lowering LDL cholesterol levels (see Chapter 4)—and that certain types of progestogen counteracted these effects more than others.[3] However, the study was not large enough to assess concrete disease endpoints, so it was impossible to say whether these hormone-related improvements would subsequently translate into a lower rate of heart attack or bone fractures.

Heart and Estrogen/Progestin Replacement Study (HERS)

Conducted at 20 centers in the United States, the Heart and Estrogen/progestin Replacement Study (HERS) tested the effect of conjugated equine estrogen plus progestin on the cardiovascular health of 2,763 menopausal women with a history of heart disease. This seminal *secondary prevention* trial found that hormone use did not prevent recurrent heart attacks or other coronary events, even though HDL cholesterol was increased by 10 percent and LDL cholesterol was reduced by 11 percent.[4] (Secondary prevention means treating persons who already have a particular disease to try to prevent the problem from recurring or worsening.) Indeed, the risk of heart attacks and heart-related deaths actually increased by 50 percent in the first year of the trial, although the elevated risk was offset by a decreased risk during the last two years of treatment. Women using hormone therapy also had an increased risk of blood clots in the veins and lungs. After the trial ended, the participants were observationally followed for nearly three more years to see whether hormone use led to more favorable heart outcomes in the longer term—it didn't.[5] The medical community was somewhat taken aback by these findings, which were published in 1998, but the real shock was to come several years later, when results from the WHI were announced.

Women's Health Initiative (WHI)

The Women's Health Initiative (WHI) is perhaps the largest and most ambitious research project of its kind. Launched in 1991 by the National Institutes of Health, the WHI was designed to define the risks and benefits of strategies that could potentially decrease heart disease, osteoporotic fracture, and breast and colorectal cancer in menopausal women aged 50 to 79. It consists of a set of four clinical trials as well as an observational study, which, taken together, have enrolled 161,809 healthy menopausal women at 40 centers across the United States. In contrast to HERS, the WHI trials are *primary prevention* trials, meaning that they are testing treatments to prevent people from developing diseases that they do not already have. One trial primarily tested the impact of dietary modification—with a goal of reducing dietary fat to 20 percent of calories and increasing fruit and vegetables—on the development of breast cancer, and another trial tested whether calcium and vitamin D supplements lower the risk of osteoporotic fracture (these results are discussed in Chapter 6).

The remaining two trials examined the effect of menopausal hormone therapy—either estrogen plus progestin (for women with a uterus) or estrogen alone (for women with hysterectomy)—on heart disease, osteoporotic fracture, colorectal cancer, and other health outcomes, and whether the possible benefits on these outcomes would outweigh possible risks from breast cancer, endometrial cancer, and blood clots.

In the estrogen-plus-progestin trial, 16,608 menopausal women with an intact uterus were assigned to take Prempro (0.625 milligrams of conjugated equine estrogen plus 2.5 milligrams of medroxyprogesterone acetate) or a placebo daily. In the estrogen-alone trial, 10,739 menopausal women who had had a hysterectomy (40 percent also had their ovaries removed along with the uterus) were assigned to take Premarin (0.625 milligrams of conjugated equine estrogen) or a placebo daily. Prempro and Premarin were chosen for study because they contain the most commonly prescribed forms of estrogen plus progestin and estrogen alone in the United States, and, in several observational studies, including the Nurses' Health Study, these drugs appeared to benefit women's health. In addition, Wyeth-Ayerst, eager to obtain FDA approval to market these medications for the prevention of heart disease (and hopeful for a favorable outcome of the trials), was willing to donate more than 100 million pills to help defray the costs of this enormous undertaking.

The WHI hormone trials enrolled study participants between 1993 and 1998 and were originally slated to end in 2005. However, the estrogen-plus-progestin trial was halted in July 2002, after an average of 5.2 years of pill taking. Rather than the expected benefit on heart disease, there was in fact a 29 percent increase* in risk of heart attacks or other cardiac events among women assigned to the Prempro group compared with those assigned to the placebo group. In addition, women in the Prempro group were more likely to develop breast cancer, stroke, and blood clots in the lungs or legs. On the positive side, Prempro was also associated with fewer hip fractures, fewer total fractures, and fewer cases of colon cancer. On balance, however, the health risks outweighed the benefits.

When clinical trials are designed, researchers include "stopping rules" that mandate that the trial be terminated when the emerging data indicate that a treatment provides a clear harm or benefit. The reason for these stopping rules is to avoid additional harm to the women assigned to the drug or, in the case of benefit, to avoid depriving the women assigned to the placebo of the benefit of the drug, as

---

*Later found to be a 24 percent increase after a few more months of follow-up. Once the decision is made to stop a clinical trial, the participants need to be notified and their medical information needs to be collected; these steps may take several months. Thus, the initial publications from the WHI estrogen-plus-progestin and estrogen-alone trials are based on a few months' less follow-up than the trials actually lasted (5.6 years and 7.1 years, respectively).

well as to ensure that study results with clear public health implications are reported in a timely way. The trial was stopped three years ahead of schedule by the study's Data and Safety Monitoring Board, an independent panel charged with monitoring the health of study participants, because of the unambiguous increase in breast cancer risk and the unfavorable overall risk-benefit ratio associated with estrogen-plus-progestin therapy observed in the study population as a whole. These findings were reported in the July 17, 2002, issue of the *Journal of the American Medical Association*.[6]

The estrogen-only trial was terminated in April 2004 after 6.8 years because of an excess risk of stroke that was not offset by a reduced risk of coronary heart disease in the hormone group. Estrogen alone also offered no clear benefit in terms of reducing risk of chronic disease overall. The results appeared in the April 14, 2004, issue of the *Journal of the American Medical Association*.[7] The WHI will continue to follow participants observationally until 2010. Among the questions yet to be answered are if and when the risks and benefits decline after use of hormone therapy ends.

Fallout from the Women's Health Initiative Hormone Trials

The publication of the WHI estrogen-plus-progestin findings, indicating unexpected adverse effects on heart disease, shook the medical community's faith in hormone therapy. Fallout from the trial was immediate. Another large trial of hormone therapy, the Women's International Study of long Duration Oestrogen after Menopause (WISDOM), was just getting under way in the United Kingdom, Australia, and New Zealand and was to have enrolled 22,000 healthy menopausal participants aged 50 to 69 to be followed for 10 years. It was abruptly canceled by its British funding agency, the Medical Research Council, shortly after the disappointing estrogen-plus-progestin results of the WHI were announced. Worldwide, menopausal hormone use plummeted. In the United States, sales of Prempro fell 52 percent, and sales of all types of estrogen-plus-progestin pills dropped 40 percent between October 2001 and October 2002. Although the WHI findings on the health effects of Premarin had not yet been released, sales of estrogen-only pills also tumbled by 20 percent during this period.

But the WHI trials are not the final word on menopause hormones. Conducting a completely comprehensive study is impossible—there are simply too many factors to consider simultaneously. Although the WHI has provided us with much valuable information and will remain the gold standard of evidence for years to come, even this study has its limitations. For one thing, the WHI hormone trials tested only standard-dose Prempro and Premarin pills, so their results may not apply to other formulations, doses, or routes of administration (such as patches or creams) of estrogen and progestogen. For another, most of the participants were in their 60s and 70s—many years past the menopausal transition. (A primary aim of the trials was to examine the impact of hormone therapy on heart disease, so the WHI sought out older women because of their higher risk of developing this outcome.) Although the trials provided clear information about the benefits and risks of hormone therapy in women over age 60 and put a halt to the increasingly common practice of starting hormone therapy in this age group for the express purpose of preventing cardiovascular disease, I believe—and a growing number of medical experts agree—that the overall WHI findings may overstate the risks for healthy younger women (those in their 40s and 50s) who begin hormone therapy closer to the onset of menopause. And, as we will see in the next chapter, a second look at the data strongly supports this notion.

Indeed, since the release of the initial WHI findings, the precipitous drop in the use of hormone therapy has slowed to some degree. Although the 38.7 million prescriptions for menopause hormones of all types during the first eight months of 2005 was less than half the 79.5 million prescriptions during the same period in 2002, the rate of decline has slowed—prescriptions fell 25 percent in 2003, 16 percent in 2004, and 10 percent in 2005. The most striking trend has been a shift away from standard-dose Premarin and Prempro to other hormone therapies. Whereas sales of Premarin fell by 19 percent and regular-dose Prempro by 32 percent in the first eight months of 2005, sales of a low-dose version of Prempro rocketed 54 percent during this period. Prescriptions for the estrogen patch Vivelle-Dot increased by 12 percent, and the use of vaginal Premarin rose by 3 percent, reflecting an emerging, although as yet untested, belief that such treatments may carry less risk than traditional hormone pills. There are few trials on alternative hormone preparations, including "natural" or "bioidentical" estrogen and progesterone. The lack of data on these agents should not be construed to mean that they are safer or more effective at reducing chronic disease than Prempro and Premarin; it simply means that more research is needed to answer these questions.

4

HORMONE THERAPY: IS IT SAFE? EVALUATING THE BALANCE OF BENEFITS AND RISKS

◉

Hormone therapy has certainly had a bumpy history. But where does that leave women who are facing the decision about whether to start (or stop) hormones today? To help you decide whether hormone therapy is the right choice for you, let's examine the most up-to-date evidence from the best available research studies on the potential benefits and risks of such therapy among women at different phases of menopause and with different health conditions. These data provide the scientific basis—or, as researchers are fond of saying, "the evidence base"—for the hormone therapy decision-making tools presented in later chapters of this book.

I should alert you at the outset—this is the "numbers" chapter. Statistics flow fast and furious here, much more so than in the rest of the book. Diligent readers will be rewarded with a better understanding of the current state of knowledge about hormone therapy than many of their healthcare providers. But if you're experiencing information overload, you can simply skip to the "Bottom Line" summaries at the end of each section—I won't be offended. If you're especially interested in knowing what the evidence is regarding hormone therapy's relationship to a particular disease—more than a dozen diseases are covered here—you can read the relevant section more carefully.

As you work your way through the chapter, you'll also find it helpful to refer to Figures 4.1 and 4.2, which summarize the major findings from the WHI estrogen-plus-progestin and estrogen-alone trials, respectively. These figures present the major findings in the total study population, as well as separately by age group. Note the much lower rates of disease in younger women.

Figure 4.1 Estrogen-Plus-Progestin Therapy and Health Outcomes by Age: Women's Health Initiative

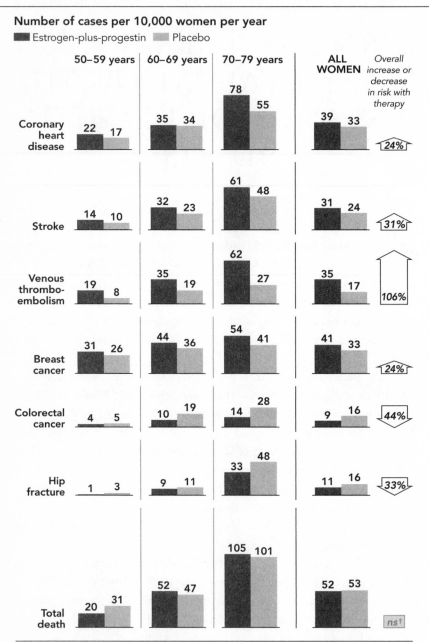

Number of cases per 10,000 women per year

† ns: No statistically significant difference between hormone therapy group and placebo group

Figure 4.2 Estrogen-Only Therapy and Health Outcomes by Age: Women's Health Initiative

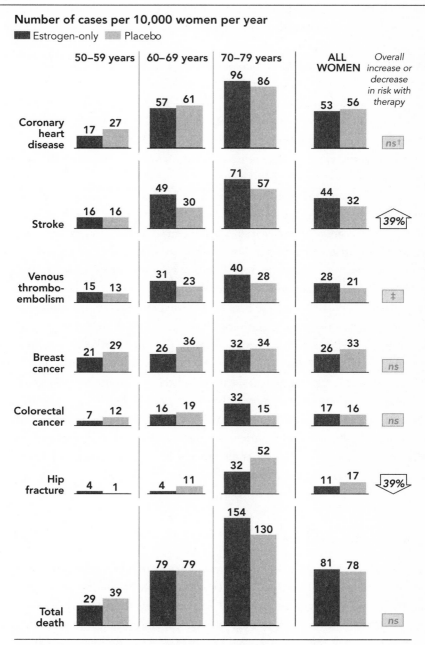

tns: No statistically significant difference between hormone therapy group and placebo group

‡Statistically significant for deep-vein thrombosis but not pulmonary embolism

CORONARY HEART DISEASE

Diseases of the blood vessels—coronary heart disease (CHD), stroke, and venous thromboembolism—are known collectively as cardiovascular disease. Each of these outcomes will be discussed in turn.

CHD is the number-one killer of women in most of the Western world. National statistics indicate that coronary heart disease affects three million women in the United States. In 2002 alone, an estimated 485,000 U.S. women had a heart attack or other coronary event, and nearly 242,000 died as a result. A 40-year-old woman has a one in three chance of developing CHD in her lifetime.

Until recently, much of the enthusiasm for menopausal hormone therapy had been due to the belief that it protected women's hearts; it was thought that this benefit would outweigh potential risks, such as breast cancer. During the past three decades, dozens of observational studies, including the Nurses' Health Study, have, in the aggregate, consistently suggested that women who take estrogen (with or without a progestogen) are 35 to 50 percent less likely to develop CHD than women who do not take menopause hormones. Yet randomized trials—most notably the Women's Health Initiative (WHI) and Heart and Estrogen/progestin Replacement Study (HERS)—have not confirmed the benefits reported in observational studies. In the WHI estrogen-plus-progestin trial, women with no history of heart disease who were randomly assigned to hormone therapy were 24 percent *more* likely to have a first heart attack or coronary death than their counterparts assigned to placebo.[1] In the WHI estrogen-only trial, women in the hormone-therapy group were about as likely to experience these events as women in the placebo group (i.e., there was no increase or decrease in risk).[2] And in the HERS trial, estrogen-plus-progestin therapy didn't protect women who had already suffered a heart attack from having a second one.[3, 4] Various explanations for the apparent discrepancy between the results from observational studies and those from clinical trials have been proposed.

The "Healthy-User" Bias

One oft-cited explanation is that women who choose to take menopause hormones tend to adhere more frequently to other types of health-promoting behaviors, such as exercising regularly and eating a healthy diet. They are therefore less likely to develop various illnesses than women who choose not to take hormones. It's also been suggested that they may have better access to medical care because hormone therapy requires visiting a doctor for a prescription. This "healthy-user" bias could obscure the true heart risk associated with menopause hormones in observational studies but would not be a problem in clinical trials because women are randomly assigned to hormone therapy. However, as shown in Table 4.1, there is strong agreement between findings from observational studies and clinical trials for many other outcomes. Some of these outcomes, most notably stroke, have similar lifestyle determinants as heart disease, arguing against healthy-user bias as the major explanation for the discrepancy in heart disease findings between clinical trials and observational studies.

So what might account for the conflicting findings? The possibilities fall into two categories—either differences in characteristics of women being studied, including body weight or age or time since menopause, or differences in the hormone therapies themselves might be responsible.

The Influence of Body Weight

One difference between hormone users in observational studies and those in clinical trials is that of body weight. The women who used hormones in the Nurses' Health Study and most other observational studies were significantly leaner than the women in the WHI.

After menopause, fat cells replace the ovaries as the body's single biggest producer of estrogen. Because their bodies tend to manufacture less estrogen than those of their heavier counterparts, lean women may be more likely to suffer from hot flashes and other menopausal symptoms, to opt for menopause hormones for symptom relief, and to benefit uniquely from such use. In the American Cancer Society's Cancer Prevention Study II, a 12-year observational follow-up of nearly 300,000 healthy menopausal women, estrogen use appeared to cut the risk of coronary death in half among the leanest women but to increase the risk by 45 percent in obese women.[5] In the estrogen-only trial of the WHI, my colleagues and I observed a similar (though less dramatic and not statistically significant) pattern; estrogen use reduced the risk of developing a coronary event by one-quarter in women with a healthy body weight but raised the risk by 10 percent in obese women. On the other hand, we found that body weight did not influence the association between hormone therapy and CHD in the WHI estrogen-plus-progestin trial. Nevertheless, the bulk of the evidence (no pun intended) suggests that hormone therapy is less likely to produce adverse heart effects in women who maintain a healthy body weight.

Table 4.1 Hormone Therapy and Health Outcomes: A Comparison of Results from the WHI Clinical Trials and Observational Studies

Outcome	Women's Health Initiative		Observational Studies	
Coronary heart disease	E+P:	▲ 24% increased risk	E+P:	▼ 36% decreased risk
	E-only:	▼ 5% decreased risk	E-only:	▼ 45% decreased risk
Stroke	E+P:	▲ 31% increased risk		▲ 12% increased risk†
	E-only:	▲ 39% increased risk		
Venous thromboembolism	E+P:	▲ 106% increased risk		▲ 110% increased risk†
	E-only:	▲ 33% increased risk		
Hip fracture	E+P:	▼ 33% decreased risk		▼ 25% decreased risk†
	E-only:	▼ 39% decreased risk		
Breast cancer	E+P:	▲ 24% increased risk	E+P:	No increase or decrease in risk (less than 5 yrs use) ▲ 63% increased risk (5 or more yrs use)
	E-only:	▼ 23% decreased risk	E-only:	No increase or decrease in risk (less than 5 yrs use) ▲ 35% increased risk (5 or more yrs use)
Endometrial cancer	E+P:	▼ 19% decreased risk	E+P:	▼ 20% decreased risk
	E-only:	Not applicable	E-only:	▲ 310% increased risk
Ovarian cancer	E+P:	▲ 58% increased risk	E+P:	No increase or decrease in risk (less than 4 yrs use)
	E-only:	Data not available	E-only:	▲ 80% increased risk (10 or more yrs use)
Colorectal cancer	E+P:	▼ 44% decreased risk		▼ 34% decreased risk†
	E-only:	▲ 8% increased risk		
Gallbladder removal	E+P:	▲ 67% increased risk		▲ 110% increased risk†
	E-only:	▲ 93% increased risk		
Dementia (among women age 65 and older)	E+P:	▲ 105% increased risk		▼ 34% decreased risk†
	E-only:	▲ 49% increased risk		
Type 2 diabetes	E+P:	▼ 21% decreased risk		▼ 20% decreased risk†
	E-only:	▼ 12% decreased risk		

E+P = estrogen-plus-progestin therapy; E-only = estrogen-only therapy

†All types of hormone therapy (oral regimens were primarily studied)

The Influence of Age or Time Since Menopause

Another major difference between participants in observational studies and those in clinical trials is when they started hormone therapy in relation to menopause onset. Women taking supplemental estrogen in observational studies typically initiate therapy shortly after entering menopause, whereas clinical trial participants are often randomized to hormones long after menses have ceased. In the United States, the average age at menopause is 51 years. In contrast, the average ages of participants recruited into the WHI and HERS hormone trials were 63 and 67 years, respectively.

When my colleagues and I took a closer look at the WHI data, we saw that age or time since menopause seemed to influence the relationship between hormone therapy and CHD. Although there was no association between estrogen-only therapy and heart disease in the sample as a whole, such therapy was associated with a heart disease risk reduction of 37 percent among participants aged 50 to 59—a statistic very similar to that observed in the Nurses' Health Study. By contrast, a risk reduction of only 8 percent was observed among 60- to 69-year-old women, and a risk increase of 11 percent was found among 70- to 79-year-old women.

The top row of Figure 4.2 shows these risks in absolute terms (and see the sidebar "How Risky Is It?"). For every 10,000 women in their 50s who took estrogen alone for one year, there were 10 fewer cases of heart disease (17 cases in the estrogen group verses 27 in the placebo group). For every 10,000 women in their 60s, there were four fewer cases of heart disease (57 cases in the estrogen group versus 61 in the placebo group). But for every 10,000 women in their 70s, there were 10 extra cases of heart disease (96 in the estrogen group versus 86 in the placebo group). An equivalent way of stating this is that the findings suggest that estrogen-only therapy prevented 10 heart disease cases per every 10,000 women aged 50 to 59 who used it for one year; prevented four heart disease cases per 10,000 women aged 60 to 69; and caused 10 heart disease cases per 10,000 women aged 70 to 79.

Because of the relatively small number of heart attacks and coronary deaths (which is how the WHI defined heart disease), especially in the younger women, these differences were not conclusive (i.e., not statistically significant). However, when other heart-related events, such as coronary bypass surgery or angioplasty, were included in the analysis, women aged 50 to 59 were significantly less likely to have heart problems on estrogen than on placebo.

Although age did not have a similar effect in the estrogen-plus-progestin trial (as can be seen in the top row of Figure 4.1), the heart disease risks associated with estrogen plus progestin steadily increased with years since menopause. Estrogen plus progestin was associated with an 11 percent risk reduction for women less than 10 years beyond menopause but was associated with a 22 percent increase in risk for women 10 to 19 years from menopause and a 71 percent increase in risk for women 20 years or more from menopause.

These findings prompted my colleagues and me to reexamine the data from earlier observational studies according to how far from menopause the participants were when they started their hormone therapy—and we found a pattern of results quite similar to the pattern in the WHI. Our new analyses of the Nurses' Health Study data, published in 2006, indicate that women who started hormone therapy within four years of menopause—a group that included more than 80 percent of the hormone users—had a lower risk of developing coronary heart disease than did nonusers, whereas those who began therapy 10 or more years after menopause appeared to receive little coronary benefit.[6]

The WHI findings also led another group of researchers, headed by Dr. Shelley Salpeter of Stanford University, to combine the data from 22 earlier (and smaller) randomized clinical trials with the data of the WHI in order to provide a comprehensive look at the influence of age on the relationship between hormone therapy and CHD. Their analysis, also published in 2006, showed that in trials that enrolled predominantly younger participants (i.e., women less than age 60 or within 10 years of menopause), hormone therapy was associated with a 30 to 40 percent reduction in the risk of CHD. On the other hand, in trials with predominantly older participants, hormone therapy had little effect on coronary risk.[7]

Why Should the Timing of Hormone Therapy Matter?

It's a good question, and to answer it, a basic understanding of the biology of coronary heart disease is required. In brief, CHD is caused by narrowing of the coronary arteries that feed the heart. Like any muscle, the heart needs a steady supply of oxygen and nutrients, which are carried to it by the blood in the coronary arteries. When these arteries become narrowed or clogged by cholesterol and fat deposits and cannot supply enough blood to the heart, the result is CHD.

Although people with compromised arteries sometimes have no outward symptoms, chest pain called angina may occur if there is insufficient blood reaching the heart. A heart attack occurs when the blood supply to a portion of the heart through a coronary artery is completely blocked. This is usually due to a sudden closure from a blood clot forming on top of a previous narrowing or by a rupture of a plaque in

How Risky Is It?

When you hear that the WHI found that taking estrogen-plus-progestin therapy for 5.6 years increased the risk of coronary heart disease by 24 percent, breast cancer by 24 percent, and ovarian cancer by 58 percent, these percentages sound big, scary, and confusing. What do the results mean for you? To answer that, it's important to recognize that there are two ways to view risk—as relative risks and absolute risks.

Medical studies generally focus on *relative risk*. It's the most common way that medical researchers compare one group of people (say, people who took a certain drug) to another (say, people who took a placebo). The relative risk is calculated by dividing the number of cases of disease that develop in the drug group by the number of cases of disease that develop in the placebo group over a given period of time, after adjusting for the fact that the two groups may not be of equal size. If the resulting ratio is 1.0, that's even odds—there's no difference between the two groups in terms of their disease risk. If the ratio is greater than 1.0—say, 1.6—then those who took the drug had a 60 percent greater risk of developing the illness. If the ratio is below 1.0—say, 0.8—then those who took the drug had a 20 percent lower risk of developing the disease than those who didn't take the drug. When researchers say that women in the estrogen-plus-progestin group of the WHI were 1.24 times more likely—or, equivalently, 24 percent more likely—to develop coronary heart disease than were women in the placebo group, this statistic is a relative risk.

The *absolute increase* (or *decrease*) *in risk* is an estimate of the actual number of excess (or fewer) cases of disease that occurs among one group (the drug group) compared to another group (the placebo group) in a given period of time. It's calculated by taking the number of cases of the disease that occur in the drug group and subtracting from it the number of cases of disease that occur in the placebo group during the course of the study—again, adjusting for the fact that the two groups may not be of equal size. This statistic gives a much better sense of personal or individual risk than relative risk does. For example, in the WHI, estrogen plus progestin raised breast cancer risk by 24 percent—this is the relative risk. But, as can be seen in Figure 4.1, that translates in absolute terms to only 8 more breast cancers among every 10,000 women who take these hormones each year compared with those who don't—41 cancers in the hormone group versus 33 cancers in the placebo group.

From the perspective of an individual woman, the impact of any drug—including hormone therapy—on any given disease obviously depends to some extent on how big the relative risk is. But it depends more on three other factors: (1) how common the disease is in

continued

the population of women for which the drug is intended, (2) at what age the disease typically occurs, and, most important, (3) what her personal risk of the disease is at baseline (before she takes the drug). Let's consider these issues in turn.

1. **How common is the disease?** A drug that increases the risk of developing a common disease by a certain percentage will have a much greater impact on a woman's health than a drug that increases the risk of developing a rare disease by that same percentage. This is true even if the rare disease is more lethal than the more common one. A hypothetical example may help to understand this point. Assume that a typical 50-year-old woman has a 1 in 10 chance of developing "disease X" over the next five years. A drug that doubled that risk—in other words, increased the risk by 100 percent—would boost that typical woman's risk to 1 in 5—a scary prospect. Now assume that a typical 50-year-old woman has a 1 in 100 chance of developing "disease Y" over the next five years. A drug that doubled the risk would boost the risk to 1 in 50—nothing to take lightly, but not quite as scary as the scenario for disease X. So before panicking when you read news stories trumpeting that a certain treatment boosts your risk of a particular disease, you first need to consider how common or rare that disease is to begin with. (If the disease is very common—*and* you are personally at high risk for it because of your age and other risk factors that you cannot change—then, and only then, do you have my permission to panic.) Figure 4.3 should give you a rough idea of how common various diseases are among U.S. women overall—but these numbers don't tell the whole story, because they don't show the powerful influence of age.

2. **How old are you?** Most chronic diseases become more common as we age. In general, women in their 50s are only half as likely to develop aging-related diseases as women in their 60s and only one-quarter as likely to do so as women in their 70s. Therefore, although the relative risks (and relative benefits) of hormone therapy tend to be similar among women in their 50s, 60s, and 70s (there are exceptions—coronary heart disease, for one), the absolute risks (and absolute benefits) associated with hormone use grow larger as women get older. Here's a hypothetical example. If hormone therapy increased the risk of a particular disease by 20 percent among women in their 50s, it might raise the absolute risk from say, 10 in 1,000 women to 12 in 1,000 women. But, with the same relative risk of 20 percent among women in their 70s, hormone therapy would increase the absolute risk from 40 in 1,000 women to 48 in 1,000 women. That is, there would be only two additional cases of disease among every 1,000 women in their 50s but eight additional cases among every 1,000 women in their 70s.

Figure 4.3 How Common, and How Deadly, Are Various Diseases in U.S. Women?

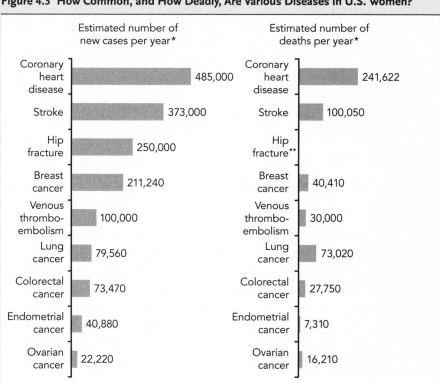

	Estimated number of new cases per year*		Estimated number of deaths per year*
Coronary heart disease	485,000	Coronary heart disease	241,622
Stroke	373,000	Stroke	100,050
Hip fracture	250,000	Hip fracture**	
Breast cancer	211,240	Breast cancer	40,410
Venous thrombo-embolism	100,000	Venous thrombo-embolism	30,000
Lung cancer	79,560	Lung cancer	73,020
Colorectal cancer	73,470	Colorectal cancer	27,750
Endometrial cancer	40,880	Endometrial cancer	7,310
Ovarian cancer	22,220	Ovarian cancer	16,210

*Coronary heart disease and stroke data are for the year 2002; cancer data are for the year 2005.
**Hip fractures often have fatal complications, but the fractures themselves are not usually classified as primary causes of death, so national data are lacking.

Data from the American Heart Association, National Osteoporosis Foundation, and American Cancer Society.

3. **What is your personal risk of disease before you take the drug?** If your personal risk of a particular disease is high to begin with (because of your age or other factors such as family history), then even a small elevation in relative risk associated with a particular drug will need to be considered carefully because it may translate into a large increase in your absolute risk of developing the disease if you take that drug. On the other hand, if your personal risk of

continued

a particular disease is low to begin with, then a small elevation in relative risk will have only a modest impact in terms of raising your absolute risk. Only a very high relative risk will boost your absolute risk substantially. (In Chapter 6, I'll show you how to calculate your personal risk of various diseases that have been linked to hormone therapy, and in Chapter 7, we'll use that information to help determine whether, from a safety perspective, hormone therapy may be a reasonable option for you.)

If you're still wondering "how risky is it?" it may help to compare the relative risks associated with hormone therapy to the relative risks associated with other exposures. For example, cigarette smoking has been linked to a 10-fold increase—in other words, a 900 percent increase—in the risk of lung cancer, and high blood pressure leads to a 4-fold increase—a 300 percent increase—in the risk of stroke. Viewed from this perspective, most of the risks of hormone therapy don't seem so large, do they?

Is your head reeling? If so, you are in good company. A study in Florida showed that many doctors, including family practitioners, internists, and even gynecologists, had only a rudimentary or muddled understanding of the Women's Health Initiative results.[8] For the most part, the doctors were correct about whether hormone therapy increased or decreased the risk of various diseases, but they greatly overestimated the degree of the increased risk for any individual woman. Indeed, their pattern of answers suggested that they had confused the relative risks with the absolute risks.

Knowing how to evaluate medical research in terms of your own risk for illness is a powerful way to help improve your chances of a lifetime of good health.

the artery, as discussed later. (By the way, cholesterol deposits and clots don't happen just in coronary arteries. Both problems can affect any artery in the body, and clots can also occur in veins. When a blockage occurs in the brain, it can cause a "brain attack," or stroke. When a clot forms in a deep leg or pelvic vein, it can travel to the lungs and choke off their blood supply. These conditions are discussed later.)

Let's take a closer look at the process.

The first step in the development of heart disease is a buildup of cholesterol in the coronary arteries. A waxy, fatlike substance produced by the liver and also consumed in food products that come from animals, cholesterol is essential for good health and serves several functions, including the repair of cell membranes and the manufacture of certain hormones.

You have undoubtedly heard of good and bad cholesterol. That's a bit of a misnomer. What makes cholesterol good or bad isn't the cholesterol itself, but the type of protein particle that attaches to and transports the cholesterol in the bloodstream. LDL particles, the major cholesterol carrier in the blood, ferry cholesterol from the liver and intestines to the parts of the body where it is needed. The problem arises when there is an overabundance of LDL particles because they deposit excess cholesterol in artery walls throughout the body. Hence, cholesterol attached to LDL has been dubbed "bad" cholesterol. HDL particles act as a cleanup crew, scavenging excess cholesterol in the bloodstream and ferrying it back to the liver so it can be safely disposed of by the body. Cholesterol attached to HDL is referred to as "good" cholesterol.

Once excess LDL cholesterol lodges in the artery wall, it is attacked by free radicals that change it into a more dangerous form known as oxidized LDL cholesterol (oxidation is similar to the processes that spoil butter and rust pipes), which kicks off a cascade of reactions that clog and stiffen the artery, a process known as atherosclerosis. The stage is set for artery-blocking blood clots, a process known as thrombosis, that can lead to a heart attack or stroke.

Atherosclerosis is heralded by the appearance of *fatty streaks* (clusters of cholesterol-laden cells) in the artery wall. This causes an early inflammatory reaction in which certain white blood cells and other components of the immune system are attracted to arteries that have been damaged by oxidized LDL. The immune cells end up trapped in the soft fatty streaks, converting them into a hard-capped *fatty plaque*. Eventually, calcium is added to the mix, forming a full-blown *atherosclerotic plaque*, which can grow larger over time. Atherosclerosis causes the artery wall to thicken and lose elasticity, narrowing the passageway through the artery and restricting blood flow. If the plaque becomes unstable, it can rupture and cause a blood clot (thrombus) to form, which leads to a heart attack or stroke. The factors responsible for plaque rupture remain unclear, but recent research has implicated a late inflammatory response.

Laboratory studies in mice, rabbits, pigs, and monkeys and randomized clinical trials in humans have shown that hormone therapy favorably affects biological processes or biochemical markers known to influence the risk of heart disease. Supplemental estrogen boosts blood levels of HDL cholesterol, lowers LDL cholesterol, and inhibits the oxidation of LDL cholesterol. Estrogen also improves the functioning of cells that line the blood vessel walls. Collectively termed the endothelium, these cells respond to estrogen by producing more nitric oxide, a substance that relaxes blood vessels, thereby increasing the ability of the vessels to dilate in response to blood flow. In addition, estrogen reduces blood levels of homocysteine, a common dietary byproduct (resulting from the metabolism of the amino acid methionine) that, when elevated, may damage the endothelium.

Estrogen also helps keep blood sugar levels under control by regulating insulin action; excess sugar in the blood can exacerbate inflammation. Indeed, clinical trials have shown that supplemental estrogen appears to reduce the risk of developing type 2 diabetes (high blood sugar). Type 2 diabetes is bad for the heart, especially in women. Whereas men with diabetes are two to three times more likely to develop heart disease than are men without diabetes, women with diabetes are three to seven times more likely to develop heart disease than their counterparts without the condition.

At the same time, however, estrogen has detrimental effects on several other biomarkers of coronary risk. Supplemental estrogen boosts blood levels of triglyceride, a type of fat that, when present in high amounts, contributes to the development of atherosclerosis. Estrogen also disrupts the delicate balance between substances that stimulate clot formation—including proteins called coagulation

Beneficial and Harmful Effects of Estrogen on the Cardiovascular System

Beneficial effects of estrogen:

- Increases HDL ("good") cholesterol*
- Reduces LDL ("bad") cholesterol*
- May prevent the oxidation of LDL cholesterol
- Improves the ability of blood vessel walls to dilate in response to blood flow by boosting nitric oxide production and reducing homocysteine levels
- Regulates blood sugar levels by boosting the body's sensitivity to insulin; reduces the risk of type 2 diabetes*

Harmful effects of estrogen:

- Increases triglycerides*
- Increases substances that promote blood clotting*
- Increases inflammation by boosting C-reactive protein and matrix metalloproteinases*

*This effect is produced by oral estrogen but to a lesser extent (or not at all) by transdermal or vaginal estrogen.

factors and viscous (sticky) blood particles called platelets—and substances that counteract this effect by promoting blood thinning. The result is that estrogen causes clots to form more easily. Estrogen may also stimulate inflammation within plaques by encouraging the production of chemicals such as C-reactive protein and matrix metalloproteinases. This can make atherosclerotic plaques in the heart and brain arteries less stable, causing them to rupture.

Estrogen taken by mouth (oral estrogen) seems to produce more of these effects than estrogen delivered through the skin (transdermal estrogen) or the vagina (vaginal estrogen). The reason is that oral estrogen must enter the digestive tract and undergo processing by the liver before entering the bloodstream, whereas transdermal patches and vaginal suppositories or rings allow estrogen to enter the bloodstream directly, without first being shunted through the liver. This "first pass" of estrogen through the liver is what appears to be responsible for boosting HDL and lowering LDL cholesterol levels, but it also triggers the release of triglycerides, clotting factors, and inflammatory factors.

As shown in Figure 4.4, it has been hypothesized that the clot- and inflammation-promoting effects of supplemental estrogen may be more problematic among women with fully formed atherosclerotic plaques in their arteries who initiate hormone therapy well after the menopausal transition, whereas women with less arterial damage who start hormone therapy early in menopause may benefit most from estrogen's favorable effect on the cholesterol profile and on blood vessel elasticity.

Animal experiments support the idea that arteries with plaques react very differently to supplemental estrogen than healthier ones do. In one series of studies, investigators induced menopause in monkeys by surgically removing their ovaries and then attempted to induce atherosclerosis by feeding them an "imprudent" diet high in fats.[9] Some of the monkeys were given conjugated equine estrogen (with or without medroxyprogesterone acetate) immediately upon ovary removal and initiation of the imprudent diet. The remaining monkeys were given these hormones only after a two-year lag (the equivalent of six years in a woman) or were not given hormones at all. Compared with the monkeys that didn't get estrogen, the monkeys that received the hormones early—and, presumably, before their arteries had advanced fatty deposits—had 70 percent less atherosclerosis, while the monkeys that didn't get estrogen right away had no reduction in atherosclerosis.

Most clinical trials examining the effect of supplemental estrogen on atherosclerosis in humans have been conducted among women who already had significant plaque buildup in their arteries at the start of follow-up and have not found estrogen to be effective in slowing the rate of plaque development. However, one

Figure 4.4 Time Since Menopause and Effect of Starting Hormone Therapy

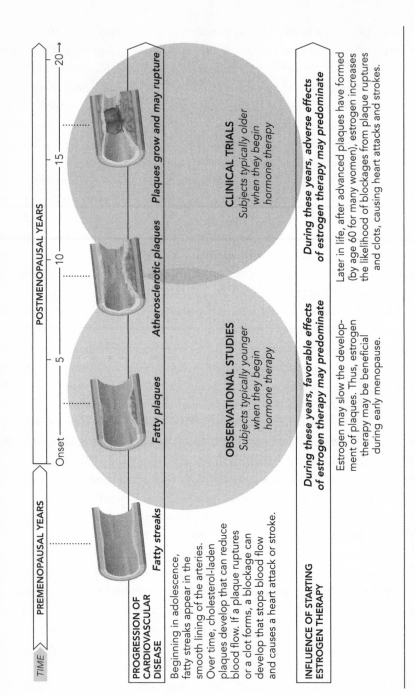

TIME

PREMENOPAUSAL YEARS

POSTMENOPAUSAL YEARS

Onset —— 5 —— 10 —— 15 —— 20 →

PROGRESSION OF CARDIOVASCULAR DISEASE   Fatty streaks   Fatty plaques   Atherosclerotic plaques   Plaques grow and may rupture

Beginning in adolescence, fatty streaks appear in the smooth lining of the arteries. Over time, cholesterol-laden plaques develop that can reduce blood flow. If a plaque ruptures or a clot forms, a blockage can develop that stops blood flow and causes a heart attack or stroke.

OBSERVATIONAL STUDIES
Subjects typically younger when they begin hormone therapy

CLINICAL TRIALS
Subjects typically older when they begin hormone therapy

INFLUENCE OF STARTING ESTROGEN THERAPY

During these years, favorable effects of estrogen therapy may predominate

Estrogen may slow the development of plaques. Thus, estrogen therapy may be beneficial during early menopause.

During these years, adverse effects of estrogen therapy may predominate

Later in life, after advanced plaques have formed (by age 60 for many women), estrogen increases the likelihood of blockages from plaque ruptures and clots, causing heart attacks and strokes.

Adapted from Manson, J. E., et al. Menopause 13 (2006): 139–47.

trial that enrolled women with fewer coronary plaques found that estrogen did slow the progression of atherosclerosis.[10] (In these studies, the rate of atherosclerotic progression is determined either via carotid ultrasound, which measures the thickness of the walls of the carotid arteries, the major arteries on each side of the neck that carry blood to the head—the thicker the artery wall, the greater the atherosclerosis—or by an angiogram, a procedure in which a catheter is inserted into an artery, dye is injected, and an X-ray of the artery is taken.)

And the pattern of findings—two distinct patterns, actually—from large clinical trials such as the WHI and observational studies such as the Nurses' Health Study fits with the hypothesis that estrogen may help if your arteries are in good shape to begin with but may make things worse if your arteries are not in good health. One pattern I've already mentioned: in both the WHI and the Nurses' Health Study, women who were older or further beyond the menopause transition when they started hormone therapy were the women most likely to experience heart problems. It is very probable that these women, on average, although they appeared outwardly healthy, had more advanced atherosclerosis than did their younger or more recently menopausal counterparts.

The second pattern is that heart problems tend to surface relatively quickly following the initiation of hormone therapy in older or sicker women but not in younger or healthier women, suggesting that the harm associated with estrogen may be primarily due to its effect on thrombosis or plaque rupture (events that happen at a relatively late stage in heart disease development and ones that can occur fairly quickly) rather than atherosclerosis (a process that begins early in the development of heart disease and one that generally takes place over many years).

In the WHI, where the majority of participants were in their 60s and 70s, women assigned to estrogen plus progestin for an average of 5.6 years were overall more likely to develop heart disease than those assigned to placebo, but most of the excess heart problems occurred within the first two years of using combined hormone therapy. Women assigned to an average of 7.1 years of estrogen alone also experienced no overall coronary benefit as compared with those assigned to placebo. In both trials, however, there was a suggestion of reduced risk among women followed for the longest periods of time—i.e., six or more years in the estrogen-plus-progestin trial and seven or more years in the estrogen-alone trial.

A similar pattern was found in HERS, whose participants all had prior heart disease, and also among the small number of women in the Nurses' Health Study who had heart disease at the start of the study. Among the latter, those using hormones for less than one year were 25 percent more likely to suffer a coronary event than those who had never taken hormones, whereas those using hormones for longer durations were about 50 percent less likely to have an event.[11]

In contrast, an early spike in coronary events associated with hormone therapy was not observed among Nurses' Health Study participants who were healthy when the study started. Interestingly, among these women, a protective role of menopause hormones was apparent even during the first few years of use.

What About the Type of Hormone Therapy Itself?

In addition to differences in timing, could differences in the particular hormone therapies looked at in observational studies and in clinical trials also play some role in explaining their divergent findings? Hormone therapies vary greatly, including the type of estrogen (what you take), its dose (how much you take), its route of administration (how you take it: pill, patch, or cream), and whether and which type of progestogen is taken concurrently. Let's consider each of these issues in turn.

Estrogen

Some have speculated that the type of estrogen studied in the WHI—conjugated equine estrogen (CEE)—may not be as beneficial as newer hormone formulations that more closely resemble the estradiol produced by the ovaries of premenopausal women; or that the dose of CEE given—0.625 milligrams per day—was too high; or that taking the CEE orally, in pill form, triggered coronary problems. Yet the Nurses' Health Study and other observational studies showing coronary benefits of estrogen primarily involved the use of oral CEE at a dose of 0.625 milligrams. Therefore, differences in estrogen formulations and dosages are unlikely to be major contributors to the divergence in findings of observational studies and clinical trials with respect to heart disease.

Although variations in estrogen formulations likely do not account for differences in the results of clinical trials and observational studies, these variations may nevertheless importantly affect risk of coronary problems. For example, to the extent that an initial increase in coronary events—particularly in women with advanced atherosclerosis—is due to release of clotting and inflammatory factors from the liver in response to oral estrogens, such problems should be lessened by use of transdermal estrogens, which enter the bloodstream without first passing through the liver. Unfortunately, because oral CEE has dominated the menopause hormone market and has been the treatment examined in 90 percent of epidemiologic studies, there aren't yet enough solid data about other estrogen formulations to allow one to draw definitive conclusions about their relative effectiveness and safety in terms of heart disease or other health outcomes. (For more information on estrogen options, see Chapter 5.)

Progestogen

Women who have not had their uterus removed and wish to take estrogen are generally advised to take either progesterone or a synthetic progestin to protect against overgrowth of the uterine lining and possible uterine cancer (see "Endometrial Cancer" later in this chapter). It is possible that progestogens have negative effects on the heart and may reduce any coronary benefit of estrogen.

Comparing the results of the two hormone trials of the WHI is somewhat helpful in disentangling the effects of estrogen from those of progestin. The increase in heart disease risk associated with estrogen-plus-progestin therapy seems to be attributable to the progestin because such an increase was not observed with estrogen alone.

That said, the women participating in the two trials differed in many ways besides the presence or absence of a uterus that could have influenced how they responded to the hormones. Most important, 40 percent of the women in the estrogen-alone trial had had their ovaries surgically removed (oophorectomy) along with their uterus, whereas less than 1 percent of women in the estrogen-plus-progestin trial had had an oophorectomy. Because the women in the estrogen-alone trial had lower levels of natural estrogen to begin with (as a result of oophorectomy), they might derive greater benefit from supplemental estrogen than the women in the estrogen-plus-progestin trial.

On the other hand, in the Nurses' Health Study, one of only a few cohorts in which the number of combination therapy users was large enough to look at its effect on heart disease, estrogen plus progestin appeared to be nearly as protective as estrogen alone against first coronary events. Compared with nonusers of hormone therapy, users of oral estrogen alone were 45 percent less likely to experience a coronary event, and users of estrogen plus progestin were 36 percent less likely to do so. Most study participants taking combination hormones reported cyclic rather than continuous progestin use, however. (In a typical cyclic therapy regimen, one takes estrogen throughout the month and estrogen plus progestogen for

10 to 14 days.) Although data are limited, some investigators have suggested that cyclic progestin therapy may be less likely than the continuous progestin therapy used in the WHI to interfere with the beneficial physiologic effects of estrogen.

Natural progesterone may also be less likely than synthetic progestins to counteract such effects. For example, results from PEPI and other trials indicate that natural progesterone is less likely than the synthetic progestin medroxyprogesterone acetate found in Prempro to negate estrogen's ability to increase HDL cholesterol levels and to dilate blood vessels. However, there are no clinical trial data showing that natural progesterone, when paired with estrogen, has more favorable effects on heart disease risk than synthetic progestins. (For more information on progestogen options, see Chapter 5.)

And the Research Continues

Two new trials are under way to address some of the unresolved clinical issues. With private funding from the Phoenix-based Kronos Longevity Research Institute, Dr. Mitchell Harman, other colleagues, and I launched the Kronos Early Estrogen Prevention Study (KEEPS) in 2005. This trial, which is slated to continue through 2010, will randomize 720 recently menopausal women—women who are no more than three years beyond the menopausal transition—to one of three regimens: low-dose oral conjugated equine estrogen (Premarin, 0.45 milligrams per day), transdermal estradiol (Climara patch, 50 micrograms per day), or a placebo. Both types of estrogen are being administered in combination with cyclic oral progesterone (Prometrium capsule, 200 milligrams for 12 days per month). The investigators will take periodic scans of the carotid and coronary arteries to measure the effects of hormone therapy on the development and progression of atherosclerosis. We will also evaluate whether low-dose estrogen and transdermal versus oral formulations have different effects on quality-of-life outcomes, including mood, fatigue, sleep quality, and sexual function; bone health; and cognition.

The Early versus Late Intervention Trial with Estradiol (ELITE) study will recruit 500 women in southern California representing two groups: those within 6 years of menopause and those who are 10 or more years beyond menopause. Within each group, the women will be randomly assigned to take oral estradiol (participants with a uterus will also use a vaginal progesterone gel) or a placebo and followed to assess the development of atherosclerosis as well as any signs of cognitive decline.

Bottom Line

There is convincing evidence that differences in age or the initial health of the participants in observational studies and clinical trials of hormone therapy may account in large part for the discrepant results between study types with regard to the effect of hormones on coronary heart disease. While women who are older, significantly past menopause, and already have heart disease or are at high risk of developing it generally should not take hormone therapy, women who are younger, have recently entered menopause, and who are not at high risk of heart disease will likely suffer no adverse coronary effects and may even benefit. This doesn't mean that newly menopausal women should take hormone therapy specifically to prevent heart disease (they shouldn't), but it does mean that, from a coronary perspective, the data can be viewed as reassuring for most women who are considering hormone therapy to relieve menopause symptoms.

STROKE

Ischemic strokes, which are caused by blockages in the brain's arteries, usually due to a blood clot, account for about 80 percent of strokes in the United States. Hemorrhagic strokes, which occur when blood vessels in the brain burst and saturate surrounding tissues with blood, account for the rest. Transient ischemic attacks (TIA) are, as the name implies, ministrokes that typically last only a few minutes. Although they do not cause permanent damage, they are often warning signs of future full-blown strokes. About one in three people who have a TIA will eventually have a more serious and debilitating stroke.

Strokes are the third leading cause of death in the United States, behind heart disease and cancer. Of the more than 373,000 strokes that occur in U.S. women each year, approximately 100,000 are fatal. Although both genders are equally likely to develop stroke, women are more likely than similarly aged men to die of it, with women accounting for more than 60 percent of stroke deaths.

Taken as a whole, observational studies show a small increase in stroke risk associated with use of menopause hormones among women with no prior history of stroke. An analysis that averaged the results across nine cohort studies, including the Nurses' Health Study, reported relatively modest—but statistically significant—risk increases of 12 percent for total stroke and 20 percent for ischemic stroke.[12]

There is some variability in the findings within and across the individual studies, however. For example, in the Nurses' Health Study, hormone therapy overall was not predictive of total stroke risk, or of stroke death.[13] Upon closer examination, women taking estrogen plus progestogen experienced a 45 percent elevation in stroke risk, while women taking estrogen alone were not at significantly increased risk. Nevertheless, the risk of stroke climbed with increasing dose of oral conjugated equine estrogen (whether or not a progestogen was also taken); whereas women taking 0.3 milligrams per day (low dose) were 46 percent *less* likely to suffer a stroke than women taking no estrogen, women taking 0.625 milligrams per day (standard dose) or 1.25 milligrams or more per day (high dose) were 35 and 63 percent *more* likely, respectively, to do so. And, focusing on stroke subtypes, hormone therapy overall was associated with a 26 percent increase in the risk of ischemic stroke but was unrelated to hemorrhagic stroke.

Other observational studies have not found an increased risk of stroke with hormone therapy, and a few have even found a reduced risk.[14] It also remains unclear whether the relation between hormone therapy and stroke differs according to age or time since menopause, as is the case for heart disease.

In the WHI, women assigned to estrogen-plus-progestin therapy were 31 percent more likely to suffer a stroke than those assigned to placebo; this elevation in risk was observed across all age groups (Figure 4.1).[15] In absolute terms, for every 10,000 women taking estrogen plus progestin, there were 31 strokes per year, compared with 24 strokes per year for women not on hormones. Estrogen-only therapy was also associated with a greater risk of stroke, but the increased risk was confined to participants aged 60 and older (Figure 4.2).[16] Indeed, there were few strokes among women in their 50s. Focusing on stroke subtypes, estrogen plus progestin increased the risk of ischemic stroke by 44 percent but had no effect on the risk of hemorrhagic stroke. Results were similar for estrogen alone.

What's the effect of hormone therapy in women who are at high risk of stroke? Two large trials have looked at this question. In HERS, whose participants were at elevated stroke risk because of prior coronary heart disease, estrogen-plus-progestin therapy was associated with a higher risk of stroke and TIA, but the association fell short of statistical significance (i.e., the role of chance could not be ruled out). In the Women's Estrogen for Stroke Trial (WEST), which followed 664 women with a history of ischemic stroke or TIA for nearly three years, participants assigned to estrogen-only therapy (oral estradiol, 1 milligram per day) were nearly three times more likely to experience a fatal stroke than were those assigned to placebo.[17] Estrogen therapy did not predict the recurrence of nonfatal stroke, but the nonfatal strokes that did occur in the estrogen group were more debilitating than were those in the placebo group.

Bottom Line

Healthy, recently menopausal women should be aware that there may be a small but real increased risk of ischemic stroke with hormone therapy. Women with a history of stroke or TIA should not take estrogen with or without progestogen because of an increased risk of recurrent stroke.

Venous Thromboembolism

Arteries bring oxygen-rich blood from the heart to the tissues, and veins bring oxygen-depleted blood to the heart and lungs, where it is reoxygenated. Just as blood clots can develop in the arteries and cause heart attacks or strokes, so too can they develop in the veins—most often in the legs or pelvis but sometimes in the arms or neck. The consequences of such clots depend upon whether they develop in veins close to the skin's surface or veins deeper in the body. Clots that develop in sur-face—or, to use the technical term, *superficial*—veins cause superficial thrombo-phlebitis, a condition in which the affected vein becomes inflamed, and the skin covering it feels tender, warm, and swollen. Superficial thrombophlebitis, which usually clears up after leg elevation (if it's the leg that's affected), moist heat, and over-the-counter nonsteroidal anti-inflammatory medications such as ibuprofen, is typically more annoying than dangerous because the likelihood that the clots will break up and be transported to the lungs is very low.

Not so for the clots that form in veins deep inside the body, a condition known as deep-vein thrombosis. If a clot breaks off from a deep vein, travels through the heart, and lodges in the lung arteries, it can choke off the blood supply to the lungs and cause a drop in the body's oxygen level, causing potentially deadly pulmonary embolism. Medical professionals use the term venous thromboembolism—usually shortened to VTE—to refer collectively to deep-vein thrombosis and pulmonary embolism. About 100,000 cases of VTE occur each year in U.S. women, most often in hospitalized and immobile patients; in the general population, the condition is quite rare.

Hormone-related exposures such as birth control pills, pregnancy, and menopausal hormone therapy have been strongly implicated as risk factors for VTE. An analysis that combined the data from 12 studies—eight case-control, one cohort (the Nurses' Health Study), and three trials (including HERS and PEPI)—found that current use of menopause hormones doubled the risk of VTE.[18]

In the WHI, estrogen plus progestin was associated with an approximate twofold increase in the risk of blood clots in the legs and lungs (Figure 4.1), while estrogen alone was associated with a 33 percent increase in risk (Figure 4.2). What does this mean in absolute terms? Eighteen of every 10,000 women taking estrogen plus progestin for one year would develop a blood clot that they would otherwise not have had they avoided estrogen (35 cases in the estrogen-plus-progestin group versus 17 in the placebo group). And 7 of every 10,000 women taking estrogen alone for one year would do so (28 cases in the estrogen-alone group versus 21 in the placebo group).

In the estrogen-plus-progestin trial, the hormone-associated relative risks of VTE were roughly similar across all age groups (Figure 4.1). On the other hand, in the estrogen-alone trial, the hormone-associated relative risks increased somewhat with age; estrogen therapy boosted the risk of VTE in women in their 50s, 60s, and 70s by 22 percent, 31 percent, and 44 percent, respectively (Figure 4.2). As with other forms of cardiovascular disease, the baseline risk of VTE—i.e., the risk of VTE in women not on hormone therapy—is much lower in younger than older women. Therefore, in absolute terms, the impact of hormone therapy on blood clots is much lower among women in their 50s than among women in their 70s.

Laboratory studies indicate that estrogen taken through the skin appears to be less clot-promoting than estrogen taken by mouth. Transdermal estrogens have traditionally been less commonly prescribed than oral ones, at least in this country, and thus many U.S. studies have insufficient data to compare the two methods of taking estrogen with respect to clotting outcomes. However, data from a large case-control study in France suggest that transdermal administration of estrogen may be safer than the oral route; current users of oral estrogen were three-and-a-half times more likely than nonusers to develop blood clots in the legs and lungs, whereas current users of transdermal estrogen had no increased risk.[19] Of note, most of the hormone users in this study took estradiol rather than conjugated equine estrogen.

A large case-control study conducted among members of a health-maintenance organization in Washington State examined whether the type of oral estrogen taken influences the risk of VTE.[20] In contrast to the French study, nearly all of the participants who used oral hormones took either conjugated equine estrogen or esterified estrogen. Current users of oral conjugated equine estrogen were 65 percent more likely to develop blood clots in the legs or lungs than nonusers, whereas current users of oral esterified estrogen had no increased risk. Although these findings are intriguing, more research is needed before we can conclude that one type or method of estrogen administration is indeed safer than another.

I should note that heredity strongly affects one's susceptibility to developing blood clots in the veins. People with a particular mutation in the genes for clotting factor V (that's "V" as in "five," and the mutation is called factor V Leiden) or clotting factor II (also known as prothrombin, and the mutation is known as the prothrombin 20210 mutation) overproduce these clot-promoting proteins, with the result that their blood forms clots very readily. Factor V Leiden, which is found in about 5 percent of the (white) U.S. population, increases the risk for VTE by five- to sevenfold. The prothrombin 20210 gene mutation, found in about 2 percent of the (white) population, increases the risk by two- to threefold. Other genetic risk factors for VTE include deficiencies in protein C, protein S, and antithrombin III, as well as antiphospholipid antibodies.

Hormone therapy is very dangerous for women who have a genetic predisposition to developing blood clots. In women with the prothrombin mutation, hormone therapy quadruples their already higher-than-usual risk. And women with factor V Leiden who take menopause hormones have a 15-fold higher risk of VTE than their counterparts who do not take hormones. For women in their 50s and 60s, this translates to 150 to 400 extra blood clots per 10,000 women per year of hormone use.

Bottom Line

Hormone therapy increases the risk of VTE and should generally not be taken by women who have a higher-than-usual risk of blood clots. These include women with a personal history of VTE; those with a strong family history of VTE; those known to carry the factor V Leiden, prothrombin 20210, or other mutations that predispose to blood clotting; and those about to have major surgery or to be rendered immobile for any other reason.

Osteoporosis and Bone Fractures

More than just a calcium repository, the human skeleton contains active cells that continuously destroy old bone and replace it with new bone in a process called remodeling, or bone turnover. (Remodeling is something you think of doing to your house every once in a while, but your body remodels your bones all the time.) An imbalance between the rate of bone destruction and the rate of new bone formation occurs with aging and accelerates after menopause, causing the bone-thinning condition known as osteoporosis (which means "porous bones"). Osteoporotic bones lose strength, become brittle, and result in an astonishing 1.5 million fractures per year in the United States. The most common fracture sites are the spine, hip, and wrist.

Although men are susceptible, osteoporosis disproportionately affects women—four of every five of its victims are female. In the United States, about 15 percent of women aged 50 and older have osteoporosis, and another 40 percent have a precursor condition known as osteopenia ("low bone mass"). The prevalence of osteoporosis rises from 4 percent among women in their 50s to 52 percent among women aged 80 and older. The skeleton of a typical 70-year-old female is about a third lighter than her 40-year-old counterpart because of osteoporosis. Nearly one of every two women past menopause will sustain an osteoporotic fracture.

Not only does osteoporosis increase the risk of breaking a bone, but broken bones don't heal well, increasing risk of future breaks and leading to all kinds of problems. Hip fractures are among the most devastating of all fracture types, as they are typically associated with not only substantial pain but also physical disability, loss of independence, hospitalization, extended nursing home stays, and an elevated risk of death. Indeed, nearly one in four patients over age 50 dies within one year of having a hip fracture, typically from pneumonia due to lack of mobility. One in three becomes a permanent nursing home resident. Only about one in three survivors are able to return to fully independent living. About 250,000 U.S. women suffer a hip fracture each year.

Osteoporotic fractures in bones other than the hip are also of great concern. Until recently, it was not believed that such fractures carried an increased risk of death, but new studies suggest otherwise. Individuals who sustain a spine fracture—both symptomatic ones that come to medical attention and asymptomatic ones that are detected only upon X-ray examination—are nearly 25 percent more likely to die in the five years following fracture than those without such fractures. About 560,000 U.S. women suffer a spine fracture each year.

Long before the "estrogen-prevents-heart-disease" hypothesis prompted widespread use of hormone therapy, the prevention of osteoporosis and consequent fractures was the main reason (besides relief of hot flashes and other menopausal symptoms) that hormones were prescribed for menopausal women. On this topic, the findings are clear-cut: estrogen slows the aging-related bone loss experienced by most women after menopause. More than 50 randomized trials, including PEPI, have demonstrated that supplemental estrogen, with or without a progestogen, rapidly increases bone density of the spine by 4 to 6 percent and of the hip by 2 to 3 percent, regardless of whether hormone therapy is initiated at the start of menopause or in old age. However, the bone-protecting effect appears to last only as long as hormone therapy is continued. In the National Osteoporosis Risk Assessment (NORA) observational study of more than 170,000 U.S. women, those who reported using hormones for 5 to 10 years after menopause and then quitting had no better bone density in the forearm or heel at age 70 than did women who reported never using hormones.[21]

Interestingly, the reduction in fracture risk associated with use of menopause hormones exceeds that expected based on increases in bone density alone. Data from observational studies indicate a 50 percent lower risk of spine fracture and a 33 percent lower risk of hip, wrist, and other fractures among current estrogen users whether or not they also take a progestogen. Similar to the findings for bone density, the fracture protection wears off rapidly after hormone use ceases, regardless of how long the hormones had been taken. For example, among 140,000 menopausal women followed for two to four years as part of the Million Women Study in the United Kingdom (more on this study later), current use of hormone therapy was associated with a 38 percent reduction in fractures, but fracture rates returned to those of never-users about one year after hormone therapy was stopped.[22] In this study, the protective effect was similar for all types of estrogen, whether taken in pill or patch form, or taken alone or with various progestogens.

Although the observational data are compelling, the first clinical trials large enough to corroborate the hypothesis that hormone therapy prevents fracture were the WHI trials. Compared with women assigned to placebo, women assigned to 5.6 years of estrogen plus progestin experienced 33 percent fewer hip fractures and 24 percent fewer total fractures.[23] For 6.8 years of estrogen alone, the corresponding risk reductions were 39 percent and 30 percent, respectively.[16] Although hormone therapy significantly reduced fracture risk in women of all ages, women aged 70 and older benefited the most in absolute terms because they had the highest risk of fracture to begin with (as can be seen in Figures 4.1 and 4.2). In fact, hip fractures were so rare among women in their 50s that the WHI investigators couldn't reliably estimate the effect of hormone therapy on hip fracture in this group.

Unfortunately, the fracture protection afforded by estrogen-plus-progestin therapy in the WHI was more than offset by its adverse impact on other health outcomes (see the last section of this chapter), even among those participants deemed to be most susceptible to fracture at the outset of the study because of their older age and other risk factors. Parallel analyses of the estrogen-alone data have not been completed, so we don't yet know whether a similar conclusion will hold for estrogen alone.

In any event, rather than give up on estrogen as an osteoporosis fighter, some researchers are now trying to determine whether ultralow doses of the hormone (with or without similarly low doses of progestogen) can slow bone loss without appreciably raising the risk of serious adverse events such as heart attack, stroke, or breast cancer in women who are well past the menopausal transition. Indeed, two small clinical trials in women aged 60 and older have found that daily doses of 0.25 milligrams of oral estradiol or 0.014 milligrams of transdermal estradiol (one-quarter of the usual doses found in the pill and patch, respectively), when taken in conjunction with calcium and vitamin D supplements, increased hip and spine bone density more than the calcium and vitamin D supplements alone.[24, 25] Importantly, the ultralow-dose hormones did not appear to cause serious adverse events. But caution is in order. These trials were not large enough to assess the overall benefits and risks of these hormones. Also, the trials lasted three years or less, so we don't know whether the treatment will remain effective and safe in the long term—an important consideration because breast cancer risk rises with longer duration of hormone use (see next section) and bone benefits dissipate once hormones are stopped. And we don't know whether the improvements in bone density associated with ultralow-dose estrogen use actually translate into a reduced risk of fracture.

Bottom Line

Hormone therapy is very effective at reducing bone loss and osteoporotic fractures. However, the bone protection lasts only as long as hormones are used. When hormones are stopped, bone loss resumes and fracture rates rise rapidly to those of women who have never taken hormones. Because the average age of women who break a hip is close to 80, one would have to stay on estrogen for many, many years to gain maximal bone benefits. Because the potential harms of long-term hormone use appear to exceed (or at least match) the bone benefits even for women who are at high fracture risk, estrogen is not recommended as a first-line strategy for preventing or treating osteoporosis.

BREAST CANCER

Coronary heart disease kills six times as many U.S. women as breast cancer, but it is breast cancer that women fear the most.

Breast cancer is the most frequently occurring cancer in women; it accounts for one of every three of their cancers. Although it still kills more women than any other cancer except lung cancer, the good news is that the number of women dying from breast cancer has been steadily declining in recent decades, a result of earlier detection and more effective treatments. Breast cancer in its early stages is often silent—it produces no obvious warning signs to prompt a visit to the doctor. But early-stage cancers that would have been missed in years past can now be detected with mammography. Tumors in the breast usually grow very slowly so that by the time one is large enough to be felt as a lump, it may have been growing for as long as 10 years. National statistics show that if breast cancer is detected while still localized, the 5-year survival rate is 96 percent—a dramatic improvement from 72 percent in the 1940s. Nevertheless, even when caught early, the rigorous demands of treatment, the possible loss of a breast, and worries about body image and cancer recurrence can be extremely traumatic for survivors of breast cancer.

How Does Breast Cancer Develop?

Before looking at the relationship between hormone therapy and breast cancer, a basic understanding of breast anatomy and how breast cancer develops is useful. The working architecture of the breast consists of *lobules*, which manufacture milk, and *ducts*, the canals that carry milk to the nipples when a woman is breast-feeding. The breast also contains fatty tissue, nerves, blood and lymphatic vessels, and connective tissue to help hold everything in place.

Throughout life, our cells are constantly dividing to create new tissue while older cells die off in a process known as apoptosis, or programmed cell death. Like all cancers, breast cancer results when the body's mechanisms for regulating the balance between the creation and death of cells do not work properly, with the result that the former process starts to outstrip the latter.

Breast cancer starts when too many cells form in the lining of the milk ducts or the lobules. If the excess cells look normal under a microscope, the overgrowth is termed *simple hyperplasia*; if they look odd, it is called *atypical hyperplasia*. (The prefix *hyper-* means "excessive" and the suffix *-plasia* means "growth.") Hyperplasia in the breast indicates a heightened breast cancer risk but is not itself cancer.

The next step, *carcinoma in situ*, occurs when the cells proliferating inside the milk ducts or lobules cross some threshold of abnormality but have not yet spread to the surrounding tissue or beyond. The term "in situ," meaning "in place," is used to describe this condition because the abnormal cells are still "in place" inside the ducts or lobules where they first developed. Despite the use of the word "carcinoma," the cells involved are not considered to be fully cancerous because they have not escaped from the ducts or lobules in which they originated. In about 30 percent of cases, *invasive breast cancer* develops when the cells eventually gain the ability to invade nearby fat tissue, enter the blood and lymphatic vessels, and travel to other parts of the body, such as the liver, lungs, and bone.

The mechanisms that regulate cell growth and division are largely controlled by our genes. If the genes are somehow damaged—by damaged, I mean that harmful mutations occur in the DNA molecules that compose the gene—cancer develops. We may inherit damaged genes from our parents, or something in the environment (e.g., exposure to radiation or to mutation-inducing chemicals, such as cigarette smoke) may damage the genes after birth.

Mutations can also arise spontaneously as a result of mistakes that are made when a cell duplicates its DNA prior to cell division. When a cell divides, it must make a copy of its DNA to pass along to the new cells that are created. Replicating detailed genetic material perfectly is complicated. The more times a cell divides, the more times the genes in it require copying, and the greater the chance for mistakes to be made—i.e., for harmful mutations to be introduced. And, as we age, the whole copying process becomes more prone to errors.

How Are Female Sex Hormones Related to Breast Cancer?

Female sex hormones are believed to influence breast cancer risk by promoting cell division at two steps in the pathway from health to cancer. First, by stimulating initially healthy breast cells to divide, estrogen and progesterone increase the likelihood that harmful mutations will arise when the genetic material inside those cells is copied to the newly created cells. Second, once mutations have already occurred and the cells have become cancerous, estrogen and progesterone promote the division of the cancerous cells, thus accelerating the growth of tumors. Laboratory studies show not only that estrogen boosts cell division, but also that cell division in the breast surges during the second half of the menstrual cycle, when progesterone levels are at their highest.

Indeed, an influence of female sex hormones on breast cancer was recognized as early as 1896, when an article in the British medical journal the *Lancet* noted that removing the ovaries led to a remission of breast cancer in some premenopausal women.[26] The importance of ovarian hormones in the development of breast cancer has since been underscored by the finding that breast cancer risk is strongly related to a woman's menstrual history. The younger you are when you start menstruating and the older you are when you stop, the higher your risk of breast cancer, presumably because the length of time that you are exposed to high levels of estrogen and progesterone is longer than that of a typical woman. Studies dating back to the 1970s have shown that women who had their first menstrual period before age 12 are 20 percent more likely to develop breast cancer than women who had their first period at age 15 or older. Similarly, a woman's risk of developing breast cancer increases by about 20 percent for every five years that her menopause is delayed.[27]

More recently, researchers have directly measured women's (naturally occurring) estrogen blood levels and correlated those levels with breast cancer risk. In an analysis of data from nine cohort studies (including the Nurses' Health Study) of menopausal women not on hormone therapy, women with the highest blood levels of estradiol were twice as likely to develop breast cancer than those with the lowest levels.[28]

What Is the Relation Between Hormone Therapy and Breast Cancer Risk?

The answer to this question depends on whether a progestogen is taken along with the estrogen, so we need to consider the two types of hormone therapy separately.

Estrogen Alone

Some observational studies have found an increased risk of breast cancer among menopausal women who take estrogen alone, with the risk most pronounced for those who take the hormone for long periods of time. In 1997, researchers at

Oxford University carried out an analysis of 51 case-control and cohort studies that included 52,705 women with breast cancer and 108,411 without breast cancer—or about 90 percent of epidemiologic data available on the topic at the time.[29] Most of the data were collected before the practice of adding progestogen to estrogen to protect against overgrowth of the uterine lining had become widespread; thus, the overwhelming majority of women in these studies—even those with an intact uterus—who took hormone therapy used estrogen alone. (Some were also using higher doses of estrogen than the oral conjugated equine estrogen dose of 0.625 milligrams that is most common today.) The analysis indicated that women who were currently using hormone therapy and had taken it for less than 5 years were not at increased risk of breast cancer, whereas women who were currently using hormone therapy and had taken it for 5 or more years (the average duration of use was 11 years) had a 35 percent increase in risk compared with women who had never used hormones.

Many researchers believe that estrogen therapy may carry less breast cancer risk among women with hysterectomy than women with an intact uterus. Natural estrogen levels tend to be lower in women with hysterectomy, even when their ovaries are not taken out along with the uterus. (Surgery to remove the uterus can cause scarring of and reduced blood flow to the ovaries, which may compromise their ability to produce estrogen.) And estrogen therapy in women may be less likely to boost breast cancer risk in women with lower rather than higher ovarian estrogen levels.

Although observational studies published in the nearly 10 years since the Oxford analysis was completed indicate that estrogen-plus-progestogen preparations raise a woman's risk of breast cancer more than estrogen-only preparations (more on this later), the majority also continue to suggest that estrogen alone can indeed be used with minimal or no increase in breast cancer risk for at least 5 years—and even somewhat longer by women with hysterectomy (who, as we now know, are the only ones who are suitable candidates to take [standard-dose] estrogen without a progestogen anyway, because they don't need the latter hormone to protect against endometrial overgrowth). For example, among 18,000 female health professionals past menopause in the Women's Health Study, current estrogen users had no increased risk of breast cancer during a 6-year follow-up period compared with women who had never used hormones, regardless of whether they'd been on estrogen for less than or for more than 5 years when the study started.[30] In analyses limited to the 29,000 women with hysterectomy in the Nurses' Health Study, my colleagues and I also found no increased risk of breast cancer associated with 5 years or even 10 years of current use of estrogen alone (for the standard oral Premarin dose of 0.625 milligrams per day), although excess risk did emerge with 15 years of use or longer.[31]

In contrast to these results, the recent Million Women Study, an aptly named investigation of—you guessed it—nearly one million 50- to 64-year-old women living in the United Kingdom, found that women who reported using estrogen alone at the start of the study and had taken it for one to four years, five to nine years, or ten or more years were 25 percent, 32 percent, and 37 percent more likely, respectively, to develop breast cancer over a two-and-a-half-year follow-up period than women who had never used menopause hormones.[32] It's hard to know what to make of the relatively rapid escalation in risk reported in this study, because the same phenomenon has not been observed in other, longer-term studies or, as described next, in the WHI trial of estrogen alone.

In the WHI, the use of estrogen alone in women with hysterectomy was not associated with an excess risk of breast cancer. To the contrary, women assigned to estrogen-only therapy were actually somewhat *less* likely to develop breast cancer than women assigned to placebo over the 6.8-year randomized treatment period.[16] It is not clear to me why such therapy would *reduce* a woman's risk of developing breast cancer. Indeed, as this book goes to press, my colleagues are conducting detailed analyses of the data to try to figure out the reason for this unexpected finding (see the sidebar "Does the Link Between Hormone Therapy and Breast Cancer Differ According to a Woman's Weight?" for one potential explanation). In any event, the WHI trial results corroborate most observational studies in suggesting that taking estrogen alone, at least for up to seven years, does not significantly raise breast cancer risk in women who have had a hysterectomy.

Estrogen Plus Progestogen

When doctors started prescribing a progestogen to prevent the development of endometrial cancer in estrogen users who hadn't had a hysterectomy, it was widely assumed that the progestogen might also protect against breast cancer. But, alas, observational studies have consistently found the opposite. Estrogen-plus-progestogen preparations seem to increase the risk of breast cancer to a greater degree than estrogen alone.

The aforementioned Oxford analysis included a small number of women who reported current use of estrogen plus progestogen; such use was associated with a

15 percent increase in breast cancer risk if the hormones had been taken for less than five years and a 53 percent increase in risk if they had been taken for five years or more.[29] Several larger studies published more recently find similar results. For example, in the Women's Health Study cohort, women taking estrogen plus progestogen for less than five years were not at appreciably higher risk of breast cancer than those who had never used these hormones, while women taking them for five or more years had a 76 percent increase in risk.[30] (The Nurses' Health Study found a 40 percent increase in breast cancer risk associated with estrogen plus progestogen but hasn't yet published findings on short- vs. long-term use of these hormones.[33])

However, a few studies—most notably the Million Women Study—have reported a somewhat higher and more rapid escalation in risk of breast cancer among users of combination therapy, with significant risks noted even among those taking hormones for less than five years.

It's important to realize that, unlike heart attacks, strokes, blood clots, and hip fractures—events that usually manifest themselves quite dramatically and demand prompt medical attention—the timeliness of breast cancer diagnoses relies heavily on whether women are regularly screened for evidence of the disease. Many scientists have pointed out that, for a variety of reasons (including the fact that they're more health conscious), women who take menopause hormones are more likely to receive regular mammograms than women who don't take hormones, and that higher rates of detection, rather than higher rates of actual disease, account for at least some of the increased breast cancer risk seen among women on hormones in observational studies. The Million Women Study has also been criticized for potential "enrollment bias." Because the study was launched as part of national breast screening initiative at a time when the potential link between hormone therapy and breast cancer was well known to the general public, it may have attracted and enrolled a disproportionate number of high-risk women on hormones who probably shouldn't have been on them to begin with and who were rightfully concerned about their breast cancer risk. These are valid criticisms, and they suggest that we should give far more credence to the results of clinical trials when considering breast cancer outcomes.

So, what are those results?

Evidence supporting the observational studies in implicating progestogen as the primary culprit in boosting breast cancer risk comes from the PEPI trial, which showed that combination therapy increased breast density (as seen on a mammogram) more than estrogen alone. High breast density is a strong risk factor for breast cancer in women past menopause. After one year of therapy, 16 to 24 percent of the women assigned to various estrogen-plus-progestogen combinations developed denser breasts, compared with only 3.5 percent of women assigned to estrogen alone and no women assigned to placebo.[34] (In the WHI, estrogen-plus-progestin also significantly increased mammographic density after one year.[35]) In addition, in a study of monkeys with surgical menopause who were treated for 30 months—the equivalent of about seven human years—with conjugated equine estrogen with or without medroxyprogesterone acetate, the combination therapy stimulated greater breast cell proliferation than did estrogen alone.[36]

In the HERS trial, four years of estrogen-plus-progestin therapy was associated with a 38 percent increase in breast cancer risk, but the increase wasn't statistically significant—the possibility that it could have occurred by chance alone could not be ruled out.[37] Moreover, there were no data provided on how long some of the participants had already been taking hormones when they entered the trial and how this may have influenced their risk of breast cancer.

The WHI estrogen-plus-progestin trial was the first trial of sufficient size and duration to permit a rigorous examination of the effect of combination hormones on breast cancer risk—and provide some clarification as to how long such therapy might be used before breast cancer risk became elevated. Women assigned to estrogen plus progestin for an average of 5.6 years were 24 percent more likely to develop breast cancer than women assigned to placebo.[38] But, importantly, the excess breast cancer risk did not begin to emerge until the fourth year of randomized treatment. Moreover, the harmful effect of estrogen plus progestin was observed only among the participants who reported that they had taken hormone therapy before enrolling in the trial—about one-quarter of the study sample—but not among those with no previous hormone use. Thus, the WHI findings provide some reassurance that women can take combination hormone therapy for up to four to five years without appreciably raising their breast cancer risk.

However, I should tell you that the breast cancers diagnosed in the WHI participants allocated to estrogen plus progestin tended to be larger and possibly more advanced than the breast cancers diagnosed in the participants allocated to placebo. The likely reason for this is that, as noted earlier, hormone therapy makes breasts appear denser on a mammogram, so it can be more difficult for the radiologist who reads that mammogram to detect precancerous changes early. After menopause, all women should have regular mammograms, but mammograms are especially important for those on hormone therapy. If you take cyclic combination therapy, which causes bleeding for a few days after stopping the progestogen, schedule your mammogram to coincide with the cessation of bleeding because the breasts temporarily become less dense at that time.

Taken as a whole, the findings on estrogen plus progestogen and breast cancer provide a strong argument for not staying on hormone therapy for more than a few years. However, if hormones are taken only for a short time, the absolute risk of breast cancer for any individual woman is relatively low. As can be seen in Figure 4.1, the WHI results imply that, if 10,000 women used estrogen plus progestin for one year, eight additional cases of breast cancer would occur (41 cases in the hormone group versus 33 in the placebo group). And absolute risks of breast cancer are lower in recently menopausal women than in women in their 60s and 70s.

Does One Type of Hormone Therapy Affect Breast Cancer Risk More than Another?

It's possible that the type of estrogen or—as is more likely—progestogen used might affect risk of breast cancer. However, there is as yet no compelling evidence that some hormone formulations are safe or even safer than others with respect to breast cancer. In the Million Women Study, the type of estrogen taken (conjugated equine estrogen versus estradiol) or the method of administration (pill, patch, or via an implant under the skin) did not make a significant difference in terms of breast cancer risk. A similar increase in breast cancer risk was also observed for different types of progestins (the most commonly used ones in the United Kingdom are norethisterone, norgestrel, levonorgestrel, and medroxyprogesterone acetate) and for both cyclic and continuous progestin regimens. Although data from a handful of other studies, including the Women's Health Study,[30] have suggested that cyclic regimens may carry less breast cancer risk than continuous ones, more research on this topic is necessary before we can conclude that this is indeed the case.

In the Million Women Study, too few participants reported the use of natural progesterone to determine whether this hormone preparation conferred less risk than its synthetic cousins, as some of its proponents have argued. Very recent data from a cohort study from France suggest that this might be the case.[39] Yet in the

PEPI trial, progesterone was nearly as likely as medroxyprogesterone acetate to boost breast density when taken in combination with estrogen.

It's also possible that lower doses of hormones have less of an adverse effect on breast cancer risk than the standard (or even higher) doses used by the majority of women in observational studies and large clinical trials.

Does Excess Breast Cancer Risk Go Away When Hormone Therapy Is Stopped?

After you stop hormone therapy, your excess risk of developing breast cancer dissipates. Data from observational studies, including the Million Women Study, consistently suggest that breast cancer risk returns to normal within 2 to 4 years, even among women who've taken hormones for more than 10 years. This issue will eventually be addressed in the WHI, but it can't be done until enough time has elapsed since the end of randomized treatment. How long dense breasts take to return to a less dense state after stopping hormone therapy is unknown.

Does the Link Between Hormone Therapy and Breast Cancer Differ According to a Woman's Weight?

Body weight appears to influence the relationship between hormone use and breast cancer risk. In the Oxford analysis, the Million Women Study, and the WHI, the adverse effect of estrogen-plus-progestin therapy on breast cancer risk was greatest among women who were not obese. Also, data from the WHI suggest that estrogen-only therapy appears to "protect" against breast cancer only for overweight women but not their leaner counterparts. (Recall that the average WHI participant was heavier than the typical woman in the general population who takes menopause hormones.)

Scientists have speculated that the estrogen levels in obese menopausal women are already naturally so high that adding more hormones has little additional impact on the

continued

breast. Restating this in terms of the estrogen-receptor concept (see Chapter 1), the estrogen receptors of an obese woman are already all filled with her own estrogen before she starts hormone therapy. But why might taking estrogen actually protect her against breast cancer? Some researchers believe that conjugated equine estrogens, at least at the traditional oral dose of 0.625 milligrams per day, may be less potent than the body's own estrogen in terms of activating (turning on) estrogen receptors in the breast. According to this view, when an obese woman takes Premarin, it may compete with and prevent some of her body's own estrogen from accessing and binding to her estrogen receptors. Once bound to the estrogen receptors, the Premarin activates those estrogen receptors to a somewhat lesser degree than her own natural estrogen would. Thus, in an obese woman, the net effect of taking Premarin may be to reduce total estrogen-receptor activation and thereby lower breast cancer risk.

The story seems to be different for a leaner woman, who has a lower natural estrogen level to begin with. If she is not on hormone therapy, she doesn't have enough estrogen to fill her estrogen receptors. When she takes Premarin, it binds to and activates her otherwise empty estrogen receptors, thus raising her total estrogen-receptor activation. But because Premarin only weakly activates estrogen receptors, her breast cancer risk is not appreciably raised in the short term.

When progestogen is added to the hormone mix, the picture becomes even more complicated. Any possible protective effect of Premarin in obese women and neutral effect of Premarin in leaner women appears to be offset in the longer term by the harmful effect of the progestogen.

I should emphasize that this idea about body weight affecting the relationship between hormone use and breast cancer is purely speculative, and research is limited. Also, irrespective of weight, women should *never* use estrogen as a strategy to reduce breast cancer risk. The astute reader will notice an apparent contradiction between the body-weight hypothesis and the hypothesis I discussed on page 94 about why estrogen-only therapy seems to carry less risk to women who have had a hysterectomy. One hypothesis implies that hormone therapy is worse for you if you have *higher* levels of your own naturally occurring estrogen, while the other hypothesis implies that hormone therapy is worse for you if you have *lower* levels of estrogen. The reality is that studies to date have not clearly been able to determine the extent to which a woman's own naturally occurring estrogen levels—whether produced by her ovaries or her fat cells—affects how she will react to hormone therapy. Given the difficulty of pinpointing the relationship, it's my opinion that any such effect is likely to be small.

Is Hormone Therapy Safe If You Have a Family History of Breast Cancer?

The WHI found that estrogen-plus-progestin therapy increased the risk of breast cancer by a similar percentage among women deemed to be at high, moderate, or low risk of breast cancer by virtue of their family history and other factors. However, because their risk is higher to begin with, women with a family history of breast cancer will have a larger absolute risk of developing the disease if they take estrogen plus progestin. These findings suggest that if you're at increased risk of breast cancer because of your family history, it may reasonable to take estrogen plus progestogen for a couple of years to relieve very severe menopausal symptoms, but use longer than that should most definitely be avoided (see Chapter 7 for more specific guidance).

Is Hormone Therapy Safe if You've Had Breast Cancer?

Although some observational studies have suggested that hormone therapy does not increase the chance of breast cancer recurring in women with a personal history of the disease, data from a recent randomized clinical trial indicate otherwise. The Hormone Replacement Therapy after Breast Cancer: Is it Safe? (HABITS) trial was designed to determine whether hormone therapy could be taken safely by breast cancer survivors who were suffering from menopausal symptoms. With an average age of 55, the trial participants were relatively young. Among those assigned to the hormone-therapy group, the specific regimen was chosen by the participants' own physicians. Researchers had originally planned to enroll 1,300 women and follow them for five years. However, the trial was halted after only 434 women had been enrolled and followed for two years, because interim analyses revealed that hormone therapy was associated with a significant three-and-a-half-fold increase in the recurrence of breast cancer.[40]

Bottom Line

Estrogen-plus-progestin therapy substantially raises the risk of developing breast cancer if taken for five or more years. Although some observational studies have found a small increase in breast cancer risk associated with five or more years' use of estrogen-only therapy, results from the Nurses' Health Study and the WHI estrogen-alone trial suggest that women with hysterectomy who take estrogen alone for seven years do not appreciably raise their breast cancer risk. Women with a history of breast cancer should not take menopause hormones for any length of time and should discuss treatment options for hot flashes and night sweats with their healthcare providers.

ENDOMETRIAL CANCER

Estrogen, whether produced by your own body or taken as hormone therapy, stimulates the growth of the endometrium—the lining of the uterus. Yet endometrial cancer almost never occurs in premenopausal women who have regular periods because the lining, which thickens every month under the influence of estrogen in anticipation of a pregnancy, is sloughed off as menstrual blood at the start of each cycle. In the process, any precancerous or cancerous cells that may have been lurking in the lining are eliminated from the body. After menopause, the uterine lining naturally tends to thin out because of lower estrogen levels, so endometrial cancer is also relatively rare even after menopause. However, if something—estrogen therapy, for example—prompts the uterine lining to grow unchecked, then any potentially dangerous cells that are present may also proliferate, setting the stage for the development of cancer.

Endometrial cancer usually announces itself early on by producing spotting or bleeding as the uterine lining grows thicker. Women who bleed unexpectedly after not menstruating for a year, as well as women in perimenopause who suddenly develop very heavy menstrual bleeding, should have a vaginal ultrasound and endometrial biopsy to check for potential problems (see Chapter 2). As in the breast, before cancer develops, the endometrial tissue goes through a precursor stage known as hyperplasia, which can be detected by looking at the biopsied tissue under a microscope. Even though hyperplasia is often referred to as precancer, the progression from hyperplasia to cancer is far from inevitable. Indeed, only 1 percent of women with untreated simple hyperplasia and about 30 percent with the most ominous-looking atypical hyperplasias will develop endometrial cancer. Hyperplasia can often effectively be treated with several cycles of a progestogen, which causes menstrual-like bleeding that sloughs off the uterine lining. And endometrial cancer itself is highly curable when caught early. A hysterectomy will do the trick if the cancer has not spread beyond the uterus.

Endometrial cancer was one of the earliest documented risks of menopausal estrogen therapy. In 1995, an analysis of data from 30 case-control and cohort studies found a tripling of risk—i.e., a 200 percent increase—of endometrial cancer in women who took estrogen for one to five years compared with women who had never used estrogen.[41] The risk climbed even higher with longer-term use, such that women on estrogen for 10 or more years experienced a 10-fold increase—i.e., a 900 percent increase—in risk. And, these risks remained noticeably elevated for many years after stopping estrogen.

To counteract the stimulatory effects of estrogen on the endometrium, doctors now routinely prescribe a progestogen to estrogen users who have not had a hysterectomy. Observational studies indicate that 10 to 14 days of progestogen use for each month of estrogen use is sufficient to protect the endometrium, especially if hormone therapy is used for less than five years. These findings are supported by results from the PEPI trial where 24 percent of women assigned to estrogen alone (0.625 milligrams of conjugated equine estrogens) for three years developed atypical endometrial hyperplasia compared with only 1 percent of the women assigned to placebo, but women assigned to estrogen plus progestogen for 12 days each month had no excess risk.[42]

Neither HERS[37] nor the WHI[43, 44] trials found an increased risk of endometrial cancer with a daily regimen of estrogen plus progestin. To the contrary, the findings from these trials hint at the possibility that women who take both of these hormones every day actually have a slightly *lower* risk of endometrial cancer than women who don't use menopause hormones.

Do Very Low Doses of Oral or Transdermal Estrogen Taken Alone Raise Endometrial Cancer Risk?

We have seen that progestogen, rather than estrogen, is the component of hormone therapy that has been most strongly implicated in the development of breast cancer. Because the sole reason for taking progestogen is to counteract the endometrial stimulation brought about by estrogen, scientists have begun asking whether the use of lower estrogen doses than are typically taken can avoid overstimulation of the uterus and the need for a progestogen, while still offering relief from menopause symptoms and/or bone protection. Recent short-term trials show that women assigned to low doses of oral (0.3 or 0.45 milligrams of CEE per day) or transdermal estrogens (0.014 milligrams of estradiol per day) for one or two years have similar—i.e., very low—rates of endometrial hyperplasia as women assigned to a placebo.[45, 46] These findings suggest that proportionately smaller doses of a progestogen—or perhaps none at all—may be all that are necessary to prevent endometrial cancer in women who use low-dose estrogen preparations—good news for women worried about breast cancer. However, these results are not conclusive, and longer-term trials are obviously needed to confirm these findings. In the meantime, current guidelines recommend use of a progestogen in all women with an intact uterus who are taking estrogen therapy.

Does Vaginal Estrogen Raise Endometrial Cancer Risk?

Although less well studied than their oral or transdermal counterparts, low-dose vaginal estrogens, which are taken for relief of vaginal symptoms but don't relieve hot flashes or night sweats, do not appear to stimulate the endometrium. There is controversy about whether vaginal estrogen at higher doses (such as that found in Femring) raises the risk of endometrial cancer. Nevertheless, you shouldn't be on vaginal estrogen—at any dose—indefinitely. It may be wise to take a "drug holiday" (go off estrogen for a few months) and/or to take a 10- to 12-day course of progestogen once every three months while using vaginal estrogen. (If you use Femring, taking a progestogen is mandatory.) If you are considering a vaginal estrogen product, discuss this issue with your healthcare provider.

If I Use Estrogen, Will a Vaginal Progestogen Protect Me Against Endometrial Cancer?

A logical question is whether a progestogen that is applied directly to the uterus or nearby vagina can protect a woman who takes estrogen against an increased risk of endometrial cancer. Short-term studies suggest that the vaginal progesterone gel Prochieve and the progestin-releasing intrauterine device Mirena, both of which were developed for other purposes, may offer the same protection against endometrial cancer as progestogens taken by pill or skin patch. The North American Menopause Society cautiously endorses Prochieve and Mirena to protect the endometrium in women who take estrogen but notes that the two products lack FDA approval for this purpose.

Bottom Line

In women who have a uterus, estrogen-only therapy dramatically boosts the likelihood of developing endometrial cancer, but adding a progestogen eliminates the excess risk. Women who have had their uterus surgically removed do not need to use—and should not use—a progestogen (for the one possible exception to this statement, see the sidebar "Other Uterine-Related Concerns").

Other Uterine-Related Concerns: Fibroids and Endometriosis

Uterine fibroids and endometriosis are two uterine-related conditions that predominantly affect pre- and perimenopausal women and appear to be related to female sex hormones.

Fibroids are pea- to watermelon-sized growths of the smooth muscle wall of the uterus. At least one in four women over age 30 has fibroids. In more than 99 percent of cases, fibroids are not life threatening and do not carry other serious health consequences, although the larger ones can cause painful pelvic pressure or abnormal bleeding. Fibroids tend to shrink and even disappear after menopause, suggesting that high levels of sex hormones are required to sustain their growth. This observation has raised concern that menopausal hormone therapy might cause fibroids to enlarge. However, although good studies on the topic are lacking, it appears that most women with a history of fibroids can take hormone therapy without fear of reactivating fibroid growth. Nevertheless, because we have no good way of predicting how any particular fibroid will respond to hormone therapy, women with a history of fibroids should ask their healthcare providers to monitor them closely for signs of fibroid growth while taking menopause hormones.

Endometriosis occurs when endometrial tissue ends up outside its rightful place in the uterus and travels to other organs in the abdomen and pelvis, including the ovaries, fallopian tubes, the ligaments supporting the uterus, bowels, and bladder. (In rare cases, endometrial tissue can grow in the lungs and more distant parts of the body.) Although endometriosis has not been linked to a higher risk of endometrial, ovarian, or other cancers, the misplaced tissue can develop into growths that cause severe pain, bloating, infertility, scar tissue, and

continued

bowel problems. An estimated 2 to 10 percent of women of reproductive age are affected by endometriosis, but, like fibroids, the condition rarely develops after menopause. Women sometimes opt for hysterectomy and oophorectomy to treat endometriosis. But even then, endometrial tissue may still lurk elsewhere. If a woman takes estrogen after her surgery to relieve hot flashes and other menopause symptoms, it may stimulate the growth of that stray tissue. For this reason, it may be advisable to take a progestogen along with the estrogen, even though there is no longer a uterus to worry about.

COLORECTAL CANCER

Cancers of the colon (also known as the large intestine or large bowel) and rectum rank as the third most common cancers among women in the United States, behind breast and lung cancer.

Data from many observational studies, including the Nurses' Health Study,[47] suggest that hormone therapy reduces a woman's chance of developing colorectal cancer by about one-third. Interestingly, this benefit doesn't seem to depend on how long hormones are taken; short-term use confers about the same degree of protection as longer-term use. The protection fades relatively quickly, however; within five years of stopping therapy, hormone users' risk of colorectal cancer returns to that of never users.

In the WHI, estrogen-plus-progestin therapy was associated with a large and significant 44 percent reduction in the risk of colorectal cancer, and this apparent benefit was observed in participants of all ages.[48] In HERS, estrogen plus progestin also appeared to protect against the development of colon cancer.[37]

In contrast to the estrogen-plus-progestin results, the WHI found that estrogen alone wasn't related to the risk of developing colorectal cancer in the study population as a whole.[16] There did, however, appear to be a beneficial effect among the youngest participants (Figure 4.2). Among women in their 50s, estrogen alone was associated with a 41 percent reduction in colorectal cancer risk, although the relation was not statistically significant—that is, the role of chance could not be ruled out. On the other hand, estrogen alone had little effect on risk of colorectal cancer among women in their 60s, while it actually doubled the risk among women in their 70s.

The ways in which hormone therapy might reduce the development of colorectal cancer are poorly understood. However, administration of estrogen decreases the production of secondary bile acids and lowers blood levels of a growth hormone known as insulin-like growth factor 1. These two compounds are thought to initiate or promote malignant changes in the cells that line the colon and rectum. Other plausible mechanisms involving estrogen receptors exist, but they are less well documented.

Bottom Line

Hormone therapy, especially estrogen plus progestogen, may lower a woman's risk of developing colorectal cancer but should not be taken specifically to prevent this disease.

OVARIAN CANCER

Although conclusive data are lacking, hormone therapy may increase the risk of ovarian cancer, a rare but often fatal disease. In a cohort of 44,000 U.S. women followed from 1979 to 1998, estrogen-only therapy was associated with an increased risk of ovarian cancer, but only after it had been taken for many years.[49] Women who used estrogen alone for 10 or more years were 80 percent more likely to develop ovarian cancer than women who had never used hormone therapy, and the risk climbed even higher after 20 years of use. The study found no increased risk of ovarian cancer among women who took estrogen plus progestin, but few participants had used the combination therapy for more than 4 years. In the American Cancer Society's Cancer Prevention Study II, women who reported 10 or more years of estrogen therapy were twice as likely to die from ovarian cancer as their counterparts who didn't take estrogen.[50] Although the risk dropped somewhat after estrogen use was stopped, it was still higher than that of women who had never used menopause hormones.

Findings from the WHI showed a 58 percent increase in the risk of ovarian cancer among women assigned to 5.6 years of estrogen-plus-progestin therapy compared with their counterparts assigned to placebo.[44] However, the findings were not statistically significant, meaning that the role of chance could not be ruled out.

The WHI results for estrogen-only therapy and ovarian cancer risk haven't yet been reported. As mentioned earlier, 40 percent of women in the estrogen-alone trial had undergone oophorectomy and would therefore be at low risk of developing this cancer. Nevertheless, it will be important to understand the effect of estrogen alone in the rest of the participants.

These data should be considered in context—fewer than 2 in 100 women will develop ovarian cancer in their lifetime. Because the risk of ovarian cancer is low to begin with, a small increase in risk associated with use of hormone therapy does not pose a threat to most women. Indeed, the WHI findings suggest that, if 10,000 women took estrogen-plus-progestin for a year, only one additional case of ovarian cancer would develop. However, if you have a family history of ovarian cancer, this issue should definitely factor into your hormone-therapy decision-making process.

Bottom Line

Long-term use of hormone therapy appears to increase a woman's risk of ovarian cancer.

GALLBLADDER DISEASE

Estrogen raises the level of cholesterol in bile, a substance produced by the liver and stored in the gallbladder. This promotes the growth of gallstones, which consist mainly of cholesterol. (As an aside: after a meal, the gallbladder squirts bile into the intestine, where it aids in the digestion and absorption of dietary fats. Unfortunately, bacteria in the intestine can convert the bile acids released by the gallbladder into the colon-cancer promoting secondary bile acids mentioned earlier.)

Gallstones are surprisingly common among women at midlife, affecting more than 1 in 10 women in their 40s and 1 in 4 women in their 50s. Indeed, medical students have long been taught that the quartet of being "female, fat, fertile, and forty" powerfully boosts gallbladder disease risk. Other risk factors include a high-fat diet and a family history of the disease. Although gallstones can be quite painful, the good news is that, if treated, they rarely lead to serious or long-lasting complications.

Large observational studies consistently report a two- to threefold increased risk of gallstones or cholecystectomy (surgery to remove the gallbladder) among women taking oral menopause hormones. For example, the Nurses' Health Study found that women who were currently using hormone therapy were twice as likely as their counterparts who had never used such hormones to undergo cholecystectomy.[51] The risk climbed even higher with longer duration of use and higher doses of estrogen. Five years after stopping hormone therapy, women who had taken hormones still had an elevated risk of cholecystectomy.

Clinical trials confirm that oral hormone therapy increases the risk of gallbladder disease. In the WHI, 5.6 years of estrogen plus progestin and 6.8 years of estrogen alone were associated with a 67 percent and 93 percent increase in cholecystectomy, respectively.[52] In absolute terms, this translates to 18 excess cases per year among 10,000 women taking estrogen plus progestin, and 31 excess cases among 10,000 women taking estrogen alone. In the HERS trial, women randomized to four years of estrogen-plus-progestin therapy had a 38 percent greater risk of developing gallbladder disease than those assigned to placebo,[53] a risk that climbed to 48 percent after three additional years of observational follow-up.[37] The PEPI trial also found a higher rate of gallbladder complications associated with menopause hormones.[42]

Bottom Line

Hormone therapy strongly increases the risk of developing gallstones, a common condition even among midlife women not on menopause hormones. However, because gallstones don't usually have lasting health consequences, gallbladder considerations don't tend to figure prominently in most women's hormone-therapy decision making.

COGNITIVE DECLINE AND DEMENTIA

One of the most commonly asked questions about hormone therapy is whether it can help ward off normal age-related memory lapses or more serious cognitive difficulties such as Alzheimer's disease and other types of dementia.

Intensive research on estrogen and memory began in earnest more than 15 years ago, when researchers showed that premenopausal women performed better on tests of certain cognitive skills—such as being able to name sequences of colors or pronounce a series of nonsense syllables fluently—during the part of their menstrual cycles when their levels of natural estrogen were highest.[54]

However, other data indicate that estrogen may not stave off memory loss. For one thing, men and women experience a similar pattern of memory change as they age, even though only women experience sharp drops in estrogen at menopause. For another, studies that have looked at whether menopausal women with higher (naturally occurring) estrogen levels do better on memory tests or are less prone to developing Alzheimer's disease than their counterparts with lower estrogen levels have not always found this to be the case.[55–58]

Yet laboratory studies in animals[59] and brain-imaging studies in humans[60] show that supplemental estrogen improves connections between neurons (nerve cells) in the brain and enhances cerebral blood flow, especially in brain areas such as the hippocampus that are involved in the formation and retrieval of memories. Estrogen also boosts certain brain chemicals such as serotonin, dopamine, and acetylcholine. These neurotransmitters are the means by which neurons communicate with each other; low levels of acetylcholine, in particular, have long been implicated in the development of Alzheimer's disease. Moreover, estrogen has antioxidant properties, which enable it to detoxify substances that otherwise might damage brain cells.

Taken in the aggregate, observational studies, most of which used a case-control study design, suggest that hormone therapy is associated with a 30 to 45 percent lower risk of Alzheimer's disease.[61, 62] However, the findings of individual studies on this topic vary wildly. Because women with memory problems (or their family members who fill out study questionnaires on their behalf) may not recall past use of hormones accurately, data from case-control studies of hormone therapy and cognitive function may be unreliable.

Therefore, scientists tend to give more credence to the results from cohort studies of cognitive decline. In the Cache County Study, which followed nearly 2,000 women with an average age of 74 for three years, participants who had ever used hormone therapy were 41 percent less likely than participants who had never used menopause hormones to develop Alzheimer's disease.[63] Upon closer examination, nearly all of the risk reduction occurred among women who had taken menopause hormones in the past. In fact, current users appeared to be at elevated risk of Alzheimer's disease unless they had been taking hormones for more than a decade. Compared with their counterparts who had never taken menopause hormones, women using hormones for 10 years or less were more than twice as likely to develop Alzheimer's disease, while women using hormones for more than 10 years were half as likely to do so. Similar findings were observed in a cohort of nearly

10,000 women aged 65 and older who were followed for four to six years as part of a study on osteoporotic fractures.[64] Women who had started hormone therapy at menopause experienced less cognitive decline—i.e., memory and thinking problems that may or may not rise to the level of full-scale dementia—than women who had never used menopause hormones, but women who began hormone therapy later in life did not.

Partly on the basis of these results, many researchers—myself included—have hypothesized that women who initiate hormone therapy in early menopause and before the onset of degenerative changes in the brain's neurons—and the blood vessels that oxygenate them—may gain cognitive benefit. (Does this hypothesis sound familiar? If you read the earlier discussion of hormones and heart disease, it should—my colleagues and I have proposed a similar idea for hormone therapy's effect on the heart.) Unfortunately, most large-scale cohort studies to date have not looked at menopausal hormone use in relation to changes in memory and thinking in women under age 65. To do so would require that researchers administer very detailed cognitive tests to detect the often subtle declines that some people experience in their 50s and early 60s. This type of testing is very time consuming, very expensive, and, in the setting of large epidemiologic studies, simply not feasible.

Nevertheless, the "timing-is-everything" hypothesis is supported by comparing the results from small clinical trials in two very different groups of women. In a series of trials conducted among healthy women in their mid-40s whose ovaries and uteruses had been surgically removed, participants who were assigned to several months of estrogen therapy immediately after the surgery were able to maintain their presurgery scores on tests of memory, while those who were assigned to a placebo showed declines.[65] Conversely, trials in older women who have already developed Alzheimer's disease show that giving them estrogen is ineffective at slowing further cognitive deterioration.[66–68]

Laboratory studies in animals also support the idea that there is a critical window of opportunity during which hormone therapy might boost brain function. In one such study, rats whose ovaries were removed at midlife received estrogen beginning either at 3 or 10 months after the surgery, or received no hormone. The rats that got the estrogen at 3 months learned to navigate a maze more quickly than the rats that didn't get the hormone. However, the rats that got the estrogen at 10 months did no better at navigating the maze than the rats not on the hormone.[65]

Findings from HERS and WHI confirm that hormone therapy, when started many years after the menopausal transition, does not forestall the development of cognitive difficulties and may, if anything, make matters worse. At the end of the HERS trial, 1,063 participants with coronary disease and an average age of 67 completed a battery of six standardized tests of memory and thinking.[69] The women assigned to estrogen-plus-progestin therapy didn't perform better on any test than did women assigned to placebo.

The WHI Memory Study tested the cognitive function of WHI participants aged 65 and older—including 4,532 women in the estrogen-plus-progestin trial and 2,947 women in the estrogen-only trial—at the beginning and end of these trials. In analyses that combined the data across the two trials, hormone therapy was associated with a 76 percent increase in the risk of developing dementia and a 25 percent increase in the risk of developing milder cognitive difficulties that may (or may not) presage dementia.[70] Looking at the two therapies separately, estrogen plus progestin doubled the risk of dementia but was unrelated to the development of milder cognitive problems,[71] while estrogen alone was associated with a slight increase in the risk of both outcomes.[70] In absolute terms, the WHI results suggest that for every 10,000 women aged 65 and older who take estrogen plus progestin for a year, 23 excess cases of dementia would develop. For estrogen alone, there would be 12 excess cases.

Among women in the WHI, as in the general U.S. population, the most frequently diagnosed type of dementia was Alzheimer's disease, which accounted for just over half of the dementia cases. Alzheimer's disease generally has an insidious onset and slowly progressive course, meaning that memory problems and other symptoms of the disease emerge gradually over many years. The follow-up interval during which dementia cases were diagnosed in the WHI was relatively short—only four to five years. This suggests that some participants may have already experienced cognitive decline at enrollment and that hormone therapy may not have actually caused their dementia but simply hastened its progression or manifestation. Indeed, the adverse impact of estrogen (with or without progestin) on cognitive function was greatest among women who performed relatively poorly on the cognitive test at the start of the trials. This finding provides additional support to the hypothesis that hormone therapy may help keep a healthy brain healthy but may exacerbate any aging-related damage to the brain that has already taken place.

Another common type of dementia is vascular dementia, which is caused by a series of strokes or TIAs that kill or damage nearby brain tissue. Vascular dementia tends to begin more abruptly and to progress more rapidly than Alzheimer's disease. The two conditions often coexist in patients, and it can be difficult to disentangle their symptoms. Although vascular dementia was less commonly diagnosed than Alzheimer's disease in WHI participants, the standard methods that doctors use to assess dementia tend to favor diagnosis of the latter disease over the former when both are present. Given the strong association between hormone therapy and stroke in the overall WHI study population, it is likely that hormone therapy packs a cognitive "double whammy" in older women by precipitating the onset of vascular dementia as well as hastening the progression of Alzheimer's disease.

Over the past decade or so, cardiologists and neurologists have come to the conclusion that what's good for the heart is (almost always) good for the brain, and what's bad for the heart is bad for the brain. Or, more precisely, what's good—or bad—for the heart and brain's blood vessels is also good—or bad—for the brain's nerve cells. The new research on menopause hormones that suggests parallel effects on heart disease and dementia—specifically, that hormone therapy may reduce risk of heart disease and forestall dementia when initiated in early menopause but boost the risk of these diseases when started many years after the menopausal transition—fits nicely with this paradigm.

Bottom Line

Although the data are not yet conclusive, there is some evidence that a woman's age or the initial health of her brain cells may determine whether hormone therapy will help preserve her memory or instead hasten the onset of memory and other thinking problems. Older women who are suffering from memory loss (as evaluated by a neurologist) should not take hormone therapy, while younger, recently menopausal women without serious cognitive difficulties will likely suffer no harmful cognitive effects and may even benefit. However, starting or staying on hormones solely to stave off the scattered thinking that many women complain of at menopause is not warranted.

TYPE 2 DIABETES

Estrogen therapy, with or without a progestogen, may reduce the risk of developing type 2 diabetes, a metabolic disorder characterized by excess glucose (sugar) in the blood that results from defects in insulin action. Insulin is a hormone produced by the pancreas.

Some of you may be unsure about the distinction between type 1 and type 2 diabetes. People with type 1 diabetes, a condition that often develops in childhood or adolescence, cannot produce insulin and must take lifelong insulin shots to remain healthy. By contrast, people with type 2 diabetes, a condition that tends to develop in midlife or later (but has recently been diagnosed at much younger ages), actually manufacture plenty of insulin, at least in the early stages of the disease. In fact, their blood insulin levels are often higher than or similar to the blood insulin levels of people without diabetes. But their cells respond sluggishly to this insulin (a condition known as insulin resistance) and therefore cannot efficiently absorb the sugar molecules that circulate in the bloodstream and that are necessary for the body to function properly. This leads to blood sugar levels that are much higher than normal. Prediabetes, also called impaired glucose tolerance, is a condition in which blood glucose levels are somewhat elevated but not high enough to be classified as full-fledged type 2 diabetes.

Type 2 diabetes is best treated with diet and exercise, and, in certain cases, medications to reduce the body's resistance to insulin. After many years of pumping out high amounts of insulin in an attempt to prod the body into using this hormone the way nature intended, the overworked insulin-making cells of the pancreas may eventually become exhausted and wear out completely. When this happens, insulin shots may be required.

Although the data are not entirely consistent, hormone therapy in menopause seems to rapidly enhance the body's ability to use insulin. For example, fasting blood tests in a randomly selected sample of participants in the WHI estrogen-plus-progestin trial indicated that blood glucose and insulin levels improved significantly during the first year of the trial in women in the hormone-therapy group but not among women in the placebo group.

In a 12-year follow-up of participants in the Nurses' Health Study, by far the largest observational study of the issue to date, my colleagues and I found that women taking hormone therapy were 20 percent less likely than women who had never taken menopause hormones to develop diabetes, after factoring out the effects of excess body weight and other potentially confounding variables.[72] (Obesity, particularly abdominal obesity, is a powerful risk factor for type 2 diabetes. Indeed, the two conditions are so closely connected that researchers have recently coined the term *diabesity* to refer to the tight link. Even small variations in body weight among those who are not obese boost diabetes risk dramatically. Thus, studies looking at the influence of hormone therapy—or other factors—on diabetes risk must carefully control for the effects of excess body weight to obtain accurate results.)

Consistent with the Nurses' Health Study findings, the WHI estrogen-plus-progestin trial also reported that hormone therapy cut the risk of type 2 diabetes by about one-fifth, even when the effects of weight changes that occurred during the 5.6-year treatment period were taken into account.[73] This translates into 15 fewer cases of diabetes per 10,000 women per year of estrogen-plus-progestin use.

Similarly, a reduction in diabetes risk associated with estrogen-plus-progestin therapy was noted in the HERS trial.[74] The WHI estrogen-alone trial also found a hormone-related reduction in diabetes risk, although the effect was not quite as large as for estrogen plus progestin.[75]

What's the Effect of Hormone Therapy in Women Who Already Have Diabetes?

If a woman already has diabetes, will taking hormone therapy improve her body's ability to use insulin and thereby reduce her blood sugar levels? Possibly, but women with type 1 or type 2 diabetes should avoid hormone therapy because they have a much higher than usual risk of developing coronary heart disease and stroke. Indeed, medical professionals often refer to diabetes as a "heart-disease risk equivalent," meaning that women who have diabetes are just as likely to experience a future heart attack or other coronary event as women who already have heart disease. And, as I noted earlier, women at elevated risk of cardiovascular disease should not take menopause hormones.

Indeed, once diabetes has developed, it alters the body's sensitivity not only to insulin but also to other hormones, including estrogen. Emerging data suggest that diabetes—both types 1 and 2—renders estrogen receptors in many organs less sensitive to the estrogen naturally produced by a woman's body. It's unclear whether estrogen taken as part of hormone therapy would be more effective than the body's own estrogen at activating these receptors in menopausal women. Women with diabetes also tend to have a higher ratio of androgens to estrogens than do women without diabetes. Some researchers believe that these two factors—a relative insensitivity to estrogen and an excess of androgen—help to explain why diabetes wipes away any protection that women ordinarily have prior to menopause vis-à-vis men in terms of coronary heart disease.

A Note About Polycystic Ovary Syndrome

An estimated 5 to 10 percent of women have polycystic ovary syndrome (PCOS), a condition that can disrupt a woman's menstrual cycle and negatively affect fertility and appearance, causing acne, excessive hair growth, and weight gain. Doctors aren't sure what causes PCOS but suspect that the core problem, as with type 2 diabetes, may be insulin resistance. Thus, their bodies try to compensate by over-producing insulin, which in turn prompts the ovaries to make too much androgen. Women with PCOS have a higher-than-usual risk of type 2 diabetes as well as cardiovascular disease and should as a general rule avoid hormone therapy.

Bottom Line

Hormone therapy may lower the risk of type 2 diabetes. However, many women at risk for diabetes are also at heightened risk for developing coronary heart disease and stroke and are therefore not good candidates for hormone therapy.

LUPUS AND OTHER AUTOIMMUNE DISORDERS

Autoimmune disorders occur when the immune system declares war on the cells, tissues, or organs it normally protects. Such disorders strike at least three times as many women as men, possibly because of the effects of female sex hormones on the immune system. Women are most vulnerable during their reproductive years. Thus, many clinicians believe that estrogen plays a critical role in activating autoimmune disorders and avoid prescribing hormone therapy for women with these conditions.

After menopause, hormone therapy may increase the risk of developing certain autoimmune disorders, including systemic lupus erythematosus and rheumatoid arthritis. Although data are limited, two observational studies—the Nurses' Health Study[76] and a national case-control study in the United Kingdom[77]—suggest that menopausal hormone therapy is associated with a doubling or tripling of lupus risk. (However, because lupus rarely develops after menopause, the absolute risk is very low.) On the other hand, observational studies of hormone therapy and rheumatoid arthritis vary greatly in their findings, with some showing an increased risk and some a decreased risk. In the Nurses' Health Study, there was no relation between hormone therapy and risk of rheumatoid arthritis.[78]

Symptoms of lupus—e.g., skin rashes, swollen and aching joints, nose or mouth ulcers, headaches, fatigue, low-grade fever, and inflammation of the sacs surrounding the heart (pericarditis) or lungs (pleuritis)—tend to wax and wane; a severe flare-up of several weeks' duration is often followed by months or years of mild or even no symptoms. Thus, a logical question is whether women who already have lupus can take hormone therapy to relieve menopause symptoms without causing their autoimmune symptoms to flare up. Few data have addressed this question, but results from a recent study offer cautious optimism. In a yearlong clinical trial that assigned 351 women with lupus to either cyclic estrogen plus progestin (0.625 milligrams of conjugated equine estrogens daily plus 5 milligrams of medroxyprogesterone acetate for 12 days per month) or placebo, hormone therapy didn't significantly increase severe flares of lupus symptoms, although it did increase milder flares.[79] On the basis of these findings, a woman who finds her hot flashes and night sweats to be more intolerable than symptoms of her particular autoimmune disorder can reasonably consider taking menopause hormones. Obviously, if she finds that such hormones precipitate a severe autoimmune flare-up, then she should stop using them.

However, another caveat is in order. Women with lupus are more prone to blood clots and to cardiovascular disease than women without lupus. And, as we've seen, hormone therapy increases the risk of blood clots. Therefore, women with lupus should determine whether they have any additional risk factors for clotting or for cardiovascular disease; if they do, they should not take hormone therapy.

Bottom Line

Hormone therapy may increase the risk of developing lupus and may cause mild flare-ups in women with the condition. Whether hormone therapy increases the risk of rheumatoid arthritis is unclear.

OTHER DISORDERS

On the basis of limited observational and clinical trial data, scientists have hypothesized that hormone therapy may affect the risk of other disorders. I mention relevant findings here for completeness' sake, but the jury is still out on these hypotheses. Much more research is needed to confirm or refute them.

Asthma

Some studies suggest that hormone therapy may increase a woman's risk of developing asthma or make her symptoms of asthma worse if she already has the condition, but others suggest the opposite. For example, hormone therapy was predictive of a twofold increase in the rate of newly diagnosed asthma in the Nurses' Health Study.[80] (Because asthma rarely develops for the first time after menopause, the absolute increase in risk was modest.) But data from another well-designed observational study of 2,353 women aged 65 and older showed that hormone therapy was associated with better lung function, both in those with healthy lungs and in those who had previously been diagnosed with asthma.[81]

Lung Cancer

In recent years, researchers have recognized that women may be more susceptible to lung cancer than men. Women who develop lung cancer do so at younger ages than men and often at lower doses of smoking. Indeed, women who have never smoked are believed to be more likely to develop the disease than men who have never smoked, although this remains controversial. These findings suggest a possible hormonal link. Reassuringly, the WHI found that estrogen-plus-progestin therapy was not associated with lung cancer risk.

Osteoarthritis

Hormone therapy may reduce the risk of osteoarthritis. However, studies of the association between hormone therapy and symptomatic osteoarthritis in the knees and hips are less consistent in suggesting a protective role for estrogen than are studies of osteoarthritis detected by radiographic imaging, which may or may not be accompanied by symptoms. In HERS, the only clinical trial to look at the issue, estrogen plus progestin had no effect on the prevalence or severity of knee pain.[82]

MENOPAUSE-RELATED SYMPTOMS

Whew! After reviewing all the risks (plus a few benefits), you may have lost sight of the main benefit—and it's a clear, unambiguous one—offered by hormone therapy, so it's worth a quick recap here: hormone therapy most definitely helps with hot flashes, night sweats, and vaginal dryness. However, whether it offers relief from other symptoms less clearly linked to the hormonal changes of menopause remains uncertain.

Hot Flashes and Night Sweats

Dozens of randomized clinical trials have shown that supplemental estrogen with or without a progestogen is extremely effective in reducing hot flashes in recently menopausal women. The WHI and HERS also show that estrogen reduces hot flashes even in older women who have experienced them for many years. Keep in mind that the purpose of these trials was to look at the relationship between hormone therapy and the long-term risk of developing various diseases, not to look at whether hormone therapy relieves menopause symptoms. Indeed, women were specifically discouraged from participating in these trials if they suffered from severe hot flashes and night sweats. Why? If they happened to be assigned to the placebo group, they would not be able to opt for hormone therapy on their own without compromising the integrity of the trial.

Still, a sizeable minority of the women in these trials did have menopause symptoms, and, for these women, hormone therapy proved to be very helpful. Of women with moderate-to-severe hot flashes at the start of the WHI, 86 percent of the women assigned to estrogen-plus-progestin reported significant symptom relief after 1 year of treatment, compared with 58 percent assigned to the placebo group.[83] (The estrogen-alone findings haven't yet been reported.) Similar results were found in HERS. Among those with hot flashes at the start of the trial, 85 percent of the women assigned to estrogen plus progestin reported relief from their symptoms, compared with 48 percent assigned to the placebo.[84] In PEPI, a trial in which most of the participants were within 10 years of menopause, women assigned to estrogen were 58 percent more likely to report relief from hot flashes and night sweats than were women assigned to placebo.[85]

Other Symptoms

The impact of hormone therapy on more general quality-of-life outcomes is less certain. In the WHI study population as a whole, women assigned to estrogen plus progestin[86] or estrogen alone[87] experienced little improvement in sleep, mood, energy, or sexual satisfaction as compared with women assigned to placebo. However, in analyses limited to 50- to 54-year-old women who reported moderate to severe hot flashes at the start of the estrogen-plus-progestin trial, hormone therapy was associated with a significant improvement in sleep, though not in mood or other symptoms.[86] In HERS, estrogen plus progestin was associated with improved mood only among those who suffered from hot flashes or night sweats at baseline.[84] In fact, women without such complaints who received hormone therapy were more likely to experience *declines* in energy than those assigned to placebo, perhaps as a result of an increased rate of heart disease and stroke (remember, these were high-risk women with prior heart disease).

So What Is the Overall Benefit-Risk Balance of Hormone Therapy?

Although hormone therapy clearly relieves hot flashes and prevents osteoporotic fractures and possibly colorectal cancer and type 2 diabetes, these benefits may for some women be offset by heightened risks of coronary heart disease, stroke, venous thromboembolism (blood clots in the legs or lungs), breast cancer, gallbladder disease, and memory and thinking disorders. My colleagues and I have used the WHI findings to provide a concise summary of the overall impact of hormone therapy, which I describe in this section. But keep in mind that the balance of benefits and risks will be different for each woman, depending on her age and health history.

Estrogen-Plus-Progestin Therapy

The WHI findings suggest that among every 10,000 women aged 50 to 79 taking estrogen plus progestin each year, there would be five fewer hip fractures and seven fewer colorectal cancers, but also six more heart attacks or other coronary events, seven more strokes, ten more pulmonary emboli (blood clots in the lungs), and eight more invasive breast cancers. To summarize the impact of hormone therapy across these important outcomes, WHI researchers created a composite outcome (a "global index") that included all of these events, plus endometrial cancer and death due to any cause. (Estrogen plus progestin didn't affect the risk of these two outcomes.) Overall, the net effect would be 19 additional harmful events per 10,000 women taking estrogen plus progestin per year.[43]

Timing Is Everything

Newly menopausal women tend to have a better benefit-risk balance with hormone therapy than women who are well past menopause

- Laboratory studies show decreased atherosclerosis in animals that are given estrogen right after menopause but not later.
- Observational studies show that women on hormone therapy have a 35 to 50 percent lower risk of coronary heart disease than women not on hormone therapy. Four of five of hormone users in such studies start their therapy within 3 to 4 years of their last menstrual period. Hormone users who start their therapy 10 or more years after menopause don't derive any heart benefit.
- Clinical trials similarly suggest that newly menopausal women do better on hormone therapy than women many years past menopause, not only in terms of CHD but in terms of the overall balance of health benefits and risks.
- Younger women have a lower baseline risk of many diseases, including CHD, stroke, venous thromboembolism, breast cancer, and osteoporotic fracture, than older women.

Therefore, although hormone therapy generally affects the relative risk of some diseases in younger and older women in a similar manner (CHD being the notable exception), the relative risks translate into a lower absolute risk of adverse outcomes in younger women.

Estrogen-Only Therapy

Analyses of the estrogen-only data of the WHI do not show a clearly favorable balance of benefits and risks for such therapy when used to prevent chronic disease among women with hysterectomy as a whole. However, unlike the results for estrogen plus progestin, the findings for estrogen alone suggest that the benefits and risks appear to be reasonably well balanced. Totaling up the impact of estrogen-only therapy on seven important outcomes—coronary heart disease, stroke, pulmonary embolism, breast cancer, colorectal cancer, hip fracture, and death—yielded a net effect of only two additional harmful events per 10,000 women on estrogen-only therapy per year.[16]

But Timing Is Key . . . and So Is Your Personal Health Profile

When you start hormone therapy will powerfully influence whether its benefits are likely to exceed its risks, or vice versa. As discussed earlier, women who were older or further from menopause were more likely than women who were younger or closer to menopause to suffer a heart attack or die of coronary causes as a consequence of being randomized to hormone therapy (as opposed to placebo) in the WHI. Given that heart disease is a large contributor to the burden of chronic disease in U.S. women, it may come as no surprise that age not only influenced the relationship between estrogen-only therapy and heart disease but also whether such therapy was useful for the prevention of chronic disease overall. Among women in their 50s, assignment to estrogen was associated with a 27 percent reduction in death, as well as a 20 percent reduction in the composite outcome of CHD, stroke, pulmonary embolism, breast cancer, colorectal cancer, hip fracture, and death. In contrast, among women in their 60s, estrogen had little effect on the composite outcome; and among women in their 70s, estrogen was associated with a slight *increase* in these adverse events. A parallel analysis for estrogen-plus-progestin therapy is not yet available.

Cognitive and quality-of-life outcomes were not included in the benefit-risk calculations. Yet, although the data aren't entirely consistent, results from observational studies and clinical trials also suggest that, as for heart disease, initiation of hormone therapy soon after menopause may help preserve memory and other cognitive abilities, whereas later initiation—that is, after degenerative changes in the brain have already begun—has a negligible or even harmful effect on cognitive function. In addition, hormone therapy provides greater quality-of-life benefits in recently menopausal women, as they tend to suffer more from hot flashes and associated symptoms than women who are many years past the menopausal transition. Taken as a whole, these findings indicate that when you start hormone therapy may critically determine its balance of benefits and risks.

This timing is critical in large part because age is such a powerful determinant of our risk of developing various diseases. But, as you will see in a later chapter, many other factors contribute to disease risk and thus influence whether hormone therapy is or is not advisable for any given woman. A one-size-fits-all recommendation is just not possible.

5

HORMONE THERAPY: A PLETHORA OF CHOICES AND THE TRUTH ABOUT BIOIDENTICAL HORMONES

◉

Long the mainstay of treatment for menopausal symptoms, supplemental estrogen remains the most effective therapy for hot flashes and vaginal discomfort. If you decide to take hormone therapy, the array of options facing you may seem bewildering. In addition to selecting a specific type of estrogen and, if necessary, progesterone or progestin (collectively known as progestogens), you will need to choose whether to take a pill, wear a patch, or use some other method of delivery. If you take a progestogen, you will also need to decide on a drug schedule—i.e., whether to take the hormone on a daily or a cyclic basis. Your menopause symptoms, medical history, and personal preferences will help determine the treatment that's best for you. Working with your healthcare provider, you can tailor the treatment to best meet your needs. Given the small but measurable health risks associated with hormone therapy, a general guideline is to use the lowest effective dose for the shortest time possible. I lay out the various options in this chapter and in Tables 5.1, 5.2, and 5.3.

THE DIFFERENT TYPES OF ESTROGEN THAT YOU CAN TAKE

Estrogens are available in many prescription preparations, both alone and in combination with progesterone or progestin. Most estrogen-only products—also known

Table 5.1 Estrogen Products

Type of Estrogen	**Pills:** For systemic relief of menopausal symptoms, such as hot flashes and vaginal discomfort	**Transdermal Products (skin patches, creams, gels):** For systemic relief of menopausal symptoms, such as hot flashes and vaginal discomfort	**Vaginal Products:** For local relief of vaginal dryness and discomfort
Conjugated equine estrogens (CEE)	Premarin		Premarin Vaginal Cream
Synthetic conjugated estrogens	Cenestin, Enjuvia		
Esterified estrogens	Menest		
17-beta-estradiol*	Estrace, various generics	Alora, Climara, Esclim, Estraderm, Estrasorb, EstroGel, Vivelle, Vivelle-Dot†	Estrace Vaginal Cream, Estring Vaginal Ring
Estropipate	Ogen, Ortho-Est, various generics		
Estradiol acetate			Femring Vaginal Ring‡
Estradiol hemihydrate			Vagifem Vaginal Tablet
Ethinyl estradiol	Estinyl		

* Bioidentical hormone

† All are skin patches except for Estrasorb (a cream) and EstroGel (a gel).

‡ Femring provides a higher dose of estrogen than other vaginal products and is intended for systemic rather than simply local relief of menopausal symptoms.

as "unopposed estrogen"—are recommended only for women who have had a hysterectomy because, without an added progestogen, they greatly increase the risk of endometrial (uterine) cancer.

Pills, patches, skin creams and gels, and one brand of vaginal ring (Femring) all contain estrogens that work systemically—i.e., throughout the whole body—to treat symptoms of menopause. With each of these estrogen products, women with an intact uterus should use a progestogen to protect against endometrial cancer. If you take systemic estrogen, you can expect hot flashes and related symptoms to

Table 5.2 Progestogen Products

Type of Progestogen	Pills	Vaginal Gel	Intrauterine Device
Medroxyprogesterone acetate (MPA)	Amen, Cycrin, Provera, various generics		
Norethindrone (norethisterone)	Camila, Micronor, Nor-QD		
Norethindrone acetate	Aygestin, various generics		
Norgestrel	Ovrette		
Megestrol acetate	Megace		
Progesterone*	Prometrium	Prochieve 4%	
Levonorgestrel			Mirena

*Bioidentical hormone

subside within the first month of treatment, although it can take up to three months to feel complete relief.

For women troubled mainly by vaginal dryness rather than hot flashes and night sweats and who want to avoid the potential health risks associated with systemic estrogen, there are estrogen products designed to have specific, localized effects on the vagina only, including vaginal creams, vaginal tablets, and one brand of vaginal ring (sold under the name Estring). Doctors disagree as to whether women who use vaginal estrogens need to take a progestogen periodically to protect the uterus. Although these products target the vagina, they do have weak systemic effects, as evidenced by small but measurable increases of estrogen levels in the bloodstream. Therefore, I believe women on vaginal estrogen, even at very low doses, should take an occasional drug holiday from the hormone or, alternatively, add a progestogen periodically—say, one week for every three months of estrogen use.

Estrogen Pills

Many types of estrogen are available in pill form, which has traditionally been the most popular method for taking hormone therapy. With the exception of Premarin,

Table 5.3 Combined Estrogen/Progestogen Products

Type of Hormones	Regimen	**Pills:** For systemic relief of menopausal symptoms, such as hot flashes and vaginal discomfort	**Skin Patches:** For systemic relief of menopausal symptoms, such as hot flashes and vaginal discomfort
Conjugated equine estrogen and medroxyprogesterone acetate	Cyclic combined	Premphase	
Conjugated equine estrogen and medroxyprogesterone acetate	Continuous combined	Prempro	
Ethinyl estradiol and norethindrone acetate	Continuous combined	Femhrt	
17-beta-estradiol and norethindrone acetate	Continuous combined	Activella	CombiPatch
17-beta-estradiol and norgestimate	Intermittent combined	Prefest	
17-beta-estradiol and levonorgestrel	Continuous combined		Climara Pro
17-beta-estradiol and drospirenone	Continuous combined	Angeliq	

all of the estrogen preparations described here are synthesized in the laboratory from plant sources.

Conjugated Equine Estrogens (CEE)

The prescription drug Premarin has for many decades been the top-selling and best-studied hormone therapy in the United States, although it has lost some ground to other formulations in the wake of the fallout from the Women's Health Initiative (WHI). Premarin is made mainly of a mix of estrogens extracted from *pregnant mares'* ur*ine* (hence the name). Its major components are estrone sulfate, equilin sulfate, and 17-alpha-dihydroequilin, which make up about 50, 25, and 15 percent of the preparation, respectively. Estrone sulfate is an estrogen produced by both humans and horses, but the latter two compounds are unique to the horses. It is unclear exactly which of the components in Premarin are responsible for its effects —both positive and negative—in menopausal women. Indeed, the FDA has never approved a generic form of Premarin because all of the active ingredients in its unique formula have not been identified. Therefore, other manufacturers cannot meet FDA generic equivalency standards.

The standard or conventional oral dose of Premarin is 0.625 milligrams per day. It's also available at two lower doses—0.3 and 0.45 milligrams—and two higher ones—0.9 and 1.25 milligrams. Most doctors recommend that you take the lowest dose needed to make your menopause symptoms manageable. Recent studies have shown that many women experience substantial relief from hot flashes and other symptoms at one of the lower doses.[1] However, women who have had their ovaries removed before they stopped menstruating may require, at least initially, the standard or even a higher dose to relieve symptoms adequately.

Other Conjugated Estrogens

Nonhorse versions of Premarin have been developed in recent years. These estrogen mixes, which are marketed in the United States as Cenestin and Enjuvia, contain many of the same components as Premarin, although the exact blend of hormones is somewhat different. The two brands received FDA approval in 1999 and 2004, respectively. Their profile of benefits and risks is believed to be similar to that of Premarin, but there are no long-term data on these products. Like Premarin, the standard dose is 0.625 milligrams per day, with lower- and higher-dose pills available.

17-Beta-Estradiol

Although it is manufactured in the lab from plants, 17-beta-estradiol—or, simply, estradiol—is a chemically exact duplicate of the estradiol that is naturally produced in great abundance by the ovaries of premenopausal women. As such, it is often referred to as *bioidentical* or *natural estrogen*, as are other manufactured products that have the same chemical structure as the body's two weaker estrogens, estrone and estriol (see also "A Closer Look at Bioidentical Hormones" later in this chapter). When first introduced, estradiol was available only by injection. In the 1970s, an oral form was developed thanks to micronization, a technique that pulverizes the hormone into tiny particles that are easily absorbed by the digestive tract. Estradiol pills, sold as Estrace or various generics, are only about 60 percent as potent as conjugated estrogen pills, so higher doses are needed to achieve the same effects. The standard oral dose is 1 to 2 milligrams per day, although a low-dose pill of 0.5 milligrams is also available. Depending on your insurance, estradiol may be less expensive than Premarin because of the existence of generic forms.

Esterified Estrogens

A mixture similar in potency to conjugated estrogens, esterified estrogens are sold in the United States under the brand name Menest, which comes in 0.3-, 0.625-, 1.25-, and 2.5-milligram tablets.

Estropipate

A form of estrone sulfate that has been stabilized by a compound called piperazine, estropipate is sold in the United States as Ogen and Ortho-Est. Both brands are available in 0.75- and 1.5-milligram doses, and Ogen also comes in a 3- and 6-milligram pill. Generic equivalents are also available.

Ethinyl Estradiol

Despite its name, ethinyl estradiol, marketed as Estinyl, has a very different chemical structure from human estradiol. It is very potent, so the standard dose is only 0.005 milligrams, or 5 micrograms. Although widely used in birth control pills, it is rarely prescribed for menopausal hormone therapy nowadays.

Estrogen Patches

Estrogen can be delivered through the skin by means of a transdermal patch. Patches are worn discreetly on the abdomen or buttock. All of the patches sold in the United States contain estrogen in the form of 17-beta-estradiol, in doses that range from 0.025 to 0.1 milligrams per day.

As you might deduce from comparing these doses to the aforementioned oral doses, estradiol taken by patch is more potent than estradiol taken by pill. Why?

A drug that is taken by mouth must first be metabolized by the liver (after passing through the digestive system), which alters its chemical structure, before entering the bloodstream and being delivered to all of the body's tissues. By contrast, a drug that is taken through the skin is absorbed directly into the bloodstream, with its chemical structure intact. When a woman takes estradiol in a pill, the liver converts it to estrone, a much weaker estrogen, before it enters the bloodstream. By contrast, when she takes estradiol in a patch, it enters the bloodstream directly— as the more powerful estradiol.

There are two types of transdermal patches: reservoir patches and matrix patches. The original patch, introduced in the 1980s and marketed as Estraderm, is a plastic disk with a small reservoir containing a solution of estradiol and alcohol. The alcohol carries the drug through a membrane in the patch and into the skin.

Introduced in 1995, matrix patches, including Alora, Climara, Esclim, and Vivelle, quickly became more popular than the reservoir patch. Estradiol is impregnated in the adhesive on the patch instead of being held in a reservoir, which permits the entire surface of the patch to stick to the skin. Matrix patches are thinner and less bulky, remain in place better, and may be less likely to irritate the skin than reservoir patches. And, unlike reservoir patches, matrix patches can be cut with a scissors, allowing you further control over the amount of hormone delivered. This technique is often used to taper off hormones.

Standard-dose patches are designed to release 0.05 milligrams of estradiol per day (roughly equivalent to 0.625 milligrams of oral conjugated estrogens or 1 milligram of oral estradiol), but nearly all manufacturers offer lower-dose (0.025 and 0.0375 milligrams per day) and higher-dose (0.075 and 0.1 milligrams per day) versions as well. As is the case for oral estrogens, many women find lower doses of transdermal estrogens to be as effective as the standard dose in relieving hot flashes.

Once the patch is affixed to the skin, it starts to release hormone. In 20 hours or so, blood levels of estradiol reach a maximum concentration—a level that remains steady for the duration of the patch's life. Most patches are worn for three or four days; Climara is kept on for a week. The Vivelle patch is available in a miniature version, the Vivelle-Dot, which may be preferred by women whose skin is sensitive to adhesives.

Interestingly, estrogen doses that may be too low to relieve menopause symptoms for most women still offer bone benefits. Indeed, one matrix patch, Menostar, which delivers a very low dose of estradiol (0.014 milligrams per day), is prescribed for osteoporosis prevention rather than symptom relief. However, if a

If You Use the Patch

- Make sure that the skin where you place the patch is clean and dry.
- To help the patch adhere better, wait half an hour after bathing before applying it. Alternatively, dry the area lightly with a hair dryer or wipe the skin with alcohol and allow it to air dry.
- Place the patch on your abdomen or buttocks, where absorption is best. Other acceptable locations are the thigh, back, or upper arm. Never apply the patch to your breast.
- Carefully pull away half the backing and apply the patch to your skin without touching the adhesive backing. Remove the rest of the backing and press that section to your skin.
- Gently rub the patch with your fingers in a circular pattern for several seconds to make sure the edges securely adhere to your skin.
- You can shower, bathe, and swim while wearing the patch. Do not use sunscreen on the skin near the patch, because it may cause too much estrogen to be absorbed.
- If the patch starts to lift while you are wearing it, apply a small piece of first aid tape to hold it in place.
- After removing the patch, apply over-the-counter hydrocortisone cream to soothe the skin. Report any redness or irritation at the site of the patch to your healthcare provider.
- Each time you apply a new patch, choose a different spot.

desire to protect your bones is the only reason you are thinking about hormone therapy, you should consider a nonhormonal option (see Chapter 6).

Estrogen Skin Creams and Gels

Like estrogen patches, estrogen creams and gels contain 17-beta-estradiol that is absorbed transdermally—that is, through the skin. One product, EstroGel, is a clear, odorless, alcohol-based gel that's delivered from a metered-dose pump. The standard dose is 0.035 milligrams. You apply the gel once a day on one arm from the wrist to shoulder. The gel dries completely in two to five minutes. Another product, Estrasorb, is a cream that you rub into your thighs, calves, and/or buttocks; it comes in individual foil packets, each containing 0.025 milligrams of estradiol. The standard dose is two packets per day. Because there are no adhesives, creams and gels don't irritate the skin as the patch sometimes can.

Estrogen Injections

Estrogen is also available in injectable form, as estradiol valerate. Before the introduction of the transdermal patch in the 1980s, injectable estrogen was commonly given to women who did not tolerate oral estrogen well, but it is rarely used now. Frequent shots are required, and most women prefer a less invasive method of taking estrogen.

Estrogen Implants

In other countries, estradiol is available as a subdermal implant—a crystalline pellet placed under the skin in a minor surgical procedure. The implant releases estradiol over several months and is replaced on a periodic basis; the procedure is similar to that used for Norplant, a progestin taken for contraception. One problem with implants is that, because the pellets are under the skin, the dose cannot easily be adjusted up or down. Also, implants may cause hot flashes to worsen when they are first inserted because they cause an estrogen spike, which is followed by a rapid drop. But an implant eliminates the daily inconveniences associated with taking a pill or wearing a patch. Although implants have been used without apparent problems in the United Kingdom and Australia for many years, there seems to be no particular push to market them in the United States.

Which Estrogen Is Better: Pill or Patch?

For estrogen, questions have tended to center more on which delivery method (pill, patch, or cream), rather than which chemical formulation, is best (but see the discussion of bioidentical hormones later in this chapter). And for progestogens, the opposite is true. Unfortunately, there are no clear answers, as surprisingly few studies have been designed to provide head-to-head comparisons between the various products.

Proponents of skin patches and skin creams point out that, unlike oral estrogens, transdermal estrogens initially bypass the liver and digestive system and enter
the bloodstream directly, in much the same way as a woman's own hormones do.
This has several advantages. Unlike oral estrogens, transdermal estrogens do not
stimulate the liver to overproduce triglycerides, inflammation factors, and blood-
clotting factors—which are believed to boost the risk of heart disease and stroke.
Moreover, transdermal estrogens, unlike oral estrogens, do not increase levels of a
protein known as sex-hormone-binding globulin. This protein binds tightly to
testosterone and renders it less biologically active, which may result in low sex
drive—a potential problem with oral estrogens (see "Testosterone Therapy" later
in this chapter). Finally, by bypassing the digestive system, transdermal estrogens
may be less likely than oral estrogens to stimulate the formation of gallstones or to
cause nausea, an occasional problem with oral therapy. And because patches deliver
estrogen in a more constant, steadier manner than do pills, other side effects, such
as headaches, may also be lessened. Thus, women who are concerned about these
issues might be better served by the transdermal route.

Proponents of estrogen pills counter that the first-pass liver effect provided by
oral estrogens dramatically improves cholesterol and blood sugar levels. This may
outweigh the adverse effects on some of the other cardiovascular risk factors and
provide protection against heart disease and type 2 diabetes. This camp also points
out that nearly all of what we know about the health effects of hormone therapy is
based on studies of oral Premarin, and that transdermal estrogens require further
study before concluding that they offer a better balance of benefits and risks. In
other words, until we have more information, they believe that it may be best to
stick with the tried and true (despite the recent questions raised about the "true"
part), rather than switch course prematurely. Finally, many women report that pop-
ping a pill is more convenient, and less irritating to the skin, than wearing a patch.

I believe that the different effects of oral versus transdermal estrogen on various risk factors make a woman's choice between the pill and patch more than just
a convenience issue. The pill might be a better choice for a woman who has a low
level of HDL (good) cholesterol, a high level of LDL (bad) cholesterol, or a borderline elevated blood sugar level (women with full-blown diabetes should avoid
hormone therapy; see Chapters 6 and 7) because studies show that oral estrogen
favorably affects these factors but transdermal estrogen does not. On the other
hand, if a woman has a high triglyceride level, any concern about a tendency toward
blood clotting, or a history of gallstones, she might want to select the patch, since
oral estrogen may aggravate these problems more than transdermal estrogen. Over-

all, there are several theoretical reasons to favor transdermal estrogen, but the absence of large-scale and long-term head-to-head studies make an across-the-board recommendation inappropriate.

What About Estrogen for Vaginal Use?

Women worried about the safety of oral or transdermal hormones may wish to consider low-dose vaginal estrogen to treat vaginal dryness, a common menopausal symptom that can cause significant discomfort and pain. Low-dose vaginal products are at least as effective, if not more so, than pills and patches for relieving vaginal symptoms, although they do not treat hot flashes and related symptoms. And, while some of the estrogen is absorbed into the bloodstream, the amount is far lower than with other methods of delivery, suggesting that vaginal estrogens may not confer the unpleasant side effects (see sidebar "Side Effects of Estrogen and Progestogen") or the long-term health risks of oral estrogens found in the Women's Health Initiative and other studies. Vaginal estrogens come in creams, tablets, or rings.

• **Vaginal creams.** Both Premarin and Estrace are available as vaginal creams. You insert the cream into the vagina daily for two weeks, then once or twice per week. To get a very low dose, you fill the standard applicator only an eighth to a quarter full. It's most convenient to apply the cream at bedtime, as it may leak out when you are standing or sitting. Estrogen cream should not be used as a lubricant before sexual intercourse, as it can be absorbed through a partner's skin.

• **Vaginal tablets.** Vagifem (estradiol hemihydrate) tablets are a somewhat less messy alternative to vaginal creams. The tablets are inserted daily at bedtime for two weeks, then twice per week.

• **Vaginal rings.** Vaginal rings are arguably the most convenient method for using vaginal estrogen, although some women find them uncomfortable. Estring is a soft, silicone-based ring impregnated with 17-beta-estradiol that fits in the vagina like a diaphragm. It delivers a low dose of estradiol (0.006 to 0.009 milligrams, or 6 to 9 micrograms) daily for three months and then must be replaced, by either the woman or her physician. Another vaginal product, Femring, is similar to Estring except that it delivers a higher, systemic dose of estrogen—comparable to that of the 0.05-milligram estradiol patch—in order to relieve hot flashes as well as vaginal dryness. Women with a uterus who use Femring must take a progestogen to protect against endometrial cancer.

The extent to which low-dose vaginal estrogen is absorbed into the bloodstream and carried to other estrogen-sensitive parts of the body such as the breast is unclear. But most studies show that the blood estrogen levels of women using vaginal preparations are much lower than the blood estrogen levels of women using oral or transdermal preparations. On the basis of these results, many doctors—myself included—believe that, for the majority of women, including those at higher-than-usual-risk for heart disease or breast cancer, the risks associated with oral or transdermal estrogen are very low (or nonexistent) with vaginal estrogen.

That said, there is controversy about whether women with a personal history of breast cancer should be exposed to even the very low estrogen levels in vaginal therapies. I would tend to discourage the use of estrogen of any kind (even vaginal estrogen) in women who have had breast cancer. But many oncologists report that their patients have safely used vaginal estrogen for short periods of time (six months or less), without a recurrence of cancer. The North American Menopause Society has not taken a stand on the topic. There are no studies on the long-term health risks of vaginal estrogen, either in the general population of women or in women who have had breast cancer.

There is no evidence that vaginal estrogen poses risks for women with a history of cardiovascular disease.

Which Dose of Estrogen Is Best for You? How Do You Know If You Need to Adjust the Dose?

Here, the answer is actually reasonably straightforward. The basic rule of thumb is to use the lowest estrogen dose that makes your menopausal symptoms tolerable and to take the hormone for as short a time as absolutely necessary, in order to minimize the long-term health risks. Small changes in dosing often make a dramatic difference in how a woman responds to treatment.

Here's how you find the best estrogen dose:

1. Take the lowest (or close to the lowest) available dose of the formulation you have chosen—for example, 0.3 milligrams of conjugated estrogen, 0.5 milligrams of oral estradiol, or 0.025 milligrams of transdermal estradiol—and monitor your symptoms for one to three months.

2. If your symptoms have not subsided to the point where you can comfortably live with them, then increase the dose slightly, and monitor your symptoms for another one to three months.

3. Repeat step 2 until either your symptoms are tolerable *or* you are taking the standard dose, whichever comes first.

Let's look at an example. A woman who had a natural menopause two years ago is experiencing eight severe hot flashes per day, so her doctor prescribes 0.3 milligrams per day of Premarin. After a month, she's still averaging close to six hot flashes per day, so her doctor ups her dose to 0.45 milligrams per day. Soon she's flashing only once per day, and she decides she can live with this.

As with most medications, compromises must often be made. Continuing the example, the woman described here may decide that even the once-daily hot flash she gets with 0.45 milligrams per day of Premarin is quite troublesome. When the dose is increased to 0.625 milligrams, her hot flashes disappear, but her breasts become quite sore—a side effect of the supplemental estrogen. What to do? The pills aren't available in dosages between 0.45 and 0.625 milligrams, but she could fine-tune her dose by taking the 0.45-milligram pill and the 0.625-milligram pill on alternate days. (Estrogen pills cannot easily be split; they may crumble if you try.) Or she could try a different type of pill, such as Estrace, which may reduce her hot flashes but may produce less breast soreness. Or she could switch to a matrix patch. Because they can be cut to produce an in-between dose, patches offer greater control over the dose, as well as a more constant stream of medication, than the pill.

But ultimately, she may still fail to hit upon a therapy that will eliminate all of her hot flashes while avoiding sore breasts. She will then need to decide which of the two problems she is more troubled by and adjust her dose up or down accordingly. It may help her to keep a daily record of symptoms and side effects, so she can more clearly track how these might relate to her estrogen dose and drug choice. Women have highly individualized responses to hormone therapy, so it's impossible to predict in advance how someone is going to react to any given dose or drug.

Many of the longer-term health risks that have been associated with hormone therapy, including stroke, blood clots, breast cancer, and possibly heart disease and gallbladder problems, appear to climb with increasing estrogen doses, so most women, especially those with intact ovaries, should not take more than the standard dose. (If your ovaries have been removed, especially if you were still having periods, you may temporarily need a higher-than-standard dose of estrogen to relieve your symptoms as your body adjusts to the sudden drop in hormones.) If your hot flashes are still bothersome at the standard dose, consider taking an anti-depressant medication (specifically an SSRI such as Effexor) along with your estrogen, rather than continuing to increase the estrogen dose.

Once you have hit upon the right dose, don't assume it will remain stable forever. For example, many women find that hot weather triggers their otherwise well-controlled symptoms, creating the temporary need for more estrogen. Conversely, as they move further away from the menopausal transition, many women find that they can slowly cut back on their estrogen without hot flashes reasserting themselves, and they can eventually stop the drug completely.

What Tests Should You Have During Treatment?

Some healthcare providers advocate blood or saliva tests to determine whether a woman has the "right amount" or "right balance" of hormones and whether to adjust her hormone dose. However, the value of these measurements is highly questionable.

For one thing, the optimal blood or saliva levels of the various estrogens in menopause have not been established. Indeed, although the monthly rise and fall of estradiol and progesterone levels associated with the menstrual cycle are no longer present, hormone levels fluctuate throughout the day as well as from day to day in menopause. For another, the hormone levels in the blood or saliva of an individual woman taking supplemental estrogen seem to be unrelated to whether she suffers from menopause symptoms or how severe those symptoms are.

Finally, blood or saliva levels have not been shown to predict a woman's likelihood of experiencing either short-term side effects (such as headaches) or longer-term risks (such as breast cancer) from hormone therapy. Therefore, as "low tech" as it sounds, the most reliable way to figure out the estrogen dose that is best for you is simply to pay attention to what your body tells you.

THE DIFFERENT TYPES OF PROGESTOGEN THAT YOU CAN TAKE

The term *progestogen* refers to a variety of pharmaceuticals that have been synthesized in the laboratory from plants and that act much like a woman's own proges-

Side Effects of Estrogen and Progestogen

Most women report that estrogen makes them feel better, but up to 10 percent of women report side effects (see Table 5.4). Breast tenderness or abdominal bloating are perhaps the most common. Some women develop nausea or experience a diminished sex drive. Taking a lower estrogen dose, or switching from oral to transdermal estrogen, can minimize these side effects. Headaches may be caused by too much or too little estrogen, so the dose may need to be adjusted either down or up. Some women develop darkened blotchy patches on their face, similar to what can occur during pregnancy.

Progestogens are more apt to produce side effects than estrogen. They can intensify some of the side effects associated with estrogen, including breast tenderness, bloating, and headaches, but they can also produce additional side effects, most notably mood changes such as mild depression, irritability, and anxiety. These mood changes are more likely in women with a history of premenstrual syndrome (PMS) or more serious mood disorders, such as depression. Side effects seem to occur more frequently with progestin than with progesterone. Progestins, especially those that are chemically similar to testosterone, are also more likely than progesterone to cause acne, greasy skin, and, occasionally, increased facial or body hair.

Women who have an intact uterus but cannot tolerate the adverse effect of progestogens may seek to take unopposed estrogen, but most doctors will not prescribe it this way because of the increased risk of endometrial cancer. To avoid the side effects of progestogen, some women with a uterus stop taking the progestogen in their prescribed hormone regimen while continuing to take estrogen. This is a dangerous practice. Any woman with an intact uterus who takes oral, transdermal, or even vaginal estrogen without periodic progestogens should have annual ultrasounds and, possibly, an endometrial biopsy to check for abnormal cell growth in the lining of the uterus.

If you do not tolerate progestogen well, ask your doctor if you can safely lower your dose, try natural progesterone or a different progestin, or try a different route of delivery. Instead of oral progestogen, try taking it via a skin patch (in combination with estrogen), or use a vaginal progesterone gel (Prochieve) or progestin intrauterine device (Mirena).

terone. It encompasses both *bioidentical* (*natural*) *progesterone*—so named because it is chemically identical to a woman's own progesterone—and *progestins*, which are chemically similar to, but distinct from, progesterone. Progestins can be further classified into those that more closely resemble either progesterone or testosterone in chemical structure.

Table 5.4 Side Effects of Hormone Therapy

Side effects of hormone therapy	. . . and how to deal with them:
Fluid retention, including swollen feet, ankles, hands, or abdomen	Reduce the dose of estrogen and/or progestogen; cut back on salt, drink plenty of water, consider taking a mild diuretic (herbal or prescription).
Abdominal bloating or gas	Lower the estrogen dose, switch to another estrogen, switch from oral estrogen to a skin patch; lower the progestogen dose, switch to progesterone or another progestin.
Breast tenderness or swelling	Cut down on salt, caffeine, and chocolate; lower the estrogen and/or progestogen dose; try a different estrogen and/or progestogen.
Nausea	Take estrogen pills with meals or in the evening with a snack; switch to a lower estrogen or progestogen dose; try a different oral estrogen; switch to a skin patch.
Headaches	Cut down on salt, caffeine, and alcohol; drink plenty of water; lower the dose of estrogen and/or progestogen; avoid medroxyprogesterone acetate; switch to progesterone; switch to an estrogen or estrogen-plus-progestogen skin patch, or take progestogen daily rather than cyclically to avoid hormone fluctuations.
Mood changes (PMS-like syndrome)	Cut down on salt, caffeine, and chocolate; drink plenty of water; lower the progestogen dose; switch to progesterone; switch to an estrogen or estrogen-plus-progestogen skin patch, or take progestogen daily rather than cyclically to avoid hormone fluctuations.
Skin irritation under patch	Keep skin under patch very clean; switch to a patch with a different adhesive; apply patch to a different area; switch to oral estrogen.

Other possible side effects include uterine bleeding; dizziness; changes in the shape of the cornea that make it difficult or impossible to wear contact lenses; lowered sex drive; blotchy, darkened patches of skin on the face; acne; or increased facial or body hair.

Although progestogens have sometimes been used alone to treat hot flashes and other symptoms, they are most often prescribed to protect against the increased risk of uterine cancer associated with using estrogen by itself. Women who have had their uterus removed are not at risk for endometrial cancer and thus have no reason to take a progestogen. However, if you have not had a hysterectomy and you wish to take estrogen therapy, your doctor will probably add progestogen to counteract estrogen's stimulatory effect on the uterus. Your doctor may write two separate prescriptions, one for estrogen and one for progestogen. Alternatively, he or she may suggest a combination prescription, which conveniently rolls both hormones into one pill or patch.

Progestogen Regimens

Nearly all women who use estrogen take it on a daily basis. However, if you use a progestogen in conjunction with estrogen, as you should to protect your endometrium, you will need to decide whether to take the progestogen on a cyclic or daily (continuous) schedule.

Cyclic combined therapy provides estrogen every day, with progestogen added for the last 10 to 14 days each month. This regimen mimics the hormone sequence of the normal menstrual cycle. The ovaries make estrogen all of the time, but progesterone is produced by the body only during the second half of the cycle, after ovulation. Indeed, 80 percent women who take hormone therapy on this schedule will have menstrual-like bleeding when the progestogen cycle ends each month, although fertility is not restored. In some women, this withdrawal bleeding, which occurs within three to four days after you stop the progestin, may taper off after a year or so.

In an early variation of this regimen, the estrogen and the progestogen were both administered in cyclic fashion. Estrogen was taken for the first 25 days each month, and progestogen was added to the estrogen on days 16 through 25, followed by 5 or 6 days of no hormones at all. This regimen is rarely used nowadays because many women complained that their hot flashes and other symptoms resurfaced on their days without estrogen.

Continuous combined therapy provides both estrogen and progestogen every day. The main advantage is that monthly withdrawal bleeds do not occur. However, about 40 percent of women do get erratic spotting or light flow while on this regimen. The timing of this "breakthrough" bleeding is unpredictable, so you may need to wear a pad throughout the month to avoid staining. The bleeding usually stops within six months. If it doesn't, or if you have heavier-than-expected bleeding (more common in recently menopausal women), your doctor will probably recommend that you have an endometrial biopsy, because irregular or heavy bleeding can be a sign of endometrial cancer.

Some medical professionals—and I am among them—have voiced concerns that the continuous use of a progestogen may account for some of the adverse effects of combination hormone therapy found in the Women's Health Initiative, especially heart disease. They note that in earlier observational studies, including the Nurses' Health Study, most women who used combination therapy took the progestogen cyclically, with no apparent increased heart disease risk. There is also the theoretical possibility that continuous use of a progestogen might raise the risk of breast cancer more than the less frequent exposure provided by cyclic use of this hormone, although rigorous evidence on this issue is scant. Nonetheless, for the above reasons, I generally favor cyclic over combined therapy, despite the inconvenience of monthly bleeding that cyclic therapy entails.

Intermittent (or *pulsed*) *therapy* is a newer regimen that provides estrogen every day, then adds progestogen intermittently in cycles of three days on, three days off. This regimen is an attempt to balance the potential health risks of continuous therapy against the benefit that daily progestogen offers in terms of minimizing bleeding. By giving the body short, frequent breaks from the progestogen, any adverse effects of continuous therapy might be avoided, yet bleeding patterns remain similar to those of women on such therapy. There is minimal research on the health effects of this regimen.

Progestins

Like estrogen, progestins are most commonly taken in pill form, although patches and a progestin-containing intrauterine device are also available.

Pills

The original—and still most frequently prescribed—progestin for menopausal hormone therapy is *medroxyprogesterone acetate* (*MPA*), which is marketed under several brand names, including Provera, Cycrin, and Amen; generic versions are also available. In the 1970s, the standard dose was 10 milligrams taken for 12 days per month, but more recent research indicates that 5 milligrams taken for 12 days per month protects the endometrium nearly as well but with fewer side effects. You can take a lower dose—2.5 milligrams—if you use MPA on a continuous schedule (i.e., every day of the month). These recommendations assume that you are taking a standard dose of estrogen (0.625 milligrams of conjugated estrogens, for example). If you take a lower dose of estrogen, you can also take a lower dose of MPA.

Two estrogen-plus-progestin pills that offer MPA as the progestin are available. Prempro, which combines Premarin with daily Provera in one pill, comes in three strengths: 0.625 milligrams of CEE plus 2.5 milligrams of MPA (the standard dose), 0.45 milligrams of CEE plus 1.5 milligrams of MPA (the low-dose version, which contains 28 percent less estrogen and 40 percent less progestin than the standard dose), and 0.3 milligrams of CEE plus 1.5 milligrams of MPA (the very low-dose version, which contains 52 percent less estrogen and 40 percent less progestin than the standard dose). Premphase, which combines Premarin with cyclic Provera in a single prescription, comes in one strength only: 0.625 milligrams of CEE plus 5 milligrams of MPA. If you want a lower dose, you need to get two separate prescriptions, one for Premarin and one for Provera.

Megestrol acetate (Megace) is a progestin that has sometimes been prescribed to relieve hot flashes in women who don't want to take estrogen. Unlike other progestins, it's not used in combination with estrogen.

Newer progestins include *norethindrone* (Micronor, Nor-QD, Camila, and various generics) and *norethindrone acetate* (Aygestin and various generics). These progestins tend to cause less breakthrough bleeding than MPA when taken daily with estrogen. They are also more potent than MPA and therefore generally prescribed at lower doses. Two combination pills use norethindrone acetate as the progestin: Activella (with 1 milligram of 17-beta-estradiol) and femhrt (with 0.005 milligrams, or 5 micrograms, of ethinyl estradiol).

Even newer progestins are *norgestimate, levonorgestrel,* and *norgestrel.* Originally developed for contraception, these progestins are used more widely in Europe for menopause than in the United States, where norgesterel is marketed as the Ovrette pill, and norgestimate is marketed in a combination pill (with 17-beta-estradiol) called Prefest for intermittent therapy. Levonorgestrel is available in the Climara Pro patch (with 17-beta-estradiol) and alone in the Mirena intrauterine device (more information in a bit).

Unlike MPA and megestrol acetate, the newer progestins are all more closely related to testosterone than to progesterone. Thus, they may be more likely to cause androgenic (testosterone-like) side effects such as acne, or greasy skin and hair, than MPA. One exception is norgestimate, which, despite its testosterone-like chemical structure, may be less androgenic than other progestins in its class.

Finally, the newest progestin expected to become available for use in menopausal hormone therapy is *drospirenone.* Laboratory studies indicate it appears to have an activity profile closer to that of natural progesterone than that of other progestins. Angeliq, a combination pill containing 1 milligram of 17-beta-estradiol plus 0.5 milligrams of drospirenone, may be introduced into the U.S. market by the end of 2006.

Skin Patches

Some progestins are available combined with 17-beta-estradiol in transdermal patches. The CombiPatch, changed twice per week, comes in two sizes: a smaller patch that delivers 0.05 milligrams of estradiol and 0.14 milligrams of norethindrone per day and a larger patch delivering 0.05 milligrams of estradiol and 0.25 milligrams of norethindrone daily. The Climara Pro patch delivers 0.045 milligrams of estradiol and 0.015 milligrams of levonorgestrel per day and needs to be changed only once per week.

Intrauterine Device

The Mirena intrauterine system is a progestin-containing device that is inserted into the uterus by a healthcare provider. Once in place, it can remain there for up to five years. Levonorgestrel is released from the device at a rate of 0.02 milligrams per day directly into the uterine lining. Originally intended for contraception, Mirena is approved by the FDA only for that purpose; taking it to protect the endometrium against the stimulatory effect of estrogen therapy is an "off-label" use. Nevertheless, short-term clinical trials suggest that it appears to be effective in doing so, and various medical organizations, including the North American Menopause Society, have given Mirena a cautious stamp of approval. The Mirena can cause breakthrough bleeding, but this typically lasts only about three months after insertion. After five months, bleeding is infrequent, and, a year after insertion, most women stop bleeding entirely. The Mirena is not recommended for women who have never been pregnant; in these women, the device causes discomfort when inserted and may later be partially or completely pushed out of the uterus. A smaller device that delivers half the dose of levonorgestrel is being developed specifically for use in menopause but is not yet available.

Progesterone

Progesterone is available in pill form or as a vaginal gel.

Pills

Like oral estradiol, oral progesterone must be micronized—broken down into tiny particles—so that it can be efficiently absorbed by the digestive tract. Before 1998, when Solvay Pharmaceuticals introduced the product commercially in the United States as Prometrium, progesterone capsules could be purchased only from compounding pharmacies (see "Custom-Compounded Hormones"). The progesterone in Prometrium is dissolved in a peanut oil base, so women with peanut allergies cannot take this drug. If you have a peanut allergy and want oral natural progesterone, you will need to purchase it from a compounding pharmacy.

Skin Patch

Progesterone cannot be delivered via a skin patch.

Vaginal Gel

Originally developed to help prevent miscarriages due to low progesterone levels during early pregnancy, vaginal progesterone gel, marketed as Prochieve, is also commonly prescribed off label to protect the uterus in menopausal women who take estrogen therapy. Based on promising results from short-term clinical trials, the North American Menopause Society has endorsed the use of Prochieve for this purpose.

Which Progestogen Is Better: Synthetic Progestin or Natural Progesterone?

Progesterone may produce fewer side effects than progestins, including breast tenderness, bloating, headaches, and, in particular, moodiness or irritability. In addition, data from the Postmenopausal Estrogen/Progestin Interventions (PEPI) trial suggest that progesterone may be less likely than progestin to interfere with estrogen's ability to boost HDL cholesterol and to dilate arteries. At the same time, the PEPI trial also found that progesterone was nearly as likely as progestin to stimulate the growth of breast cells when taken in conjunction with estrogen. On the other hand, very recent findings from a French observational study of women using combination hormones suggest that progestin may be more likely than progesterone to boost breast cancer risk.[2] But, other than this one study, few large-scale investigations have directly compared the effects of progestins and progesterone on actual disease endpoints. Still, I think it may be prudent to opt for progesterone over progestin where possible.

A CLOSER LOOK AT BIOIDENTICAL HORMONES

In the wake of the disappointing results of the WHI trials, there has been growing interest in bioidentical hormones as a safer alternative to Premarin and Prempro. Many women may intuitively perceive bioidentical hormones to be better or safer than other hormones, even though they may not know exactly what a bioidentical hormone is. The confusion partly arises from the fact that the term is used in two different ways.

All scientists and most healthcare providers use the term *bioidentical hormones* to refer to hormone therapies that provide hormones that are an exact molecular match to those made naturally in our bodies. Women make three types of estrogen (17-beta-estradiol, estrone, and estriol), as well as progesterone, testosterone, and other hormones. Thus, bioidentical hormones are drugs that provide one or more of these hormones as the active ingredient.

Many of the government-approved prescription drugs discussed in this chapter contain bioidentical estradiol (Estrace and generic oral tablets, all estrogen skin patches, EstroGel and Estrasorb skin cream, Estrace vaginal cream, and Estring vaginal ring) or bioidentical progesterone (Prometrium capsule and Prochieve vaginal gel). It is possible that these products offer a better balance of long-term benefits and risks than other hormone options such as Premarin and Prempro. But we simply don't know if this is the case, because large-scale trials haven't been done and the science to prove it just isn't there yet.

If you prefer to use bioidentical hormones, then feel free to do so. Indeed, for the reasons discussed in the previous sections, I do tend to favor the use of natural progesterone over synthetic progestins and also believe that transdermal estradiol may have some advantages over oral forms of estrogen. However, until we have solid data from randomized clinical trials that indicate otherwise, the conservative and prudent approach is to assume that all hormone formulations confer a roughly similar balance of benefits and risks.

Custom-Compounded Hormones

Although scientists define the term differently, many consumers and some health-care providers sometimes use the term *bioidentical hormones* to refer only to custom-mixed cocktails of these hormones, prepared according to an individualized prescription from a doctor. Although hormone compounding has been popular in Europe for years, interest in the United States surged only after the WHI results cooled the ardor for Prempro and Premarin. An estimated two million U.S. women now rely on customized hormone products to treat symptoms of menopause.

Custom-compounded bioidentical hormones may offer benefits for women who cannot use a commercially available medication. For example, a patient may be allergic to an ingredient (such as peanut oil in Prometrium) or may require a dose or product mixture not produced by a pharmaceutical company. However, there may also be risks.

- Custom-compounded preparations do not have government approval because individually mixed recipes lack testing to prove that they are absorbed appropriately by the body or provide predictable hormone levels in blood or tissue.

- Preparation methods differ from one pharmacy (and pharmacist) to another, so patients may not receive consistent amounts of medication. In addition, inactive ingredients vary, and contaminants may be present. In 2001, the government purchased and tested 29 products, including hormone preparations, from compounding pharmacies and found that one-third of the samples fell short of standard quality benchmarks. In some cases, the actual potency of the products was much less than the purported potency.

- Expense may be an issue. Many custom-compounded products are classified as experimental drugs and therefore are not covered by health insurance.

Some women may request custom-compounded hormones because they are misled by claims that are not backed up by rigorous scientific research. I'd like to comment on two commonly promoted products.

Estriol

One bioidentical estrogen available only through a compounding pharmacy is estriol, a weak estrogen with 5 to 10 percent the strength of estradiol. Estriol is typically mixed with estradiol and estrone in an oral capsule or skin cream. The usual proportions are 80 percent estriol, 10 percent estradiol, and 10 percent estrone. This mixture is often called Tri-Est. Estriol alone is sometimes used as a vaginal cream.

Naturopaths and compounding pharmacies sometimes promote estriol as providing the benefits of patented estrogen products without increasing certain risks, such as cancer. Proponents have claimed that using estriol may actually prevent breast cancer. Although it is a weak estrogen, estriol can still have a stimulatory effect on the breast and uterine lining. Until more is known, women with a uterus who take estriol should also take a progestogen to protect the uterus. Studies have not determined what effect estriol has on breast cancer risk.

Progesterone Skin Creams

Progesterone skin creams, which are available only through compounding pharmacies, are well absorbed through the skin, but the preparations are often not standardized, so it's hard to know exactly how much progesterone you are getting. If you take estrogen, progesterone skin creams or gels may not adequately protect your uterine lining and should not be used for this purpose.

Some naturopaths and medical authors (most notably the late Dr. John Lee, whose hormone books have been recent bestsellers) advocate using custom-compounded progesterone cream alone, without estrogen, to relieve hot flashes and other menopausal symptoms. However, there has been little research on whether it's effective in doing so, and, more important, zero research on potential long-term risks of this approach. I, along with the majority of doctors, don't recommend it.

An over-the-counter product marketed as "wild yam cream" contains an inactive precursor of progesterone that cannot be metabolized by the human body. Given that it contains no active hormones, wild yam cream is not likely to harm you, but it won't help your menopause symptoms, either. I wouldn't waste my money on it.

TESTOSTERONE THERAPY

Androgens are male hormones, but women's bodies make them too, though in significantly lower amounts. Like men, women produce both a strong androgen, testosterone, and several weaker androgens, including androstenedione and dehydroepiandrosterone (DHEA). About 40 percent of a woman's androgens are made by her ovaries and the rest by her adrenal glands. The ovaries produce testosterone, and the adrenal glands, which sit atop the kidneys, produce the weaker androgens, which are converted to testosterone after they reach their destination in tissues.

Unlike estrogen levels, which fall sharply at menopause, the decline in testosterone occurs gradually over a longer period of time. Testosterone levels peak in early adulthood and then decline slowly and steadily, leaving women in their 40s with about half the testosterone they had in their 20s. Androgens do not disappear completely, however. The ovaries and adrenal glands manufacture them throughout life.

Symptoms associated with fluctuating or low estrogen, such as hot flashes and vaginal dryness, can be hard to ignore, but those produced by the loss of testosterone may go unrecognized because there is no abrupt drop in androgens at menopause. Some signs, such as fatigue and vaginal dryness, are similar to those related to estrogen loss. But testosterone depletion may cause other changes, including thinning body hair—particularly in the armpits and pubic region—and a lowered sex drive. As androgen levels decline, a woman's sexual interest and pleasure can wane. It doesn't occur in every menopausal woman, but loss of libido is particularly likely in women who have had their ovaries removed surgically or who have adrenal insufficiency. Women who are upset by their decreased desire may wonder if testosterone can help.

Do Studies Show Improved Sex Drive?

Medical research offers volumes of data on the effects of estrogen therapy in menopausal women, but no comparable body of information exists on testosterone. Most of what we know comes from small studies or individual cases. Proponents of testosterone therapy claim that it increases sex drive and well-being, improves mood, decreases fatigue, and strengthens bone. Of these, testosterone's effect on libido has received the most attention.

Results from clinical trials show that supplemental testosterone improves sexual function—sexual desire, arousal, and ability to have orgasms—in women after menopause. The earliest studies, conducted in the 1980s and 1990s, used high, injected doses that, while boosting sexual function, also caused masculinizing side effects, such as acne, excess facial and body hair, and a lowered voice, as well as liver problems and unfavorable cholesterol levels. More recent, larger clinical trials of oral[3] or transdermal[4-6] testosterone have found that lower doses—those designed to bring women's testosterone levels more in line with the premenopausal norm—can improve sexual response without producing these side effects, at least in the short term.

For example, a series of three trials tested the effect of an experimental testosterone skin patch in healthy women who said that their sexual pleasure had declined after their ovaries were removed. All the women were taking estrogen therapy and all were in stable, long-term relationships. In the largest and longest of these trials, 533 women wore a patch with 300 micrograms of testosterone or an inactive placebo patch for six months.[5] During the study, they didn't know which patch they were wearing. Compared with those assigned to the placebo patch, the women assigned to the testosterone patch had sex more often and enjoyed it more. Similar results were found in the two smaller trials.

Androgen Products

Compared with estrogen options, testosterone therapies for women are limited.

Testosterone Pill

The only testosterone drug approved by the FDA for use in women is the Estratest pill, and it's approved only to treat hot flashes. But many doctors prescribe it as a remedy for flagging libido. Estratest is a combination of esterified estrogens (1.25 milligrams) with methyltestosterone (2.5 milligrams). Methylation is a process that enables the testosterone to be absorbed by the digestive tract. Estratest HS (half strength) contains half-doses of each hormone. Estratest is usually prescribed daily for 21 consecutive days followed by seven days without medication. To get a lower dose, you can take the pills every other day. Premarin is also sold in a combination pill with 5 or 10 milligrams of methyltestosterone. Unfortunately, these doses may be too high for the majority of women.

Testosterone Patches and Creams

As with estrogen, testosterone absorbed through the skin goes directly into the bloodstream, thus avoiding first-pass liver effects. Rather than a methylated compound, the testosterone in patches and creams is identical to the testosterone produced by the body. For these reasons, it's possible that a patch or cream—or an intramuscular injection—might be safer to use than a pill. Two skin patches (Androderm, Testoderm), a gel (AndroGel), and injectable testosterone are available by prescription, but the FDA has approved these only for men because they deliver a testosterone dose that is far too high for women.

Some doctors do prescribe AndroGel for their female patients, instructing them to rub no more than a quarter of a 2.5-gram packet per day into the skin of the lower abdomen. (Unfortunately, supplemental testosterone doesn't work on an as-needed basis, so you can't take it only before a romantic interlude.) Patches and gels that contain testosterone doses suitable for women are currently being tested in clinical trials, such as those described earlier, but have not yet gained FDA approval. Low-dose testosterone creams are available (with a prescription) from compounding pharmacies; the risks of using custom-compounded products detailed previously also apply here.

DHEA Pills

Over-the-counter supplements of the testosterone precursor DHEA have been promoted by naturopaths as effective in reducing menopause symptoms, improving sexual function, and increasing well-being in women, but there are little data to back up these claims. One small trial of DHEA found that it increased sexual interest and satisfaction in women with adrenal insufficiency,[7] but another trial in such women found no effect.[8] DHEA does not appear to boost the libido of women with intact ovaries. Pharmacologic studies have shown that the DHEA content of supplements is inconsistent and varies enormously.

Should You Take Testosterone?

The women most likely to benefit from testosterone therapy for menopause symptoms or low sexual desire are those with a drastically reduced natural supply of the hormone. You may be a reasonable candidate for supplemental testosterone if your ovaries have been surgically removed; you have Addison's disease, in which the adrenal glands do not function adequately; or you have a disorder of the hypothalamus or pituitary gland, both of which regulate ovarian and adrenal function.

Because testosterone treats some of the same symptoms as estrogen, the standard procedure is to try estrogen therapy first, adding testosterone only if estrogen does not work. Indeed, most medical authorities, including the North American

Menopause Society, recommend that menopausal women never take testosterone by itself, without estrogen. Paradoxically, estrogen pills reduce the amount of testosterone available to the body, because the liver responds to oral estrogen by upping its production of a protein called sex-hormone-binding globulin that makes testosterone less active biologically. Estrogen patches do not have this effect.

However, there are no data on whether supplemental testosterone remains effective or safe if taken for longer than six months or if taken by women who are not also using estrogen therapy. If you take testosterone or DHEA in any form, you'll need regular blood tests to monitor your androgen levels and to pick up any unfavorable changes in cholesterol levels and liver function. Some women may be particularly sensitive to testosterone and susceptible to its masculinizing effects. If you are, or if the dose is too high, you may notice side effects—acne, increased body hair, weight gain (particularly in the belly area), bursts of anger or aggression, or, more rarely, a deeper voice and clitoral enlargement. (These don't happen overnight but occur gradually over time.) It is also unknown whether testosterone therapy increases the risk of breast, uterine, or ovarian cancer; cardiovascular disease; or blood clots. However, very recent data from the Nurses' Health Study suggest that it may indeed increase risk of breast cancer, and there are theoretical reasons for concern about increased cardiovascular risk. To my way of thinking, the potential risks of testosterone therapy outweigh the known benefits for the vast majority of women.

6

WHAT'S YOUR HEALTH PROFILE? HOW TO CALCULATE — AND REDUCE — YOUR PERSONAL RISK OF FIVE HEALTH OUTCOMES ASSOCIATED WITH HORMONE THERAPY

◉

I will now show you how to figure out your risk of developing five common aging-related health outcomes that have been linked in some way to hormone therapy: coronary heart disease, stroke, venous thromboembolism, breast cancer, and osteoporosis. In the next chapter, you will use this information to weigh the benefits and risks of hormone therapy in light of your personal health profile.

I'd like to emphasize that no woman should start (or continue) hormone therapy for the express purpose of preventing cardiovascular disease or any other chronic disease. However, if a woman is considering hormone therapy for treatment of menopausal symptoms, estimation of her risk of other health conditions can help her decide if she's a good candidate for hormone therapy. Generally, the best candidates for hormone therapy are women at low baseline risk of cardiovascular disease. For women whose menopausal symptoms last longer than a few years, decisions about duration of hormone therapy use can be influenced by a woman's risk of breast cancer and osteoporosis.

As you are no doubt aware, calculating an individual's risk of disease is an inexact science. No one can predict with perfect accuracy which of us will develop which disease and when we will develop it. But large research studies have shown that people with certain risk factors are more likely than those without those factors to develop specific diseases. Risk factors include aspects of personal behavior (diet and physical activity, for example), the environment (such as air or water pollution), or inborn traits (biological predispositions carried in our genes). Scientists are constantly carrying out research to refine our understanding of which risk factors relate to a disease and how much they impact it. One risk factor relevant to nearly all diseases is age; in general, the risk of disease doubles every 10 years beginning at about age 40.

Keep in mind that even women with no known risk factors for a particular disease do sometimes get that disease. Conversely, women with many risk factors for a disease may never get it. For certain diseases, risk-factor calculations simply indicate whether your chance of getting a particular disease is higher or lower than other women in your age range, but they don't attempt to provide a precise numerical estimate of your risk. Nevertheless, knowing your risk factors can help you make important medical decisions—such as whether to take hormone therapy—and identify other strategies that you can adopt to boost your chances of living a long and healthy life.

CORONARY HEART DISEASE

Let's look at how to calculate—and reduce—your personal risk of coronary heart disease (CHD).

What Are the Risk Factors for Coronary Heart Disease?

Many factors are known to increase the risk for CHD, which results from atherosclerosis, or the accumulation of fatty plaques in artery walls that causes arteries to narrow. If a blood clot or plaque rupture blocks a narrowed artery leading to the heart, it can cause a heart attack. The more risk factors a woman has, the greater the likelihood that she will suffer a heart attack. Some risk factors are beyond one's control, including increasing age and a family history of heart disease. Women with a father or brother who developed heart disease before age 55 or a mother or sister who developed heart disease before age 65 are at increased risk. Race is also a factor, with black women being more likely than white women to develop heart disease, although it is not clear whether the racial difference can be accounted for by other risk factors that are within one's control. The majority of factors that contribute to heart disease, such as an unfavorable cholesterol profile, high blood pressure, and high blood sugar can, in fact, be controlled or modified by making simple changes in your lifestyle—quitting smoking, increasing physical activity, losing excess weight, and improving your diet—and, if necessary, taking certain medicines.

In 2004, the American Heart Association adopted the slogan "Know Your Numbers" to improve the public's awareness of heart health. Let's review 11 numbers—listed in Table 6.1—that are worth knowing.

The fats in your bloodstream are collectively known as lipids, the most important of which are *LDL (bad) cholesterol* and *HDL (good) cholesterol*. The lower your LDL and the higher your HDL, the lower your chances of having a heart attack. *Total cholesterol* is a useful general indictor. High *triglycerides* may pose a problem, especially in combination with excess weight, high blood sugar, and low HDL.

Table 6.1 Numbers to Know for Your Heart's Health

Indicator	Ideal	When to Worry[a]	How Often Should It Be Measured?[b]	Write Your Number Here
Lipids			Every 5 years	
Total cholesterol	Under 200 mg/dL	240 mg/dL or higher		
HDL (good) cholesterol	Above 60 mg/dL	40 mg/dL or lower		
LDL (bad) cholesterol	Under 100 mg/dL[c]	160 mg/dL or higher[d]		
Triglycerides	Under 150 mg/dL	200 mg/dL or higher		
Blood pressure			Every year[e]	
Systolic (top number)	Under 120 mm Hg	140 mm Hg or higher		
Diastolic (bottom number)	Under 80 mm Hg	90 mm Hg or higher		

continued

Table 6.1 Numbers to Know for Your Heart's Health, *continued*

Indicator	Ideal	When to Worry[a]	How Often Should It Be Measured?[b]	Write Your Number Here
Body measurements			At every physical exam	
Body mass index (BMI)	Under 25 kg/m²	30 kg/m² or higher		
Waist circumference	Under 30 inches	35 inches or higher		
Fasting blood sugar[f]	Under 100 mg/dL	Over 125 mg/dL	Every 3 years	
Hemoglobin A1c[g]	Under 7%[g]	Over 8%[g]	Every 3 to 6 months[g]	
C-reactive protein (CRP)[h]	Under 2 mg/L	3 mg/L or higher	Not determined	

a When to take action beyond lifestyle changes. These numbers may be different for people with diabetes, heart disease, stroke, or other medical issues.

b More often for persons at increased risk of heart disease

c For persons who have an LDL cholesterol level of below 100 mg/dL but are at high risk of heart disease by virtue of other risk factors, a goal of below 70 mg/dL is recommended.

d This depends on how many other risk factors are present; for people with a lot of other risk factors, an LDL over 130 suggests the need for treatment with cholesterol-lowering medications; for others, an LDL of 160 or more, or 190 or more, does so.

e Every 2 years for healthy persons under age 40

f Persons with blood sugar levels of 100 to 125 mg/dL have prediabetes, and those with blood sugar levels of 126 mg/dL or higher have full-blown diabetes.

g For persons with diagnosed diabetes

h CRP screening is recommended for people at moderate risk of heart disease by virtue of other risk factors.

Your blood pressure is composed of two measurements: *systolic pressure* (the top number of a blood pressure reading, or your pressure when your heart contracts) and *diastolic pressure* (the bottom number, or your pressure when your heart relaxes). The higher each one is, the greater the chance that your arteries are suffering damage—and of you having a heart attack or stroke.

Excess weight—especially at the waist or abdominal area—adversely affects heart health. *Body mass index* (*BMI*) is a measure of weight in relation to your height. To calculate your BMI, multiply your weight in pounds by 703. Divide that number by your height in inches, and then divide again by your height in inches. Or, if you don't want to do the math, use the weight-for-height chart in Table 6.2.

To measure your *waist circumference*, hold a tape measure at the level of your navel and circle your torso with it. Be sure to measure below, not at, the narrowest part of your abdomen.

Diabetes, which is characterized by high blood sugar, is a chronic disease that injures the heart and blood vessels. *Fasting blood sugar* gives you a snapshot of your blood sugar at one point in time, while *hemoglobin A1c* offers a time-lapse look over several weeks. Although the hemoglobin A1c test is traditionally reserved for people who already have a diagnosis of diabetes, some doctors now recommend it for people at higher-than-usual risk for diabetes and heart disease.

Within the last decade, other substances in the blood, including C-reactive protein, homocysteine, lipoprotein(a), and fibrinogen, have also been linked to an increased risk of heart disease. Of these, *C-reactive protein* (*CRP*) has received the most publicity. An elevated CRP level is a signal of active, low-grade inflammation, a process that has been implicated in heart disease. However, it is still unclear what level of CRP puts you at elevated risk and whether controlling it will help lower your risk. This marker may be most helpful in assessing disease risk in persons already determined to be at moderate risk on the basis of established risk factors.

Having more than one risk factor for heart disease is especially worrisome, because risk factors tend to "gang up" to worsen each other's effects. One potent cluster of risk factors—an increased waist circumference, high triglycerides, low HDL cholesterol, high blood pressure, and high blood sugar—is referred to as the *metabolic syndrome* or by its older name, syndrome X. National surveys indicate that about 27 percent of adults in the United States have this syndrome,[1] which is associated with a sharply increased risk of developing diabetes, heart disease, and stroke.

How Do I Estimate My Risk of Developing Coronary Heart Disease?

Armed with the knowledge of some of these key numbers, you can use the tool in Table 6.3 to estimate how likely you are to have a first heart attack or be diagnosed with coronary heart disease in the next 10 years. I adapted the tool from one developed by investigators with the Framingham Heart Study, the world's longest-running

Table 6.2   What's My Body Mass Index?

Height	Body weight in pounds																
4'10"	91	96	100	105	110	115	119	124	129	134	138	143	148	153	158	162	167
4'11"	94	99	104	109	114	119	124	128	133	138	143	148	153	158	163	168	173
5'0"	97	102	107	112	118	123	128	133	138	143	148	153	158	163	168	174	179
5'1"	100	106	111	116	122	127	132	137	143	148	153	158	164	169	174	180	185
5'2"	104	109	115	120	126	131	136	142	147	153	158	164	169	175	180	186	191
5'3"	107	113	118	124	130	135	141	146	152	158	163	169	175	180	186	191	197
5'4"	110	116	122	128	134	140	145	151	157	163	169	174	180	186	192	197	204
5'5"	114	120	126	132	138	144	150	156	162	168	174	180	186	192	198	204	210
5'6"	118	124	130	136	142	148	155	161	167	173	179	186	192	198	204	210	216
5'7"	121	127	134	140	146	153	159	166	172	178	185	191	198	204	211	217	223
5'8"	125	131	138	144	151	158	164	171	177	184	190	197	203	210	216	223	230
5'9"	128	135	142	149	155	162	169	176	182	188	196	203	209	216	223	230	236
5'10"	132	139	146	153	160	167	174	181	188	195	202	207	216	222	229	236	243
5'11"	136	143	150	157	165	172	179	184	191	197	208	215	221	228	235	242	250
6'0"	140	147	154	162	169	177	184	191	199	206	213	221	228	235	242	250	258
6'1"	144	151	159	166	174	182	189	197	204	212	219	227	235	242	250	257	265
6'2"	148	155	163	171	179	186	194	202	210	218	225	233	241	249	256	264	272
6'3"	152	160	168	176	184	192	200	208	216	224	232	240	248	256	264	272	279
6'4"	156	164	172	180	189	197	205	213	221	230	238	246	254	263	271	279	287
BMI	**19**	**20**	**21**	**22**	**23**	**24**	**25**	**26**	**27**	**28**	**29**	**30**	**31**	**32**	**33**	**34**	**35**
	Healthy Weight						Overweight					Obese					

epidemiologic study. The original Framingham tool, a version of which is on the Web at www.nhlbi.nih.gov/about/framingham/riskabs.htm, assigns points on the basis of your age, total cholesterol level, HDL cholesterol, blood pressure, diabetes status, and smoking status. However, recent research indicates that the tool may underestimate a woman's risk for heart disease because it doesn't take into account other known or strongly suspected risk factors for heart disease, such as a high BMI, physical inactivity, and family history. To address this concern, I've incorporated these risk factors into the tool presented here to provide what I believe to be a more comprehensive and accurate estimate of risk. The points are then totaled and converted into a 10-year risk, which can be interpreted as the likelihood that you will develop or die from heart disease in the next 10 years. A risk greater than 20 percent is considered high; a risk between 10 and 20 percent is moderate; a risk between 5 and 10 percent is low; and a risk less than 5 percent is very low.

You may notice that not all of the risk factors discussed in the previous section are included in the risk assessment tool. Don't take that to mean that these risk factors are not important; it really means that researchers haven't agreed on a satisfactory way of combining all of the numbers to predict risk across a sufficiently wide swath of the female population. So how can you use your knowledge of these additional numbers to assess your heart disease risk? If, after calculating your risk using the tool, you find your coronary heart disease risk score is on the borderline between two risk categories (that is, you are within a percentage point or two of a neighboring risk category), you may wish to use any unfavorable measurements on risk factors not included in the tool (e.g., triglycerides, waist circumference, CRP) to nudge yourself into the next highest risk category. In this manner, you will err on the side of caution when considering your heart disease risk profile vis-à-vis your hormone-therapy decision. (And this advice also holds for the use of the stroke and breast cancer tools presented later.)

Knowing your coronary heart disease risk may motivate you to make lifestyle changes and will help your doctor determine whether to prescribe certain medications to lower your risk. Nearly everyone can benefit from making healthy changes.*

---

*An interactive tool developed by my colleagues at the Harvard School of Public Health on the basis of data from the Nurses' Health Study and the Health Professionals Follow-Up Study, a parallel study of more than 51,000 U.S. male health professionals who have been tracked since 1986, provides an alternative estimate of your risk of developing the diseases discussed in this chapter and offers personalized tips for prevention. The Harvard tool, which can be found on the Web at www.yourdiseaserisk.harvard.edu, incorporates an even broader array of potential risk factors than does the modified Framingham tool to assess your risk of heart disease and stroke, as well as diabetes, certain types of cancer, and osteoporosis. The Harvard tool does not provide a specific percentage but instead estimates your risk of developing these diseases compared with a typical woman of the same age.

But the urgency and intensity of such changes depend on how close you are to the top of the heart attack risk chart. The greater your risk, the greater the payoff from prevention efforts—and the less likely you are to be a suitable candidate for hormone therapy.

Table 6.3 Estimating Your 10-Year Risk of Coronary Heart Disease

Find your point score in Boxes A through I, and then add up these points to get your point total. Look up your point total in Box J to find an estimate of your 10-year risk of coronary heart disease. A risk greater than 20 percent is considered high; a risk of 10 to 20 percent is moderate; a risk of 5 to 10 percent is low; and a risk of less than 5 percent is very low. This tool is an adaptation of the Framingham Coronary Heart Disease Risk Score for women.[2,3] It is most accurate for women aged 30 to 74. The tool is intended for use only by women without a previous history of heart disease. If you already have been diagnosed with heart disease—that is, if you have had a heart attack, angina, angioplasty procedure, or coronary bypass surgery—do not use this tool to calculate your risk. You are at higher-than-average risk of having another heart attack or other coronary event, and you are not a good candidate for menopausal hormone therapy. The same goes for women who have been diagnosed with diabetes. Even if your blood sugar is well controlled, you are still at elevated risk of coronary heart disease and should therefore not take hormone therapy.

Box A

Age (years)	
20–34	−7 points
35–39	−3 points
40–44	0 points
45–49	3 points
50–54	6 points
55–59	8 points
60–64	10 points
65–69	12 points
70–74	14 points
75–79	16 points

Box B

Total cholesterol	Age (years)				
(mg/dL)†	20–39	40–49	50–59	60–69	70–79
Less than 160	0 points	0 points	0 points	0 points	0 points
160–199	4 points	3 points	2 points	1 point	1 point
200–239	8 points	6 points	4 points	2 points	1 point
240–279	11 points	8 points	5 points	3 points	2 points
280 or more	13 points	10 points	7 points	4 points	2 points

*Most recent total cholesterol value. Add 2 points if you take a statin or other prescription cholesterol-lowering medication to achieve the above value.†

Box C

Smoking status	Age (years)				
	20–39	40–49	50–59	60–69	70–79
Nonsmoker	0 points	0 points	0 points	0 points	0 points
Smoker	9 points	7 points	4 points	2 points	1 point

Box D

HDL cholesterol (mg/dL)	
60 or more	−1 point
50–59	0 points
40–49	1 point
Less than 40	2 points

Box E

Systolic blood pressure (mm Hg)	Not taking blood pressure medication	Taking blood pressure medication
Less than 120	0 points	0 points
120–129	1 point	3 points
130–139	2 points	4 points
140–159	3 points	5 points
160 or more	4 points	6 points

continued

Table 6.3 Estimating Your 10-Year Risk of Coronary Heart Disease, *continued*

Box F†

Body mass index (kg/m²)	
Less than 25	0 points
25.0–29.9	2 points
30 or more	4 points

Box G†

Physical activity	
Do you walk or perform other moderate-intensity activity for at least 30 minutes per day on most days of the week, or at least 3 hours per week?	
Do you perform vigorous physical activity such as jogging for at least 20 minutes per day on 3 or more days of the week, or at least 1 hour per week?	
Yes to at least one question	−2 points
No to both questions	0 points

Box H†

Family history of heart disease	
Did your biological father or brother have a heart attack before age 55?	
Did your biological mother or sister have a heart attack before age 65?	
No to both questions	0 points
Yes to at least one question	2 points

Box I†

Diabetes	
If you have diabetes, you are at high risk of heart disease. Diabetes is considered to be a heart disease "risk equivalent." Relying on the points you have tallied above will underestimate your risk. Therefore, disregard the points from the above boxes and give yourself 23 points.	

Box J

Point total	10-year risk of developing coronary heart disease	Risk category
Less than 9	Less than 1%	
9	1%	
10	1%	
11	1%	
12	1%	Very low risk
13	2%	
14	2%	
15	3%	
16	4%	
17	5%	
18	6%	Low risk
19	8%	
20	11%	
21	14%	Moderate risk
22	17%	
23	22%	
24	27%	High risk
25 or more	30% or more	

† These are the items that I added to the original Framingham coronary heart disease risk assessment tool. A portion of the elevation in heart disease risk associated with a high BMI, lack of physical activity, and a family history of heart disease is reflected in other variables in this risk prediction tool because excess body weight and lack of physical activity lead to unfavorable cholesterol and blood pressure levels, which in turn affect heart disease risk. Moreover, family members tend to share genetic and environmental factors that influence all of the other variables (except age) in the tool. My revisions also incorporate information about the use of cholesterol-lowering medication.

What Can I Do to Protect Myself Against Coronary Heart Disease?

Epidemiologic studies suggest that more than 80 percent of CHD in women can be prevented by making relatively simple lifestyle changes. Adopting these changes is your first line of defense against heart disease (see Figure 6.1)—and also against stroke, diabetes, and many types of cancer.

Don't Smoke

Nicotine constricts blood vessels and, together with carbon monoxide in tobacco smoke, reduces the oxygen in your blood and damages blood vessel walls, making clots more likely to form. Your chance of having a heart attack doubles if you smoke as few as one to four cigarettes per day and increases sixfold if you are a heavy smoker. If you stop smoking, your risk of heart attack drops by 50 percent within one to two years, and, after five years, your risk approaches that of nonsmokers. Regular exposure to smoke from someone else's cigarettes is also bad for your heart and lungs. If you live with someone who smokes, encourage him or her to quit.

Be Physically Active

Aim for 30 minutes or more of moderate-intensity physical activity, such as brisk walking or biking, on most, and preferably all, days of the week. Alternatively, try to get at least 20 minutes of vigorous exercise, such as running or racquet sports, at least three times per week. In several observational studies of midlife and older women, those who walked briskly for at least two to three hours per week—or burned an equivalent amount of energy through more vigorous exercise—cut their risk of coronary heart disease by 30 to 40 percent. Exercise doesn't need to be a "production number" involving structured workout sessions at the gym; incorporating several short bouts of activity into your daily routine (e.g., taking walks during lunch or coffee breaks or using the stairs instead of the elevator) may be sufficient to obtain the recommended amount of activity. The use of a pedometer may also encourage daily activity—10,000 steps per day is a reasonable goal. In addition to aerobic exercise, consider strength training (exercising with arm and/or leg weights) for 20 minutes two to three times per week to boost metabolic rate and help maintain a healthy body weight.

Figure 6.1 Importance of Lifestyle in Preventing Coronary Heart Disease in Women

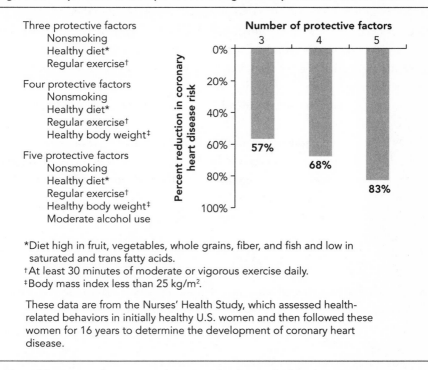

*Diet high in fruit, vegetables, whole grains, fiber, and fish and low in saturated and trans fatty acids.
†At least 30 minutes of moderate or vigorous exercise daily.
‡Body mass index less than 25 kg/m².

These data are from the Nurses' Health Study, which assessed health-related behaviors in initially healthy U.S. women and then followed these women for 16 years to determine the development of coronary heart disease.

Adapted from Stampfer, M. J., et al. New England Journal of Medicine 343 (2000): 16–22.

Eat a Heart–Healthy Diet

Include in your diet a variety of fruits, especially deeply colored fruits; vegetables, especially dark green, leafy vegetables; whole grains, including whole-grain breads (products labeled "100 percent whole-grain" are best), whole-grain pastas, brown rice, oatmeal, bran, and popcorn; low-fat or nonfat dairy products; and fish, nuts, legumes (dry beans and peas), and other sources of protein low in saturated fat such as poultry and lean meats.

Data from observational studies suggest that you can get up to 25 to 35 percent of your daily calories from fat and still have a diet that's good for your heart. But here's the catch: most of the fat must be "good" fat—i.e., monounsaturated and polyunsaturated fats. "Bad" fat—i.e., saturated and trans fats—should be eaten only in moderation or not at all. Specifically, saturated fats should be limited to 7 percent or less of your daily calories, and trans fats should be avoided altogether. One way to boost your intake of good fat while cutting back on the bad is to substitute canola, olive, or other (nonhydrogenated) vegetable oil for butter whenever possible. See Table 6.4 for help in distinguishing good and bad fats.

Limiting your intake of salt and other forms of sodium will help keep your blood pressure at a healthy level. Avoid liberal use of the salt shaker and other major sources of dietary salt, including canned foods and commercially prepared dishes such as frozen dinners.

Drinking modest amounts of alcohol, such as one glass of wine or one 12-ounce beer per day, may lower a woman's risk of heart disease by 20 to 40 percent. Women who do not currently drink should not begin drinking for heart benefits. Although moderate alcohol consumption may reduce heart disease and diabetes, it also raises your risk of breast and other cancers, high blood pressure, stroke, and bone loss.

Maintain a Healthy Body Weight

Aim for a body mass index of between 18.5 and 24.9 (see Table 6.2) and a waist circumference of less than 35 inches. Persons with BMI of 25 to 29.9 are consid-

Table 6.4 Distinguishing Good and Bad Fats

	Effect on Heart Disease Risk Factors	Main Food Sources
Good fats		
Monounsaturated fats	Do not raise LDL, do not lower HDL cholesterol	Canola oil Olive oil Nut oils, nuts, nut butters Avocado
Polyunsaturated fats* Omega-6 fats	Do not raise LDL, may lower HDL cholesterol	Corn oil Vegetable oil (nonhydrogenated)
Polyunsaturated fats* Omega-3 fats†	Have blood-thinning properties, may lower triglycerides	Oily fish (salmon, sardines, trout, herring) Flaxseed, flaxseed oil Walnuts, walnut oil

	Effect on Heart Disease Risk Factors	Main Food Sources
Bad fats		
Saturated	Raise LDL and may lower HDL cholesterol	Full-fat dairy products (butter, cheese, whole milk) Red meat (beef, veal, lamb, pork) Coconut oil
Trans‡	Raise LDL and lower HDL cholesterol	Stick margarine Commercially prepared deep-fried foods (such as donuts and some french fries) Commercially prepared baked goods (such as crackers, cookies, and chips)

*Polyunsaturated fats are divided into omega-6 fats and omega-3 fats. Both omega-6 and omega-3 fats are essential for heart health. For optimum health and disease prevention, a balance of one to four times more omega-6 than omega-3 fats is generally recommended. A typical U.S. diet, however, tends to contain 10 to 30 times more omega-6 than omega-3 fats, suggesting that most of us should cut back on the omega-6s and increase the omega-3s.

†Omega-3 fats can be further subdivided into three categories: eicosapentaenoic acid, docosahexaenoic acid, and alpha-linolenic acid—quite a mouthful—so they're generally referred to as EPA, DHA, and ALA, respectively. There is an ongoing debate in the scientific community as to whether EPA and DHA, the omega-3 fats found exclusively in oily fish, offer greater protection against heart disease and stroke than ALA, the omega-3 fat found in non-marine foods such as flaxseed and walnuts. The answer is not yet clear, but aiming for two servings of fish per week may be prudent. Recent concerns about environmental contaminants such as methylmercury and polychlorinated biphenyls (PCBs) in fish are less relevant to women past menopause than women in their child-bearing years.[4]

‡As of 2006, food manufacturers are required by the federal government to list trans fats along with saturated fats on nutrition labels. However, if the suggested serving size on the package has less than 0.5 grams of trans fat, the manufacturer may legally claim a trans fat content of zero. The most reliable way to tell if trans fat is present is to check the ingredient list; if the phrase "partially hydrogenated vegetable oil" or "vegetable shortening" appears, then trans fats are indeed lurking in the food.

ered overweight, and those with BMI of 30 or greater are obese. If your BMI is in one of these categories, don't despair. Losing just 5 to 10 percent of your body weight favorably affects cholesterol, blood pressure, blood sugar, and other risk factors for heart disease. For most women, reducing food intake by 500 calories per day, or a reduction of 300 calories in combination with 30 minutes of moderate physical activity such as brisk walking, will result in a weight loss of one to two pounds per week. Controlling calories is best achieved by reducing portion sizes; minimizing snacks, desserts, and sugar-sweetened beverages; limiting high-fat foods; and increasing fruit and vegetable intakes.

Reduce Stress and Treat Depression

Chronic stress and depression are now recognized as risk factors for heart disease. In a case-control study of 6,300 women from many countries, experiencing habit-

A Possible "Prescription" for Weight Loss or Maintenance

Diet

- Pay attention to portions; avoid supersizing.
- Set regular times to eat: three meals and no more than two snacks per day.
- Limit saturated and trans fats.
- Increase daily intake of fruits and vegetables: at least five, aim for seven to nine servings.
- Aim for two to three servings of whole-grain food per day.
- Limit sweetened beverages; drink water or nonfat or 1 percent milk.

Exercise

- Take the stairs whenever possible.
- Purchase a pedometer and aim for 10,000 steps per day.
- Display an "exercise prescription" in a visible place.
- When you drive, park in a space far away from the door and walk.
- If you take public transportation, get off a stop early and walk.
- Walk on your lunch break.
- Consider strength training for 20 minutes two to three times per week.

Why Are We So Fat?

Currently, two of three U.S. adults are overweight or obese, compared with just one in four in the 1960s. Why? National surveys indicate that our average daily calorie intake has crept steadily upward during the past three decades. From 1971 to 2000, the daily calorie intake of the typical woman rose 22 percent, from 1,542 to 1,877 calories, while the typical man increased his intake by 7 percent, from 2,450 to 2,618 calories.[5] Meanwhile, physical activity levels have remained fairly constant—and disconcertingly low—at least through the 1990s. Indeed, 73 percent of women and 66 percent of men do not meet the current recommendation of 30 minutes of leisure-time physical activity on most days of the week, and 41 percent of women and 35 percent of men engage in no leisure-time physical activity at all.[6] Taken together, these two factors likely account for the rising prevalence of obesity in our country.

What Are the Health Risks of Excess Body Weight?

The cardiovascular health risks of obesity are shown in Figure 6.2. Excess body weight also boosts your risk of several types of cancer, including colon, breast, uterine, and kidney cancer; data from the American Cancer Society's Cancer Prevention Study II suggest that 15 to 20 percent of cancer deaths are attributable to overweight and obesity.[7]

Figure 6.2 Relative Risks of Various Cardiovascular Conditions, According to Body Mass Index, After 14 to 16 Years of Follow-Up, Nurses' Health Study

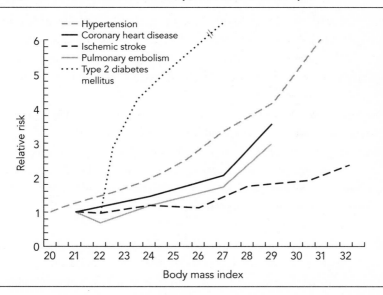

ual stress at home or at work was associated with a 75 percent increased risk of heart attack.[8] To manage stress, choose health-promoting strategies such as physical activity, adequate sleep, meditation, or other relaxation techniques rather than unhealthy ones such as smoking and overeating. For depression and chronic anxiety, seek the help of a healthcare professional.

Know Your Numbers

Schedule and keep appointments with your primary healthcare provider to monitor the indicators listed in Table 6.1 on a regular basis. In many instances, adopting the heart-healthy behaviors outlined in this chapter will go a long way toward achieving the ideal values listed in the table. For example, poor eating habits and excess weight gain are leading causes of type 2 diabetes, a disorder that is becoming alarmingly common in this country. (It is estimated that one of every three persons born in 2000 will develop the disease in their lifetime if current trends continue.[9]) Left untreated, diabetes can lead to heart attack, stroke, and other debilitating diseases. Women with diabetes are three to seven times more likely than women without diabetes to develop heart disease. If you have been diagnosed with diabetes, diet, exercise, and medication are essential to regulate your blood sugar level and to control your risk factors for cardiovascular disease.

What Medications Are Available to Lower Heart Disease Risk?

Women who are considered to be at highest risk for developing heart disease, including those who already have cardiovascular disease, diabetes, or chronic kidney disease, are most likely to benefit from drug therapy. Drugs that lower blood pressure or favorably affect cholesterol levels have been shown to prevent heart attacks or increase survival in high-risk women.

Antihypertensive medications lower blood pressure. If, after attempting the lifestyle changes detailed here, your blood pressure stays at 140/90 mm Hg or higher (130/80 mm Hg or higher if you have diabetes), your doctor will likely prescribe one of these drugs. Because different patients respond differently to these medications, you may need to go through a trial period to find out which drug works best for you with the fewest side effects.

- *Diuretics*, or "water pills," are often the first medication chosen. Diuretics help the kidneys eliminate excess salt and water from the body. This decreases blood volume, so your heart has less to pump with each beat, which in turn lowers blood pressure. Common diuretics include chlorothiazine (Diuril) and hydrochlorothiazide (Hydrodiuril).

• *Beta blockers* lower blood pressure by slowing the heart rate and reducing the force of the heartbeat, lightening the heart's workload. Beta blockers are recommended for women who have had a heart attack or have ongoing angina (chest pain). Common beta blockers include atenolol (Tenormin), metoprolol (Lopressor), nadolol (Corgard), propanolol (Inderal), timolol (Blocadren), and bisoprolol (Zebeta).

• *Angiotensin-converting enzyme (ACE) inhibitors* interfere with the body's production of angiotensin II, a chemical that causes the arteries to narrow. These medications, as well as *angiotensin receptor blockers (ARBs)*, are often of benefit for people with congestive heart failure or diabetes. Common ACE inhibitors include benazepril (Lotensin), captopril (Capoten), enalapril (Vasotec), lisinopril (Zestril), and quinapril (Accupril). Common ARBs include irbesartan (Avapro), losartan (Cozaar), olmesartan (Benicar), and valsartan (Diovan).

• *Calcium channel blockers* slow the movement of calcium into the smooth-muscle cells of the heart and blood vessels. This reduces the force of the heartbeat and increases blood vessel dilation, lowering blood pressure. Because calcium channel blockers also slow nerve impulses in the heart, they are also prescribed for arrhythmia (irregular heartbeat). Common calcium channel blockers include diltiazem (Cardizem, Cartia), amlodipine (Norvasc), felodipine (Plendil), and nifedipine (Procardia).

Cholesterol-lowering drugs may be prescribed individually or in combination with one another.

• *Statins* reduce LDL cholesterol and triglyceride levels in the blood by blocking an enzyme that is necessary for the liver to manufacture cholesterol. Recent studies show that statins are helpful in preventing heart attack in high-risk patients, even when their LDL cholesterol levels are already below 100 mg/dL. Common statins include atorvastatin (Lipitor), fluvastatin (Lescol), lovastatin (Mevacor), pravastatin (Pravachol), simvastatin (Zocor), and rosuvastatin (Crestor).

• *Niacin* is available as a prescription drug that reduces LDL cholesterol and triglyceride levels while also raising HDL cholesterol levels. Niacin can also be purchased as a dietary supplement; however, because this form of niacin can vary widely in strength and composition, it should *not* be used as a substitute for prescription niacin.

• *Fibrates*, such as gemfibrozil (Lopid) and clofibrate (Atromid-S), lower triglycerides and, to some extent, can help raise HDL cholesterol.

Aspirin and other antiplatelet drugs, which prevent blood from clotting, are effective in preventing recurrent heart attacks in men and women with a history of heart disease, treating heart attacks in men and women, as well as preventing first heart attacks in healthy men. Until recently, it was not known whether aspirin also prevented first heart attacks in healthy women. To answer this, my colleagues and I conducted the large Women's Health Study, a 10-year clinical trial of low-dose aspirin (100 milligrams every other day) in 40,000 initially healthy women aged 45 and older. Much to our surprise, we found that aspirin was *not* effective in preventing first heart attacks in these women, except for women aged 65 and older.[10] However, aspirin was effective in reducing the overall risk of stroke. On the basis of our results, aspirin is not routinely recommended for heart disease prevention for healthy women below age 65 who are at low or average cardiovascular risk.

The long-touted benefit of *vitamin E and other antioxidant vitamin supplements* for preventing or treating heart disease has also been called into question by recent clinical trials. For example, the Women's Health Study, in addition to testing aspirin, also tested whether vitamin E supplements reduced the risk of a first heart attack in otherwise healthy women and found that they did not.[11] Most studies of these vitamins in high-risk men and women have also been disappointing. Pending the outcome of a few ongoing clinical trials, antioxidant vitamin supplements are no longer recommended for the prevention or treatment of heart disease. Two other nutritional supplements—*folic acid* and *omega-3 fats* (e.g., fish-oil capsules)—are recommended by some doctors for those at moderate or high risk of heart disease, with the caveat that data from large clinical trials are still needed to support such a recommendation. As this book goes to press, my colleagues and I have begun analyzing data from the recently concluded Women's Antioxidant/Folate Cardiovascular Study, a 10-year clinical trial of the benefits and risks of folic acid and antioxidant vitamins in 8,200 women at high risk of heart disease.[12] The results of this trial should provide additional guidance for high-risk women and their doctors regarding vitamin supplementation.

STROKE

Let's look at how to calculate—and reduce—your personal risk of stroke.

What Are the Risk Factors for Stroke?

Not surprisingly, because both are diseases of the arteries, stroke and coronary heart disease share many risk factors. However, the relative importance of their shared risk factors varies to some degree. Along with age, the most powerful risk factor for stroke is high blood pressure. Smoking also boosts your stroke risk, as do diabetes and certain heart disorders, especially atrial fibrillation and left ventricular hypertrophy. Atrial fibrillation is a heart rhythm disorder in which the upper pumping chambers—the atria—of the heart quiver instead of beating effectively, which can let the blood pool and clot. If a clot breaks loose from the chamber wall, enters the bloodstream, and lodges in an artery leading to the brain, a stroke results. Atrial fibrillation accounts for about 15 percent of strokes, and people with atrial fibrillation are five to seven times more likely to have a stroke than those without the condition. Left ventricular hypertrophy is a thickening of the walls of the heart's left lower pumping chamber—the left ventricle—of the heart; it is most commonly a result of, and is an indicator of, chronically elevated blood pressure. Left ventricular hypertrophy can also lead to heart failure (as the heart becomes enlarged, it loses some of its pumping ability), another risk factor for stroke. Other types of heart disease, including CHD, heart valve disease, and some types of congenital heart defects also raise the risk of stroke. Transient ischemic attacks—ministrokes lasting for only a few minutes or hours—are often warning signals that a full-blown stroke will happen in the near future.

Other risk factors include a family history of stroke; stroke appears to run in some families, although it's not clear whether this is due to genetics and/or shared lifestyle factors. Physical inactivity, excess body weight, and high alcohol intake (defined as more than one drink per day for women) can raise blood pressure and thus stroke risk. An adverse lipid profile—high LDL, low HDL, high triglycerides—raises the risk of stroke by raising the risk of heart disease but does not reliably predict risk of future stroke in people without heart disease or prior stroke. The use of birth control pills sharply increases stroke risk in women who smoke but has less of an effect on stroke risk in their nonsmoking counterparts.

How Do I Estimate My Risk of Having a Stroke?

To allow you to calculate your 10-year risk of stroke, I again adapted a tool from
one developed by investigators with the Framingham Heart Study (Table 6.5). The
point assignments for the stroke risk assessment tool are not the same as for the
CHD tool, reflecting the differing importance of certain risk factors for the two
conditions. Your risk can be interpreted as the likelihood that you will develop or
die from stroke in the next 10 years. A risk greater than 20 percent is considered
high; a risk between 10 and 20 percent is moderate; a risk between 5 and 10 percent is low; and a risk less than 5 percent is very low.

What Can I Do to Protect Myself Against Stroke?

Experts now believe that stroke is as preventable as heart attack. Nearly all of the
recommended strategies to prevent heart attack also prevent stroke. The most
important steps you can take to prevent stroke are to control your blood pressure
by maintaining a healthy body weight, getting adequate physical activity, avoiding
a high-salt diet, and taking antihypertensive medications as needed. Somewhat surprisingly, although cholesterol is a less potent predictor of stroke than of CHD,
clinical trials of the cholesterol-lowering statin drugs show that they are as effective in preventing stroke as they are in preventing coronary heart disease.[14]

Although my colleagues and I did not find that habitual use of low-dose aspirin
prevented heart disease in healthy women younger than age 65 in the Women's
Health Study, we did find that it was associated with a moderate reduction in stroke

---

Table 6.5 Estimating Your 10-Year Risk of Stroke

Find your point score in Boxes A through J and then add up these points to get your point
total. Look up your point total in Box K to find an estimate of your 10-year risk of stroke. A
risk greater than 20 percent is considered high; a risk of 10 to 20 percent is moderate; a risk
of 5 to 10 percent is low; and a risk of less than 5 percent is very low. This tool is adapted
from the Framingham Stroke Risk Profile for women.[13] It is most accurate for women aged 55
to 84. The tool is intended for use only by women without a previous history of stroke. If you
already have had a stroke, do not use this tool to calculate your risk. You are at higher-than-
average risk of having another stroke, and you are not a good candidate for menopausal hormone therapy.

Box A

Age (years)	
56 or younger	0 points
57–59	1 point
60–62	2 points
63–64	3 points
65–67	4 points
68–70	5 points
71–73	6 points
74–76	7 points
77–78	8 points
79–81	9 points
82–84	10 points

Box B
If you are *not* taking blood pressure medication:

Systolic blood pressure (mm Hg)	
95–106	1 point
107–118	2 points
119–130	3 points
131–143	4 points
144–155	5 points
156–167	6 points
168–180	7 points
181–192	8 points
193–204	9 points
205 or more	10 points

continued

Table 6.5 Estimating Your 10-Year Risk of Stroke, *continued*

If you are taking blood pressure medication:

Systolic blood pressure (mm Hg)	
95–106	1 point
107–113	2 points
114–119	3 points
120–125	4 points
125–131	5 points
132–139	6 points
140–148	7 points
149–160	8 points
161–204	9 points
205 or more	10 points

Box C

Smoking status	
Nonsmoker	0 points
Smoker	3 points

Box D

Diabetes	
No	0 points
Yes	3 points

Box E

Have you been diagnosed with atrial fibrillation?	
No	0 points
Yes	6 points

Box F

Have you been diagnosed with left ventricular hypertrophy?	
No	0 points
Yes	4 points

Box G

Have you been diagnosed with heart disease (other than atrial fibrillation or left ventricular hypertrophy)?	
No	0 points
Yes	2 points

Box H*

Body mass index (kg/m²)	
Less than 25	0 points
25.0–29.9	2 points
30 or more	4 points

Box I*

Physical activity	
Do you walk or perform other moderate-intensity activity for at least 30 minutes per day on most days of the week, or at least 3 hours per week?	
Do you perform vigorous physical activity such as jogging for at least 20 minutes per day on 3 or more days of the week, or at least 1 hour per week?	
Yes to at least one question	−2 points
No to both questions	0 points

Box J*

Family history of heart attack or stroke	
Did your biological father or brother have a heart attack or stroke before age 55?	
Did your biological mother or sister have a heart attack or stroke before age 65?	
No to both questions	0 points
Yes to at least one question	2 points

continued

Table 6.5 Estimating Your 10-Year Risk of Stroke, *continued*

Box K

Point total	10-year risk of developing stroke	Risk category
1	1%	
2	1%	
3	2%	
4	2%	
5	2%	Very low risk
6	3%	
7	4%	
8	4%	
9	5%	
10	6%	Low risk
11	8%	
12	9%	
13	11%	
14	13%	Moderate risk
15	16%	
16	19%	
17	23%	
18	27%	High risk
19 or more	32% or more	

*These are the items that I added to the original Framingham stroke risk assessment tool. A portion of the elevation in stroke risk associated with a high body mass index, lack of physical activity, and a family history of heart disease or stroke is reflected in other variables included in this risk prediction tool. This is because excess body weight and lack of physical activity lead to unfavorable blood pressure levels, which in turn affect stroke risk. Moreover, family members tend to share genetic and environmental factors that influence all the other variables (except age) included in the tool. Although diabetes is given only 3 points, it is considered a heart disease "risk equivalent" (see coronary heart disease section).

risk.[10] However, aspirin is not a totally benign drug. Because it acts as a blood thinner, aspirin carries some bleeding risks, such as bleeding in the gastrointestinal tract. Indeed, a closer look at the Women's Health Study data showed that while aspirin significantly lowered the risk of ischemic stroke, it also increased the risk of hemorrhagic stroke. Because hemorrhagic strokes are much less common than ischemic strokes, the effect of aspirin on overall stroke risk was favorable—still, this highlights the need to check with your doctor before considering a low-dose aspirin regimen.

There are medications that can decrease your risk of stroke if you have a higher-than-usual risk of having one because of heart problems. For example, if you have atrial fibrillation, your doctor may prescribe the blood-thinning medication warfarin (Coumadin) or aspirin to prevent clots from forming in the heart and traveling to the brain, where they could cause an ischemic stroke. Also, a medication may be prescribed to control the heart rhythm. Left ventricular hypertrophy is best treated by controlling blood pressure.

Venous Thromboembolism

Deep-vein thrombosis refers to blood clots that form in the veins deep in the legs, pelvis, or, more rarely, the arms or neck. If a clot breaks off from a vein and lodges in the lungs, it can cause pulmonary embolism. Together, deep-vein thrombosis and pulmonary embolism are formally referred to as venous thromboembolism (VTE) or, more informally, as blood clots in the deep veins or lungs. Let's look at how to calculate—and reduce—your personal risk of VTE.

What Are the Risk Factors for Venous Thromboembolism?

Heredity strongly affects one's susceptibility to developing blood clots in the deep veins and the lungs. If you have a strong family history of VTE, you may be at increased risk, and your doctor may recommend tests to look for certain genetic mutations (such as factor V Leiden and prothrombin 20210) or blood protein deficiencies (such as in proteins C and S) that predispose to clots. Having lupus also raises your risk for VTE.

Additional risk factors for VTE include prolonged immobility (due to long airplane flights, for example), recent surgery, and other bodily traumas such as bone fracture. Indeed, media coverage of several high-profile cases of collapse and death from pulmonary embolism that occurred on or shortly after long airplane flights has raised awareness of the condition. Immobility raises VTE risk because blood returning to the heart through the veins is largely driven by muscle contractions in the legs; in the absence of contractions, the blood is more likely to pool and clot. Surgery and trauma increase risk both because they are associated with immobility and because they lead to inflammation and activation of the body's clotting systems. Illnesses such as cancer, chronic obstructive pulmonary disease, and heart failure also raise the risk of VTE.

In epidemiologic studies, obesity is the lifestyle factor most consistently implicated in the development of VTE. Physical inactivity and smoking may also be risk factors. Hormonal exposures, such as birth control pills and pregnancy, raise the risk of VTE.

Are You at Elevated Risk of Venous Thromboembolism?

Scientists have not developed a formal tool to estimate your numerical risk of developing VTE. But here are some items to consider when evaluating your risk.

Have you ever had a blood clot in the deep veins or lungs that required treatment with blood-thinning injections (such as heparin) or pills (such as warfarin [Coumadin])?*   Yes / No

If yes, was the clot a result of any of the following:

Use of birth control pills, pregnancy, previous menopausal hormone therapy, or raloxifene (Evista)?*   Yes / No

Immobility: prolonged sitting, such as on a long airplane flight, or prolonged bed rest not connected to surgery?   Yes / No

Surgery or other bodily trauma, such as bone fracture?   Yes / No

Chronic illness, such as cancer?*   Yes / No

My doctor could not figure out the cause of my blood clot.* Yes / No

Do you carry a potentially harmful mutation in a gene that controls clotting (such as factor V Leiden), or do you have protein C or S deficiency?*   Yes / No / Don't know

Has a biological first-degree relative (parent, sibling, or child) ever had a blood clot in the deep veins or lungs?	Yes / No / Don't know
Does a biological first-degree relative (parent, sibling, or child) carry a potentially harmful mutation in a gene that controls clotting (such as factor V Leiden)?*	Yes / No / Don't know
Do you have lupus?	Yes / No
Is your body mass index 30 or more?	Yes / No
Are you physically inactive?	Yes / No
Do you currently smoke cigarettes?	Yes / No

If you answered yes to any of these questions, especially those with an asterisk, you are at heightened risk of VTE, and you may be more likely than other women to develop blood clots in your deep veins or lungs if you take hormone therapy.

What Can I Do to Protect Myself Against Venous Thromboembolism?

Maintaining a healthy body weight, keeping physically active, and avoiding smoking are the best strategies. Long-haul air travelers can greatly reduce their risk by walking the aisles and frequently flexing and stretching their leg muscles while on board the aircraft.

BREAST CANCER

Let's look at how to calculate—and reduce—your personal risk of breast cancer.

What Are the Risk Factors for Breast Cancer?

Age is a strong risk factor for breast cancer. Rates are generally low in women under 40, start to increase after 40, and are highest in those 70 and older. The average age at which breast cancer is diagnosed is 62 (see the sidebar " 'One in Eight Women' "). Having a family history of breast or ovarian cancer increases your risk, especially if your relative was diagnosed at an early age or more than one relative has had breast or ovarian cancer.

Currently, much research is being done to learn more about cancer-susceptibility genes, such as *BRCA1* and *BRCA2* (*BR*east *CA*ncer genes 1 and 2). Certain mutations in these genes are more frequently found in families and ethnic groups— Ashkenazi Jews, to be specific—that have a relatively high incidence of breast and ovarian cancer. However, it is estimated that only 5 to 10 percent of all breast cancers result from inherited mutations in *BRCA1* and *BRCA2* genes. Most breast cancers arise in women without a family history of the disease. Even in families with multiple cases of breast cancer, only about half of the cases are attributable to inherited genetic mutations. Race is also a factor, with white women more likely to develop breast cancer than black or Asian women.

Having had a breast biopsy that showed a change in cell tissue known as atypical hyperplasia increases breast cancer risk, as does having dense breasts as determined by mammography. Height is also a risk factor, with tall women more likely to develop breast cancer than their shorter counterparts. Scientists aren't sure why. One reason may be that tall people grow faster during their childhood. Faster growth means a greater proliferation of cells than average, with accordingly greater potential for harmful mistakes in DNA replication to occur. Exposure to ionizing radiation at a young age (e.g., for treatment of childhood cancer) also increases breast cancer risk by damaging DNA.

Many risk factors for breast cancer appear to operate at least partly through their influence on female sex hormones. A host of reproductive factors have been linked to breast cancer. The younger you were when you started menstruating and the older you were when you entered menopause, the greater your breast cancer risk, presumably because the number of years that you are exposed to high levels of estrogen is longer. Having children before the age of 35—and breast-feeding them for at least a year (combined across all children)—are each independently associated with a lower risk of developing breast cancer after menopause. (For about 10 years or so after she gives birth, a woman actually has an elevated breast cancer risk, probably because of the higher risk of genetic mutation that accompanies the rapid division of breast cells during pregnancy. But in the longer run, the changes in breast cells brought about by pregnancy and lactation render them less susceptible to cancer-causing agents. Delivering a first child after age 35 increases breast cancer risk because a woman's breast cells have likely already sustained some aging-related DNA damage, which will be amplified when cell division increases during pregnancy.) Having your ovaries surgically removed lowers your risk of breast cancer by drastically decreasing your estrogen exposure.

Estrogen- and progestogen-containing medications, such as birth control pills and menopausal hormone therapy, also increase breast cancer risk, but as we've seen, at least for menopause hormones, the risk is greatest among long-term users. (Some data have suggested that the increased risk of breast cancer associated with birth control pills is limited to long-term use before a first pregnancy.)

The relationship between obesity, physical activity, and breast cancer is complicated but likely depends on sex hormones as well. Obesity after menopause, especially if the extra pounds were gained at midlife, increases the risk of breast cancer. National cohort studies suggest that, compared with women of normal weight, overweight women are 30 percent more likely to develop breast cancer, and obese women are 50 percent more likely to do so. Indeed, 23 percent of postmenopausal breast cancers in the United States seem to be attributable to overweight and obesity.[7] However, carrying around excess body weight before menopause actually seems to lower the risk. A possible explanation is that, during the reproductive years, heavier women tend to have more irregular and fewer ovulatory menstrual cycles than thinner women; they may thus have lower levels of ovarian hormones. But after menopause, fat cells replace the ovaries as the main source of estrogen, so obesity emerges as a stronger predictor of breast cancer risk. On the other hand, physical activity in early life has been linked to a reduced breast cancer risk later on, whereas physical activity after menopause seems to have less of an effect. A high level of physical activity may delay the onset of puberty and may otherwise lower ovarian estrogen levels in menstruating women. After menopause, not only fat cells but also muscle cells are a primary source of estrogen, so physically active women may produce more estrogen than sedentary women, all else (e.g., excess fat) being equal.

Consuming more than one alcoholic drink per day on a regular basis substantially increases breast cancer risk. There are two purported reasons for this: alcohol is known to boost estrogen levels in the bloodstream and to decrease the body's stores of folate and vitamin A. Data from large observational studies, including the Nurses' Health Study, suggest that a high intake of folate, a nutrient important for the manufacture and repair of DNA, may reduce risk of breast (and colon) cancer in women, especially those who drink alcohol.[15] Women who eat at least three servings of vegetables per day—most of which are rich in vitamin A, such as carrots, broccoli, and winter squash—or a low-fat diet also appear to be at lower risk of breast cancer in such studies, although the data are not entirely consistent.[16, 17] There

"One in Eight Women"

You have probably heard the oft-quoted statistic from the National Cancer Institute (NCI) that one in eight women will develop breast cancer in her lifetime. At family gatherings, business meetings, and outings with friends, women looked around the room and wondered who the one in eight would be. Many women didn't realize that the statistic covers a life span of 85 years or more. The likelihood that a woman will develop the disease is much lower at midlife than it is in old age.

To show women that one in eight is not a static figure, the NCI calculated the probability of developing breast cancer according to age groups:

If Current Age Is:	The Likelihood of Developing Breast Cancer in the Next 10 Years Is:
20	1 in 1,985
30	1 in 229
40	1 in 68
50	1 in 37
60	1 in 26
70	1 in 24
Lifetime risk	1 in 8

Keep in mind that these figures are averages; some women have a lower and some a higher chance of developing breast cancer. Also keep in mind that a one-in-eight lifetime chance in developing breast cancer also means a seven-in-eight chance of living a life free of breast cancer.

appears to be little association between the consumption of omega-3 fats and breast (or other) cancers.[18] The relationship between soy and breast cancer is controversial (see the sidebar "What's the Scoop on Soy?"). More research is needed to confirm or refute the role of dietary factors other than alcohol in breast cancer risk.

Large randomized clinical trials of diet and breast cancer are few and far between. In 2006, my colleagues and I published the results of the Women's Health

What's the Scoop on Soy?

Soy has attracted considerable attention not only for its potential role in improving hot flashes in menopausal women but also for the possibility that it protects against both heart disease and breast cancer. As discussed in Chapter 2, soy and other phytoestrogen-rich foods have long been thought to act like naturally occurring selective estrogen receptor modulators (SERMs) in the human body. That is, in some tissues, such as the blood vessels, phytoestrogens may mimic or amplify the action of our own estrogen, whereas in others, such as the breast, they may block it. If soy sounds too good to be true . . . well, as the saying goes, it probably is.

Soy and Heart Disease

Besides phytoestrogens, soy is also rich in protein, polyunsaturated fats, fiber, minerals, and vitamins. Evidence from the most recent clinical trials of the effect of soy on heart disease risk factors (lipids and blood pressure) suggests that other components—not phytoestrogens—in soy may be responsible for any protection that this food might confer against heart disease.[19] But these trials also show that you'd need to eat a tremendous amount of soy— half or more of your daily protein intake—to produce a modest reduction in your LDL cholesterol, and that soy has little effect on blood pressure or other lipids. Scientists now believe that any heart benefit of soy results from the fact that it tends to replace unhealthy protein sources that are high in saturated fat, such as red meat. In any event, boosting your soy intake to a high level after menopause may not be advisable because of newly emerging concerns about breast cancer.

Soy and Breast Cancer

The estrogen-blocking activity of phytoestrogens might, in theory, reduce breast cancer, because our own estrogen stimulates the growth and multiplication of breast cancer cells. However, the actual relationship between soy and breast cancer risk is murky. The studies are all over the map—literally and figuratively. International studies show that Japanese women living in Japan who eat lots of soy have low rates of breast cancer. But the simplistic explanation is almost certainly wrong. Breast cancer rates have been low throughout Asia (at least until recently), and soy isn't a staple in many Asian countries. This suggests that other factors, such as differences in body weight, amount of physical activity, childbirth patterns, or other components of lifestyle or nutrition, are the real culprit.

continued

Some—though not all—observational studies have found that high soy intake is associated with reduced breast cancer risk in premenopausal women but not in postmenopausal women, which suggests that soy can affect different tissues differently at different life stages. The estrogen-blocking activity of phytoestrogens may be most beneficial for young women, whose breast tissue is bombarded by more powerful human estrogens. However, a high-phytoestrogen intake later in life, as estrogen production wanes, may not provide the same protection—and may even promote breast cancer by turning on estrogen receptors in the breast that would have otherwise sat empty. Indeed, studies of animals, as well as of human breast cells cultured in the lab, suggest reason for caution as they show that soy promotes the proliferation of breast cells in some circumstances but inhibits it in others. It is not yet clear which study results are most applicable to free-living humans. In light of this uncertainty, I'll repeat the advice I gave in Chapter 2: if you'd like to try soy to relieve hot flashes, you should do so. But don't go overboard with soy; eat it only in moderation.

Initiative dietary modification trial—the largest and longest randomized clinical trial of diet and breast cancer risk undertaken to date.[20] We randomly assigned 48,835 women aged 50 to 79 to one of two groups. The first group was given intensive dietary counseling to restrict total fat to 20 percent of calories and boost fruit and vegetable intake to at least five servings daily. The second group was instructed to follow their usual diet. After eight years, we found that the WHI eating plan didn't significantly lower the risk of breast cancer in the study population as a whole. Nevertheless, the eating plan was associated with a significant reduction in breast cancer risk among the women who had been eating a lot of fat when they enrolled in the trial. This finding provides support to the idea that reducing dietary fat may be beneficial to breast health.

Incidentally, we also found that the WHI eating plan, which focused on total fat reduction but not specifically on upping the ratio of good to bad fats, did not reduce the risk of coronary heart disease.[21] This result shouldn't be all that surprising, because, as I noted previously, observational studies suggest that the type of fat one eats is a more important driver of heart health than how much fat is eaten. (Indeed, the women who restricted saturated and trans fats the most *did* have a suggestion of heart benefit.)

How Do I Estimate My Risk for Developing Breast Cancer?

I adapted an assessment tool developed by my colleague Dr. Graham Colditz and others at the Harvard School of Public Health to provide an estimate of your lifetime risk of developing breast cancer (see Table 6.6).

What Can I Do to Protect Myself Against Breast Cancer?

Compared to heart disease, breast cancer may be less amenable to prevention by lifestyle changes that are initiated after menopause. However, maintaining a healthy body weight and/or avoiding midlife weight gain, engaging in moderate-intensity physical activity for at least 30 minutes per day, limiting alcohol to no more than one drink per day, having high intake of fruits and vegetables, and, possibly, taking folic acid supplements are recommended to reduce breast cancer risk.

Healthy women should be screened for breast cancer with mammography once every one to two years beginning at age 40, or earlier if there are particular risks or concerns. Studies show mammographic screening is especially important for those aged 50 to 69. Women should also do breast self-exams and have their healthcare provider do a manual breast exam during routine physical checkups. See your doctor if you discover a suspicious lump or skin changes in your breasts. If you opt to take menopause hormones, being extra vigilant about monitoring the health of your breasts and having regular mammography is vital.

The selective estrogen receptor modulators tamoxifen (Nolvadex) and raloxifene (Evista), which block estrogen receptors in the breast, and aromatase inhibitors, such as anastrozole (Arimidex) and letrozole (Femara), which block the conversion of androgen to estrogen in fat, muscle, and other tissues, have been found to prevent breast cancer in high-risk women and/or prevent recurrent breast cancer in women with a history of the disease. If you are taking one of these drugs because of breast cancer concerns, you are likely not a candidate for menopausal hormone therapy.

OSTEOPOROTIC FRACTURE

Let's look at how to calculate—and reduce—your personal risk of osteoporotic fracture.

Table 6.6 Estimating Your Lifetime Risk of Breast Cancer

The adapted* Harvard Breast Cancer Risk Index[22] is most accurate for women aged 40 or older who have not had any type of cancer (except nonmelanoma skin cancer) in the past. If you have a personal history of breast cancer or are known to carry the harmful BRCA1 or BRCA2 gene mutation, you have an elevated risk of recurrent or new cancer and should not use this tool because it will underestimate your risk.

Family history (questions refer to biological relatives only)

1a. Has your mother had breast cancer?	Yes=30 No = 0
1b. Has one or more of your sisters had breast cancer?	Yes, 1 sister has had breast cancer=30 Yes, 2 or more sisters have had breast cancer=60 No=0
1c. Has one or both of your grandmothers had breast cancer before age 80?	Yes, 1 grand-mother has had breast cancer=15 Yes, both grand-mothers have had breast cancer=30 No=0
1d. Has one or more of your aunts had breast cancer before age 80? (Do not include in-laws, who are biologically unrelated to you.)	Yes, 1 aunt has had breast cancer=15 Yes, 2 or more aunts have had breast cancer=30 No=0
2. Are you age 60 or older?	Yes = 10 No = 0
3. Are you physically active 3 or more hours each week?	Yes = 0 No = 10
4. Are you taller than 5 feet 7 inches?	Yes = 5 No = 0
If you have not gone through menopause, skip to question 6. 5. Is your body mass index 30 or greater?	Yes = 10 No = 0
6. Do you have more than 7 drinks of alcohol per week? (One drink is 1 beer, 1 glass of wine, or 1 shot of other alcohol.)	Yes = 5 No = 0
7. Do you take a multivitamin with folic acid every day?	Yes = 0 No = 5
8. Is your ethnic background Ashkenazi Jewish?	Yes = 5 No=0
9. Did your menstrual periods start at age 12 or earlier?	Yes = 5 No=0

If you are under age 55, skip to question 11.

10. Did you start menopause when you were age 55 or older?	Yes = 5 No = 0
11. Have you given birth to one or more children?	Yes = 0 No = 5

If you have never given birth, skip to question 14.

12. Did you give birth to your first child at age 35 or older?	Yes = 10 No = 0
13. Have you breast-fed for 12 months or more (combined for all pregnancies)?	Yes = 0 No = 5
14. Are you currently using or have you previously used birth control pills?	Yes = 5 No = 0
15. Are you currently taking menopausal hormone therapy?	Yes, estrogen alone for 5 years or more = 5 Yes, estrogen plus progestogen for 5 years or more = 10 No, or for less than 5 years = 0
16. Have you had a breast biopsy that showed a change in cell tissue known as atypical hyperplasia?	Yes = 10 No = 0

Point total	Risk category	Risk compared to the average woman of the same age
0–15	Below average	Risk is one-half to three-quarters that of the average woman
20–25	Average	Risk is that of the average woman
30–55	Slightly above average	Risk is one and one-half times that of the average woman
60 or more	Much above average	Risk is three to five times that of the average woman

*Questions about family history of breast cancer and menopausal hormone therapy have been modified, and a question on age has been added. Questions about the use of tamoxifen and raloxifene and about prophylactic bilateral mastectomy (surgical removal of both breasts in the absence of breast cancer) have been omitted because of a lack of general applicability to the population of women considering menopausal hormone therapy.

Other variables are not included in this risk assessment tool either because researchers cannot accurately determine how much these factors contribute to the calculation of risk for an individual woman or because the evidence linking them to breast cancer risk is not conclusive.

A somewhat different version of this tool can be found at the website www.yourdiseaserisk.harvard.edu.

What Are the Risk Factors for Osteoporosis and Osteoporotic Fracture?

The risk factors for osteoporosis and related bone fractures are well established. Having a parent with osteoporosis or who has broken a bone after age 50 puts a woman at increased risk. Women with smaller, more delicate body frames are higher risk than those with larger, thicker bones. Because they have less bone mass to start out with, small-framed women can afford to lose very little of it without greatly boosting their susceptibility to fracture. Leaner women are also at greater risk for bone thinning and fracture than their overweight counterparts, for three reasons. The bones of obese women benefit from a greater supply of estrogen after menopause, from the workout they get supporting the excess weight, and from the cushioning effects of fat after a fall. However, obesity is not an unalloyed boon to the skeleton; it is the leading cause of knee and hip osteoarthritis in U.S. women.

A lifetime diet that is low in calcium increases osteoporosis risk, as does physical inactivity or extended bed rest, cigarette smoking, and high alcohol intake (more than one drink per day). Certain prescription medications, most notably corticosteroids and anticonvulsants, are notorious for their bone-robbing qualities. Aromatase inhibitors, which are used to treat breast cancer by reducing estrogen, also increase the risk of osteoporosis. Women whose ovaries have been surgically removed are at increased risk of osteoporosis.

Compared with white women, black women are at much lower risk of suffering a hip fracture, whereas Hispanic and Asian women are at higher risk.[23] Scientists believe that this is due not only to racial and ethnic differences in body size and weight but also to differences in how their skin responds to the sun and in their diets. Sunlight is a major source of vitamin D, which is essential for the body to process calcium efficiently. After differences in body size are factored out, darker-skinned people may be less able to manufacture vitamin D from the sun's rays and hence less able to use the calcium taken in via diet. Also, many Asians are intolerant of lactose, a sugar found in calcium-rich dairy foods; avoiding such foods may increase their risk.

Last, your risk of sustaining an osteoporotic fracture depends not only on your bone mass but also on how likely you are to lose your balance and take a spill. The weaker your leg muscles are, the more prone you may be to falling. One quick test of leg strength and balance is to see whether you can rise from a chair without using your arms. Worsening eyesight, dizzy spells, and sedation—alcohol, sleeping pills, and tranquilizers are common culprits—also raise the risk of falls.

How Do I Estimate My Risk of Developing Osteoporotic Hip Fracture?

An assessment tool developed by investigators with the Study of Osteoporotic Fractures, a cohort study of women aged 65 and older, provides an assessment of your risk of developing an osteoporotic hip fracture, the most disabling of all osteoporotic fracture types (see Table 6.7).

Is There a Test for Osteoporosis?

Osteopororosis refers not only to a reduction in bone mineral density (BMD)—synonyms are bone density, bone quantity, or bone mass—but also a reduction in the quality of bone that remains. However, because BMD accounts for 70 percent of bone strength, many researchers consider it the best single proxy for osteoporosis.

The best way to determine your bone density is to have a test called dual-energy x-ray absorptiometry (DEXA). It uses very low doses of radiation to measure the amount of bone in your hip and spine, and in some cases, your forearm—the sites where osteoporotic fractures are most likely to occur. Only a fraction of the radiation dose of a standard chest X-ray is necessary. The test takes only 15 minutes or so, and you don't even have to undress for it.

Bone density results are expressed as a T-score. Your T-score reflects how your bone density compares to a standard—the average value in healthy women aged 20 to 30, the age decade at which bone density is at its peak. Each bone measured will have its own T-score.

The lower your T-score, the less dense your bone (see Figure 6.3). For those familiar with the mathematical concept of the "standard deviation," a T-score of -1 or greater indicates that your bone density is no more than 1 standard deviation below that of the typical woman aged 20 to 30; you are considered to have normal bone density. A T-score of between -1 and -2.5 indicates that your bone density is between 1 and 2.5 standard deviations below that of the standard; you are considered to have osteopenia, or low bone density, but not full-blown osteoporosis. A T-score of -2.5 or lower indicates that your bone density is at least 2.5 standard deviations below that of the standard, and you are considered to have osteoporosis ("porous bones"). If the explanation is confusing, keep in mind that osteopenia and osteoporosis simply refer to varying stages of bone loss.

Studies of menopausal women show a strong relationship between low bone density and an increased future risk of fracture. Still, BMD isn't the only determi-

Table 6.7 Estimating Your Five-Year Risk of Osteoporotic Hip Fracture[*24]

	Points
1. What is your age?	
Less than 65	0
65–69	1
70–74	2
75–79	3
80–84	4
85 or more	5
2. Have you broken any bones after age 50?	
Yes	2
No/don't know	0
3. Has your biological mother had a hip fracture after age 50?	
Yes	2
No/don't know	0
4. Do you weigh 125 pounds or less?	
Yes	2
No	0
5. Do you smoke cigarettes?	
Yes	1
No	0
6. Do you usually need to use your arms to assist yourself in standing up from a chair?	
Yes	2
No/don't know	0
If you have a current hip bone mineral density (BMD) assessment, then answer the next question. **7. BMD: total hip T-score**	
T-score greater than or equal to −1	0
T-score between −1 and −2	2
T-score between −2 and −2.5	3
T-score less than −2.5	4
Point total	

*Some modifications have been made to the original instrument. Other factors that increase risk are use of steroids, low calcium and vitamin D intake, low physical activity level, and having a biological father with hip fracture after age 50.

If Hip T-Score Is Not Known:			If Hip T-Score Is Known:		
Point total	**5-year risk of hip fracture**	**Risk category**	**Point total**	**5-year risk of hip fracture**	**Risk category**
0–1	<0.6%	Very low	0–2	<0.4%	Very low
2	1.4%	Low	3–4	0.9%	Low
3	2.1%	Average	5	1.9%	Average
4	3.2%	High	6–7	3.9%	High
5 or more	8.2%	Very high	8 or more	8.7%	Very high

nant of fracture risk, as women with similar BMD scores can have very different levels of fracture risk. For example, an 80-year-old woman with a low BMD score has a much greater risk of fracture than a 60-year-old woman with the same score. And half of all fractures occur in people who don't have full-blown osteoporosis as defined by BMD measurements (see Figure 6.4).

Medical authorities, including the U.S. Preventive Services Task Force, the National Osteoporosis Foundation, and the North American Menopause Society, recommend that all women aged 65 and older be screened for osteoporosis with a bone density test, regardless of their risk factor status. There is less of a universal consensus on screening guidelines for younger women, but many authorities agree that menopausal women at elevated risk for osteoporotic fracture by virtue of their family history or other risk factors should be screened at age 60 or perhaps even

Figure 6.3 What's Your T-Score?

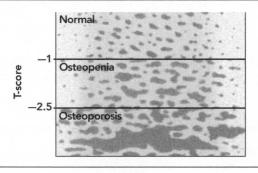

A T-score ranging from −1 to −2.5 is classified as osteopenia, while a T-score of −2.5 or lower is classified as osteoporosis. The lower your score, the more porous your bone.

Figure 6.4 Relationship Between Age, Bone Density, and Fracture Risk in Menopausal Women

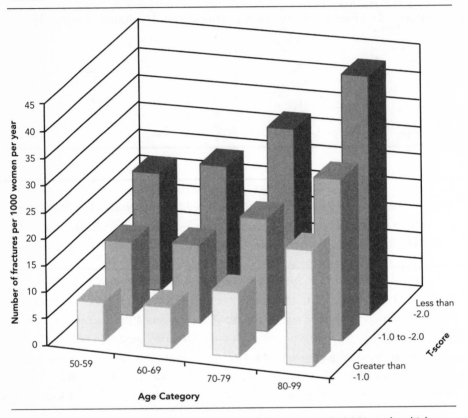

These data are from the National Osteoporosis Risk Assessment (NORA) study, which assessed bone density in 170,000 U.S. menopausal women aged 50 to 99 and then followed them for three years for the development of bone fracture.

From Siris, E. S., et al. Osteoporosis International 17 (2006): 565–74. (with permission)

earlier. Testing is needed at most every two years. In women with normal bone density, a longer interval—five years, for example—is likely to be sufficient.

What Can I Do to Protect Myself Against Osteoporosis and Osteoporotic Fracture?

The fundamentals of osteoporosis prevention are adequate calcium, vitamin D, and weight-bearing exercise, plus medications as needed.

Get Enough Calcium

Recommended daily intakes of calcium are listed in Table 6.8. Ideally, calcium requirements should be met by food sources, but most midlife women consume only 700 milligrams of calcium daily, much less than the recommended level of 1,200 milligrams. Good food sources of calcium are listed in Table 6.9 and include dairy foods; canned oily fish with bones, such as sardines or salmon; calcium-fortified orange juice; calcium-fortified cereal; and certain dark green, leafy vegetables, such as broccoli, collard greens, and kale. (Some other calcium-containing greens, including spinach, are less desirable as calcium sources because they also contain oxalic acid, which interferes with calcium absorption.)

Some women have difficulty achieving the recommended intake of calcium from diet. Women who are lactose intolerant, follow a vegetarian diet that excludes dairy products, or have poor eating habits should take a calcium supplement. The two most common forms are calcium carbonate (Caltrate, Os-Cal, Rolaids, Tums, or Viactiv) and calcium citrate (Citracal). Calcium carbonate requires stomach acid for proper absorption, so it should be taken with food or soon after a meal. By contrast, calcium citrate does not require stomach acid for absorption and thus can be taken without food. This may be more convenient, but it can also be more expensive, because it takes more calcium citrate than calcium carbonate to get the same dose of actual (elemental) calcium. Trying to figure out exactly how much actual calcium is contained in supplements can be confusing. Read the labels carefully and check with your doctor if you're unsure. Taking too much calcium can increase the risk of kidney stones, impair kidney function, and interfere with the absorption of other minerals.

The body can't assimilate more than about 500 milligrams of calcium in any two-hour period, whether from food or supplements. Therefore, you'll need to

Table 6.8 Recommended Daily Intakes of Calcium and Vitamin D

Age	Calcium*	Vitamin D†
19–50	1,000 mg	200 IU
51–70	1,200 mg	400 IU‡
70 or more	1,200 mg	600 IU‡

*Not to exceed 2,500 mg

†Not to exceed 2,000 IU

‡Recent studies suggest that 600 to 800 IU may be preferable.

Table 6.9 Foods High in Calcium*

Food	Serving size	Calcium content (mg) per serving
Yogurt, low-fat, plain	1 cup	415
Yogurt, low-fat, fruit-flavored	1 cup	245–384
Sardines, canned in oil, with bones	3 ounces	324
Milk, skim	1 cup	302
Milk, 2% milk fat	1 cup	297
Milk, whole	1 cup	291
Gruyère cheese	1 ounce	287
Swiss cheese	1 ounce	272
Figs, dried	10 figs	269
Tofu, raw, firm	½ cup	258
Calcium-fortified cereals†	¾ cup	250
Cheddar cheese	1 ounce	204
Calcium-fortified orange juice	6 ounces	200
Mozzarella cheese, part-skim	1 ounce	183
Salmon, pink, canned, solids with bone	3 ounces	181
Collards, cooked from frozen, chopped	½ cup	179
American cheese, processed	1 ounce	174
Blackstrap molasses	1 tablespoon	172
Creamed cottage cheese	1 cup	126
Sardines, canned in oil	2 sardines	92
Parmesan cheese, grated	1 tablespoon	69
Mustard greens	½ cup	52
Kale, boiled	½ cup	47
Broccoli, boiled	½ cup	36

*Sources: Pennington, J. A. T., et al. *Food Values of Portions Commonly Used*, 17th edition. Philadelphia: Lippincott, 1998, and http://ods.od.nih.gov/factsheets/calcium_pf.asp.

†Some cereals contain 1,000 milligrams of calcium per serving.

space out your calcium intake throughout the day. If you take calcium carbonate, which requires food for optimal absorption, take it with the meal that has the least amount of dairy in it, or take it midmorning or midafternoon with a piece of fruit or other healthy snack. Women who take iron supplements will need to take their iron separately from their calcium supplements, as iron interferes with calcium absorption.

Get Enough Vitamin D

To ensure effective calcium absorption, you must get adequate vitamin D. An excellent source of vitamin D is sunlight. Exposing 40 percent of one's skin to the sun for 20 minutes a day without sunscreen helps most women make enough to meet the daily requirement. However, this may increase the risk of skin cancer and is obviously not a practical option for those in northern climes in winter. Vitamin D can also be obtained through food. Good dietary sources of vitamin D include fortified milk (1 cup contains 98 IU) and cereal; oily fish, such as sardines and salmon (one serving contains between 250 and 360 IU); and cod liver oil (1 tablespoon has 1,360 IU). Vitamin D supplements are a third option. But check with your healthcare provider before taking supplements. Doses in excess of the recommended upper limit can cause gastrointestinal problems and raise blood levels of calcium, resulting in confusion and heart rhythm abnormalities.

Although a wealth of data from observational studies and randomized clinical trials shows that calcium and vitamin D supplements slow bone loss and prevent the development of osteoporosis in menopausal women, evidence that these supplements reduce hip fracture is actually quite sparse. To fill the research void, my colleagues and I undertook a clinical trial of calcium and vitamin D as part of the WHI. To do this, we recruited 36,282 of the women who were already enrolled in the aforementioned WHI dietary modification trial and assigned them to a calcium-and-vitamin-D supplement (the daily dose was 1,000 milligrams elemental calcium and 400 IU of vitamin D) or to a placebo pill. We then followed the women for seven years to see who would develop hip fracture. At the end of the trial, we found that the women assigned to calcium-and-vitamin-D supplements had experienced less bone loss at the hip and were 12 percent less likely to have had a hip fracture than those assigned to placebo.[25] To be frank, the overall reduction in hip fracture was disappointingly small and not statistically significant—it could have been a chance finding. But among the women aged 60 and older, the intervention was associated with a significant 21 percent reduction in hip fracture. And when we looked only at the participants who took their study pills faithfully, we found that women on the calcium-and-vitamin-D supplements were 30 percent less likely to have had hip fracture than those on the placebo pills—a still larger, and statistically significant, effect.

Do Weight-Bearing Physical Activity and Strength Training

Observational studies have shown that midlife and older women with higher levels of physical activity, including walking, experience a 30 to 40 percent reduction in risk for osteoporotic fractures compared with their inactive counterparts. Physical activity enhances bone formation in response to mechanical forces from muscle contraction and also lowers the risk of falling by improving muscle strength, balance, and mobility. Aerobic weight-bearing and nonaerobic weight-resisting (also known as strengthening) activities—i.e., those that work against gravity—are best at stimulating the growth of new bone tissue and preventing bone loss. Aerobic weight-bearing activities include walking, jogging, climbing stairs, dancing, and, as a general rule, other physical activities where your feet touch the ground. (Swimming and biking are good for overall fitness and reduction of cardiovascular disease, but they are not weight-bearing and thus are not useful in building bone.) Aim for at least 30 minutes per day of aerobic weight-bearing activity. Strengthening activities—exercising with arm and/or leg weights or with resistance bands—should also be performed on a regular basis to keep your bones in top shape; aim for 20 minutes per day two to three times per week. It is discouraging to note that in a recent national survey, only 16 percent of U.S. women aged 45 to 64 years and less than 10 percent of women aged 65 and older reported ever engaging in strengthening exercises.[6]

Consider Medications

Until recently, long-term estrogen (combined with a progestogen in women who have a uterus) was the mainstay of medication-based efforts to prevent osteoporosis in menopausal women. But with the new understanding of the overall balance of benefits and risks of hormone therapy brought about by the WHI and other recent studies, medical authorities—myself included—are now encouraging women who have been taking menopause hormones primarily to protect their bones to consider alternative approaches, including redoubling their efforts on the exercise front, ensuring adequate calcium and vitamin D, and, where appropriate, taking nonestrogen prescription medications.

When is it appropriate to consider prescription medications for the prevention or treatment of osteoporosis? There is some controversy about exactly how low a T-score you need to qualify, but the following guidelines are reasonable:

- Women with osteoporotic hip or spine fracture or who have hip or spine T-scores worse than −2.5 are considered to have osteoporosis and are candidates to take medications approved for the treatment of osteoporosis.

- Women with hip or spine T-scores from −1.5 to −2.5 and at least one risk factor for fracture (e.g., body weight less than 125 pounds, current smoker, lifelong low calcium intake, or a history of osteoporotic fracture in a first-degree relative) may be candidates to take medications approved for the prevention of osteoporosis.

- Women with hip or spine T-scores from −1.5 to −2.5 but with none of the risk factors listed in this chapter, or with hip or spine T-scores from −1 to −2 with one or more risk factors should repeat their bone density test in two to five years, ideally on the same machine. If a comparison of the two test results suggests that you are losing bone at a more rapid clip than expected by your doctor, you could consider taking a medication approved for the prevention of osteoporosis.

If you aren't in one of these three groups, your best bet is to focus on getting adequate calcium, vitamin D, and regular bone-stressing exercise. And let me repeat—these basic strategies are still essential even if you do take osteoporosis medications. In the WHI, for example, estrogen-plus-progestin therapy was about 60 percent more effective at protecting against hip fractures in women who reported daily calcium intakes of at least 1,200 milligrams compared with those who reported lower calcium intakes.

Most FDA-approved osteoporosis drugs are antiresorptive agents—that is, they slow the breakdown (resorption) of bone by interfering with the activity of osteoclasts (see the sidebar "Bone Remodeling"). Drugs in this class include bisphosphonates, raloxifene, and calcitonin, as well as estrogen. All antiresorptive drugs have been shown to reduce the risk of spine fracture in clinical trials; some also reduce hip and wrist fractures.

Estrogen is the top choice for osteoporosis prevention only for those women who are already taking the hormone to relieve severe menopausal symptoms. But estrogen is approved only to prevent osteoporosis, not to treat it. If you have been diagnosed with osteoporosis, you should consider another medication to strengthen your bones, even if you're already on estrogen.

Bisphosphonates are typically the drug of choice to prevent osteoporosis among high-risk menopausal women who aren't on estrogen to cool their hot flashes; and these drugs are also the preferred treatment option for most women with osteoporosis, regardless of their estrogen-therapy status. Although they can cause nausea or heartburn, these drugs have few serious side effects when taken properly. (That said, bisphosphonates have very recently been implicated in a rare complication called osteonecrosis of the jaw—more on this in a bit.) Alendronate (Fosamax) and risedronate (Actonel) are available as a daily or once-per-week pill. Ibandronate (Boniva) is available as a daily or once-per-month pill. The pills must be taken on an empty stomach (that is, first thing in the morning) with a full glass of water. Then you must remain upright (standing or sitting) and eat and drink nothing else for at least 30 minutes (60 minutes for Boniva) to ensure absorption and to prevent dangerous irritation of the esophagus and stomach. (An injectable form of Boniva given every three months, which avoids these problems, is also available for the treatment of osteoporosis. The injections must be administered by a healthcare provider.) Fosamax and Actonel reduce the risk of spine, hip, and wrist fractures by 40 to 50 percent. Boniva reduces the risk of spine fractures by a comparable amount, but data on its ability to reduce hip or wrist fractures are less compelling.

Within the past year or so, reports have begun to surface linking bisphosphonates to an increased risk of osteonecrosis of the jaw, a condition in which the jawbone deteriorates and dies. Most of the individuals who have experienced this complication are cancer patients taking one of two potent injectable bisphosphonates, zoledronic acid (Zometa) and pamidronate (Aredia). (Bisphosphonates are sometimes prescribed for cancer patients whose tumors cause excessive osteoclast activity. When cancer has spread to the bone, these drugs can reduce bone pain, cancer-related fractures, and dangerously high blood levels of calcium.) However, a few cases have also occurred in noncancer patients who have taken less potent oral bisphosphonates for five or more years to prevent or treat osteoporosis. Although it's not yet clear who is susceptible to developing this drug-related complication, more than half of reported cases occurred after a major dental procedure such as a tooth extraction. Therefore, it may be prudent to have a thorough dental exam before starting bisphosphonate treatment and to avoid dental or oral surgery while taking the medication.

Raloxifene (Evista) is a SERM with estrogen-like effects on the bone and anti-estrogen effects on the breast and uterus. It is approved for both the prevention and treatment of osteoporosis. It reduces spine fractures by 40 to 50 percent but does not seem to be effective in reducing hip and wrist fractures. Possible side effects include hot flashes, leg cramps, and blood clots, which make it less than ideal for women with menopause symptoms and a higher-than-usual risk of VTE.

Calcitonin (Miacalcin, Calcimar, and Fortical) is a hormone preparation that produces a modest reduction in spine fracture risk. It is approved only for the treatment of osteoporosis in women who are at least five years past menopause. The drug is taken by injection or nasal spray. Side effects include nausea and flushing. As a nasal spray, it can cause a runny nose or nosebleed.

In contrast to antiresorptive drugs, which slow bone breakdown but have limited bone-building ability, anabolic drugs stimulate bone formation by increasing the activity of cells known as osteoblasts. To date, one such drug has received approval from the FDA for the treatment (not prevention) of osteoporosis—teraparatide (Forteo), a synthetic form of parathyroid hormone. In a 19-month clinical trial among women with previous spine fractures, the drug cut the risk of new spine fractures by an impressive 65 percent and nonspine fractures by 53 percent. Taken as a daily injection, Forteo is expensive, costing about $600 per month. In animal studies, rats on the drug for two years showed an increased risk for bone cancer. Although tumors have not been reported in human studies, the FDA has ruled that Forteo should not be taken for more than two years because it lacks a long-term track record for safety and effectiveness.

OTHER DISORDERS

As you learned in Chapter 4, hormone therapy has been linked to other disorders—for example, it may reduce the risk of colorectal cancer and type 2 diabetes, increase the risk of ovarian cancer, and, depending on when you start it, either decrease or increase the risk of memory and thinking problems. However, there is much less

Bone Remodeling: The Interrelationship Between Calcium, Vitamin D, and Other Hormones

Bone remodeling (also known as turnover) involves two stages: bone breakdown (resorption) and bone formation. Calcium—an element essential for proper cell function throughout the body, including muscle contraction, transmission of nerve signals, and blood clotting—is stored in bone. When it's needed in the body, bone-destroying cells, called *osteoclasts*, attach to the bone surface and break it down, leaving cavities in the bone. Then bone-building cells, called *osteoblasts*, move in and release collagen and other proteins into these cavities and stimulate bone mineralization. The osteoblasts then join with calcium and other substances to form new bone material to replace what was lost. (Osteoblasts that remain part of the matrix are called *osteocytes*.) Up until age 30 or so, the bone-building osteoblasts are more active than the bone-destroying osteoclasts; after that, the osteoclasts tend to gain the upper hand.

A number of the body's hormones, estrogen and progesterone among them, regulate bone remodeling via their effects on calcium. The key players are parathyroid hormone from the parathyroid glands, calcitonin from the thyroid gland, and vitamin D from the skin. (Yes, unlike other vitamins, vitamin D is actually a hormone.)

The parathyroid glands in the neck regulate the level of calcium in the bloodstream. When the calcium level gets too low, these glands secrete parathyroid hormone. This hormone converts vitamin D from its inactive to its active form, which helps the intestine to absorb calcium from food and prompts the kidneys to retain calcium rather than excreting it in the urine. Parathyroid hormone also directs the osteoclasts to break down more bone and release calcium into the bloodstream. (Oddly, although sustained elevations in parathyroid hormone reduce bone density, single daily injections of the hormone, which raise hormone levels in a pulsed fashion, actually increase the activity of osteoblasts more than the activity of osteoclasts and therefore boost bone density. Recognition of this paradoxical effect, first reported in humans in 1980, paved the way for the development of Forteo as an osteoporosis treatment.) Conversely, when the body's available calcium has reached an adequate level, calcitonin from the thyroid gland quiets down the osteoclasts, slowing bone destruction. To the detriment of our bones, calcitonin levels tend to drop off as we go through menopause.

Estrogen appears to benefit bone by blocking the actions of parathyroid hormone on osteoclasts and by boosting the production of calcitonin. It also helps maintain adequate levels of vitamin D. Progesterone seems to benefit bone by counteracting the effect of certain adrenal hormones known as glucocorticoids. Activated in times of stress (and responsible for the well-known fight-or-flight response), glucocorticoids heighten the bones' normal sensitivity to parathyroid hormone and vitamin D to ensure calcium is quickly delivered to all parts of the body that need it. Unlike estrogen and progesterone, androgens such as testosterone directly stimulate the formation of new bone by activating the osteoblasts. Their higher androgen levels are one reason why men have higher bone mass than women do.

evidence that consideration of these conditions (in contrast to the five conditions that I reviewed in this chapter) will be helpful in guiding decision making about hormone therapy. Nevertheless, if you have particular concerns about any of these disorders, you should definitely raise these concerns with your healthcare provider.

Once you've completed the hard work of assessing your risk factors and estimating your risk of the five diseases discussed in detail in this chapter, you can use your results to determine whether or not you are good candidate for hormone therapy. Let's move on to Chapter 7.

7

Putting It All Together: Should I Start Hormone Therapy? Should I Stop?

◉

Since the publication of the Women's Health Initiative (WHI) results, not only have many women either stopped or become reluctant to use menopausal hormone therapy, but many healthcare providers and researchers—myself included—have been forced to rethink their recommendations regarding the use of menopause hormones. Virtually all professional organizations concerned with the medical issues of midlife and older women, including the North American Menopause Society, the American College of Obstetricians and Gynecologists, and the American Heart Association, now advise that hormone therapy not be used to prevent heart disease, stroke, or other forms of cardiovascular disease. Indeed, the FDA now requires that estrogen and estrogen-plus-progestogen preparations carry labels that warn against the use of these products for cardiovascular disease protection. The labels for estrogen-plus-progestogen products additionally highlight the increased risks of heart attack, stroke, blood clots in the lungs and legs, and breast cancer found in the WHI. And the U.S. Preventive Services Task Force and the Canadian Task Force on Preventive Health Care, agencies with a mandate by their respective federal governments to review available scientific data and provide advice about various medical therapies, recommend that estrogen (with or without a progestogen) not be taken solely for the purpose of preventing chronic diseases of aging.

At the same time, acknowledging that menopause hormones are far and away the most effective treatment available for the relief of troublesome menopausal symptoms, mainstream medical organizations have urged physicians and other healthcare providers to adopt an individualized approach to hormone therapy—that is, to tailor their advice and prescribing practices to the health profile and personal preferences of each of their patients. Yet, as of this writing, these organizations have provided scant guidance to physicians on how to go about making these patient-by-patient recommendations. Indeed, many doctors readily admit that they're confused about how to decide if a woman is a good candidate for hormone therapy. And, many women who turn to their doctors for advice about hormone therapy find that their doctors are unable or reluctant to move beyond the general guideline—i.e., take the lowest dose of menopause hormones possible for the shortest period of time—in addressing their particular situation.

In this chapter, I provide the personalized guidance that you may be seeking—guidance that will help you work more effectively with your healthcare provider to decide if hormone therapy is right for you. From a strictly medical perspective, whether you should start—or continue—menopausal hormone therapy depends on the answers to only two questions. The first—and relatively straightforward—question is, "Are hot flashes, night sweats, or symptoms of vaginal dryness causing major disruptions in my life?" If the answer is no, stop here; you have no compelling reason to take menopause hormones and you should not do so.

However, if the answer is yes, then you will need to ask yourself a second—and more complicated—question: "Given my personal health history, will menopausal hormone therapy lead to a favorable—or at least neutral—balance of benefits and risks?" If the answer is no, stop here; you should definitely not take menopause hormones. If the answer is yes, then you may be an appropriate candidate for hormone therapy.

But there is a third question to be answered, one that falls outside the purview of strictly medical considerations. If—and only if—a careful weighing of the benefits and risks of hormone therapy suggests that you are a reasonable candidate for hormone therapy from a medical point of view, you must then look inward to your own values and preferences to guide your decision. Simply put, the question is, "Am I at ease with the decision?" Keep in mind that, despite our society's tendency to "medicalize" menopause, it is not an "estrogen-deficiency disease" but rather a natural and universal stage of female life to which your body is perfectly capable of adjusting on its own without help from supplemental hormones. Therefore, if taking prescription estrogen seems uncomfortably like treating a natural physical process as if it were an illness, then hormone therapy may not be the right choice for you.

Together we'll work through these questions in detail. But here's an overview of important aspects of the hormone decision-making process.

- **Starting hormone therapy:** A key consideration in your initial decision making is where you are in the menopausal transition. At the risk of sounding like a broken record, let me repeat—timing is everything. Most doctors agree that if you are still menstruating, even if your periods are highly erratic, menopausal hormone therapy is not appropriate because of the risk of estrogen overload. A better option would be low-dose birth control pills, which not only reduce hot flashes and night sweats but also control menstrual bleeding and provide contraception (see the sidebar "Making the Switch").

Once you have entered menopause, two key factors—your age and how long it's been since your last menstrual period (5 years or less, 6 to 10 years, or more than 10 years)—will play a major role in determining whether you are a good candidate for menopause hormones or not. However, you will need to reevaluate your decision at regular intervals (at annual physical exams, for example), because for all women, the balance of benefits and risks shifts over time—with increasing duration of hormone use (independent of age) and as you grow older (independent of how long you've used hormones).

- **Duration of hormone therapy:** The majority of women who opt for oral or transdermal hormones, which work systemically (i.e., throughout the body) to relieve hot flashes, night sweats, and associated symptoms, should plan on taking such hormones for only a short period of time—ideally two to three years, and generally no more than five years for estrogen plus progestogen or seven years for estrogen alone. (Recall that unless you've had a hysterectomy, you should not take estrogen without a progestogen.) There are two reasons for these time limits. First, hot flashes and night sweats tend to peak in the first couple of years after one's last menstrual period and then subside, which suggests that most women won't need hormone therapy for hot flash control after that time. Second, the risk of breast cancer rises with longer-term use of hormones (particularly estrogen plus progestogen), which eventually tips the overall balance of benefits and risks into unfavorable territory for most women.

That said, a small percentage of women do continue to suffer from intolerable hot flashes for years after menopause, and these women have difficulty when they try to stop their hormone therapy. Provided that a woman's risks of heart attack, stroke, and venous thromboembolism (VTE) all remain relatively low (if they weren't low to begin with, she shouldn't have been on hormones in the first place) *and* she is not at above-average risk of breast cancer, then extending estrogen-only therapy for up to 3 more years—for a total of 10 years—should not pose too much danger. Indeed, taking estrogen for this length of time will provide significant bone benefits to a woman at high risk of osteoporosis, and the potential reduction in her fracture risk will likely outweigh any breast cancer concerns. However, extending estrogen-plus-progestogen therapy beyond 5 years is less advisable, because the risk of breast cancer escalates more rapidly with combination hormones than with estrogen alone.

• **Deciding whether to use vaginal estrogen:** Deciding whether to use and how long to take vaginal estrogen is much easier than making these decisions about systemic (oral or transdermal) estrogen; there are far fewer health variables to consider. Prescribed only for relief of vaginal dryness and its associated symptoms, vaginal estrogen can safely be used by most women, regardless of their health history, with the exception of those with a history of breast cancer or endometrial cancer. And unlike systemic estrogen, vaginal estrogen can be taken for an indefinite period of time—that is, there seems to be no upper limit on how long you can safely use it. Nevertheless, women with a uterus will need to take an occasional break from vaginal estrogen and/or add a progestogen periodically—say once every three months—to protect against the possibility of developing endometrial cancer.

One caveat: the Femring vaginal ring delivers a higher dose of estrogen than other vaginal products and is intended for systemic use—i.e., to relieve hot flashes and night sweats as well as vaginal dryness. In your decision making, consider Femring to be equivalent to transdermal estrogen.

Data from the WHI and other recent studies provide a solid foundation for formulating a decision-making strategy about hormone therapy. My recommended approach is diagrammed in the flowchart in Figure 7.1. As you read the next sections of the book, you should refer to the flowchart to help keep your decision-making process on track.

QUESTION 1: HOW DEBILITATING ARE MY SYMPTOMS?

Hormone therapy is very effective for alleviating the "core" menopause symptoms of hot flashes, night sweats, and vaginal dryness—and may help disruptions in sleep, mood, self-confidence, memory and concentration, and sex life, to the extent that these are consequences of the core symptoms. Are hot flashes or night sweats

Making the Switch from Contraceptive Hormones to Menopausal Hormone Therapy

While going one year without a menstrual period confirms the arrival of menopause for most midlife women who are not taking birth control pills, it's impossible to assess the natural pattern of menstrual cycles in women who take contraceptive hormones.

If you're a sexually active woman who has been using birth control pills to treat perimenopausal symptoms, how will you know when it's time to come off these hormones and—provided that you're suffering from hot flashes—make the transition to menopausal hormone therapy? You'll need to switch from a hormonal to a barrier method of contraception to see if your period occurs spontaneously. If it does, you can go back on hormonal contraceptives and try going off again in six months to a year. If it doesn't (i.e., you go six months or more without a period), then you're probably past menopause and can safely begin menopausal hormone therapy. To be sure, some doctors recommend blood tests to check your FSH level; if two tests performed at least one month apart both show a level above 30 IU/ml, you've likely reached menopause.

When should you first attempt to make the switch? It largely depends on your age, the age at which your mother or other close female relatives experienced (natural) menopause, and how long you've been taking birth control pills to treat perimenopausal symptoms. Because the average age of menopause in the United States is 51 years, you should try coming off the hormonal contraceptives at that age—unless your family history suggests you'll have an earlier or later menopause, in which case you can adjust the timetable accordingly. In addition, because the average length of time between the appearance of the first perimenopausal symptoms and one's last menstrual period is four years or so, you should try stopping the birth control pills no more than four years after you first started taking them to alleviate your perimenopausal symptoms.

Women who smoke, have current liver disease, or have a history of blood clots, breast cancer, increased risk of cardiovascular disease, or unexplained vaginal bleeding should not take birth control pills.

bothersome, uncomfortable, or embarrassing enough to interfere on a regular basis with your day-to-day activities, interactions with others, or peace of mind? Do hot flashes or night sweats seem to be disrupting your sleep, your mood, or your ability to remember or concentrate? Has vaginal dryness curtailed your enjoyment of sex and created friction—outside the bedroom—with your partner? If you

Figure 7.1 Hormone Therapy (HT) Decision-Making Flowchart[a]

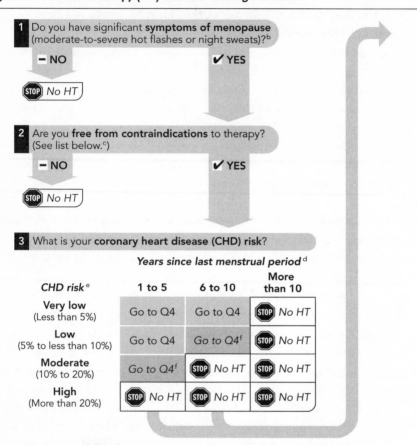

a. Reassess each step at least once every 6 to 12 months (assuming ongoing personal preference for HT).

b. Women who have vaginal dryness without moderate-to-severe hot flashes or night sweats may be candidates for vaginal estrogen; see Chapter 7 text.

c. Major contraindications include unexplained vaginal bleeding; current liver disease; history of venous thromboembolism due to pregnancy, birth control pills, or unknown cause; blood clotting disorder; history of breast or endometrial cancer; and history of coronary heart disease, stroke, transient ischemic attack, or diabetes. For other contraindications, including high triglycerides (400 mg/dL or more); current gallbladder disease; and history of venous thromboembolism due to past immobility, surgery, or bone fracture, oral HT should be avoided but transdermal HT may be an option (see 'f' below).

d. Women more than 10 years past menopause are not good candidates for starting (first use of) HT.

e. Ten-year risk of heart disease, based on modified Framingham Coronary Heart Disease Risk Score (see Chapter 6).

f. Avoid oral HT. Transdermal HT may be an option because it has a less adverse effect on clotting factors, triglyceride levels, and inflammation factors than oral HT.

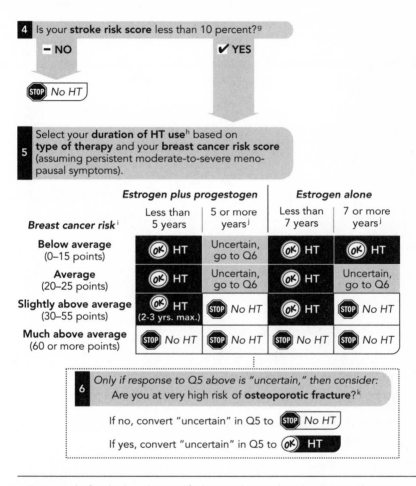

4 Is your **stroke risk score** less than 10 percent?[g]

– NO   **✔ YES**

(STOP) *No HT*

5 Select your **duration of HT use**[h] based on **type of therapy** and your **breast cancer risk score** (assuming persistent moderate-to-severe menopausal symptoms).

	Estrogen plus progestogen		Estrogen alone	
Breast cancer risk[i]	Less than 5 years	5 or more years[j]	Less than 7 years	7 or more years[j]
Below average (0–15 points)	(OK) HT	Uncertain, go to Q6	(OK) HT	(OK) HT
Average (20–25 points)	(OK) HT	Uncertain, go to Q6	(OK) HT	Uncertain, go to Q6
Slightly above average (30–55 points)	(OK) HT (2-3 yrs. max.)	(STOP) No HT	(OK) HT	(STOP) No HT
Much above average (60 or more points)	(STOP) No HT	(STOP) No HT	(STOP) No HT	(STOP) No HT

6 *Only if response to Q5 above is "uncertain," then consider:* Are you at very high risk of **osteoporotic fracture**?[k]

If no, convert "uncertain" in Q5 to (STOP) *No HT*

If yes, convert "uncertain" in Q5 to (OK) **HT**

g. Ten-year risk of stroke, based on modified Framingham Stroke Risk Score (see Chapter 6).

h. HT should be continued only if moderate-to-severe menopausal symptoms persist. The recommended cutpoints for duration are based on results of the Women's Health Initiative estrogen-plus-progestin and estrogen-alone trials, which lasted 5.6 and 7.1 years, respectively. For longer durations, the balance of benefits and risks is not known.

i. See risk assessment tool in Chapter 6. Risk factors scored as multiples of 5.

j. Try to reduce HT doses. If progestogen is taken daily, avoid extending duration. If progestogen is cyclical or infrequent, avoid extending duration more than 1–2 years. For estrogen alone, avoid extending duration more than 2–3 years.

k. See risk assessment tool in Chapter 6. Very high risk = risk score of 8 or more if hip T-score is known; or 5 or more if hip T-score is unknown. For duration guidelines , see 'j' above.

answered no to these questions, then there is no compelling reason for you to take menopause hormones. If you answered yes to at least one of these questions—and have already tried the lifestyle changes (or other nonhormonal strategies) discussed in Chapter 2—you may be a suitable candidate for hormone therapy, provided that your health profile is satisfactory.

Here is a chart that will help you gauge your symptoms:

Evaluating Your Menopausal Symptoms

How much does it bother you?

	Not at all	A little bit	Quite a bit	Extremely
1. Hot flashes/sudden flushes of warmth	_____	_____	_____	_____
2. Night or day sweats/cold sweats	_____	_____	_____	_____
3. Dry vagina/painful intercourse	_____	_____	_____	_____
4. Trouble getting to sleep or staying asleep/daytime exhaustion or fatigue	_____	_____	_____	_____
5. Mood swings/irritable, anxious, or depressed feelings	_____	_____	_____	_____
6. Memory and concentration problems/ "scattered thinking"	_____	_____	_____	_____

If you answered "quite a bit" or "extremely" on items 1 or 2, especially if you also answered in this way on at least one of items 3, 4, 5, or 6, then you may be a candidate for systemic (oral or transdermal) hormone therapy, if your health profile is acceptable. You'll need to continue to Question 2 to evaluate your health status.

If you answered "quite a bit" or "extremely" on item 3 but not on items 1 or 2, then you are a candidate for vaginal estrogen provided that you have no personal history of breast or endometrial cancer.

If you did not answer the symptom questionnaire as described in the preceding two paragraphs, then your menopausal symptoms are probably not severe enough to justify the use of hormone therapy. Nevertheless, if you are on the fence, you should continue to Question 2 to evaluate your health status.

QUESTION 2: GIVEN MY PERSONAL HEALTH HISTORY, WILL SYSTEMIC HORMONE THERAPY LEAD TO A FAVORABLE—OR AT LEAST NEUTRAL— BALANCE OF BENEFITS AND RISKS?

In the last chapter, I showed you how to figure out your risk of developing five major diseases that have been most closely linked to systemic hormone therapy: coronary heart disease (CHD), stroke, VTE, breast cancer, and osteoporotic fracture. We will now use that information to weigh the benefits and risks of systemic hormone therapy in light of your personal health profile.

I'll state right off the bat that systemic hormone therapy—oral and transdermal estrogen—is simply too risky to take if you have any of the following conditions ("contraindications"): vaginal bleeding of unknown origin, current liver disease (hormone therapy can cause dangerous elevations in certain liver enzymes), a history of breast cancer or endometrial cancer, a history of CHD (i.e., heart attack, angina, coronary bypass surgery, or angioplasty), a history of stroke or transient ischemic attack, or diabetes. In addition, most women who have had a VTE (blood clots in the veins of the legs, or the lungs) should steer clear of hormone therapy, but there's a bit of a gray zone here. I discuss the factors that you need to consider in the next section.

Oral hormone therapy should also not be taken if you have a high triglyceride level (400 mg/dL or more) or current gallbladder disease. Oral estrogen may push triglyceride levels higher, which can lead to a very serious condition called pancreatitis, or inflammation of the pancreas. And oral estrogen raises the amount of cholesterol contained in bile, which promotes the growth of gallstones (see Chapter 4). However, transdermal therapy (or Femring) may be an option, as it is thought to be less likely to cause these problems. If the rest of your health profile checks out in a satisfactory manner, you can discuss the possibility of transdermal estrogen with your doctor.

If you have one or more of the contraindications to hormone therapy, or if you simply prefer not to take hormones, you can try a selective serotonin reuptake inhibitor (SRRI, such as Effexor, Paxil, or Prozac), gabapentin (Neurontin), clonidine (Catapres), black cohosh, or soy to relieve your hot flashes and night sweats, and you can use vaginal estrogen to treat vaginal dryness. And this advice holds as you work your way through the hormone-therapy decision-making process. If at any point you determine that you are not a good candidate for hormone therapy, you can try one or more of these strategies to relieve your menopausal symptoms. If you have a history of breast or endometrial cancer, check with your doctor before upping your soy consumption, taking black cohosh, or using vaginal estrogen.

How to Use Venous Thromboembolism Risk Considerations to Guide Your Hormone-Therapy Decision

Hormone therapy increases the risk of blood clots in the deep veins and lungs. A woman with a history of venous blood clots requiring treatment with blood-thinning medications should generally avoid menopausal hormone therapy. However, the strength of this recommendation depends to some extent on the reason for her prior blood clots.

If you developed a blood clot while taking birth control pills, while pregnant, or while taking menopausal hormone therapy in the past, you are susceptible to forming clots in reaction to estrogen and/or progesterone. You should definitely steer clear of hormone therapy. Ditto if your doctor could not pinpoint the reason for your clot.

If you developed a blood clot as a result of prolonged immobilization or in reaction to a bodily trauma, such as surgery or bone fracture, you are not an ideal candidate for menopause hormones. That said, you could still consider taking hormone therapy if your menopausal symptoms are absolutely intolerable, but you should be aware that your risk of developing a clot in reaction to such therapy is not negligible. Oral hormones should be avoided, but transdermal hormones might be an option to discuss with your doctor because patches are less likely to boost your body's production of substances that promote blood clotting. And if you again become immobile for any length of time, have surgery, or experience another bodily trauma, you must stop hormone therapy until at least three months after regaining your mobility or making a complete recovery. Actually, this precaution is a good idea for *all* women who are currently on hormone therapy, but it is essential for those women with a personal history of blood clots.

If you have a family history of blood clots, especially if two or more close relatives have had them, then you may have an inherited clotting disorder. If genetic or other blood tests show that you have such a disorder, then you should definitely not take any type of systemic hormone therapy. (Genetic tests include those for factor V Leiden and prothrombin 20210 mutations; blood tests include those for protein C and protein S deficiencies, and for lupus.) However, most women with a family history of blood clots have not had tests to look for inherited disorders. In the absence of this information, I would strongly advise that you err on the side of caution and avoid hormone therapy if at all possible. But, if you do try hormone therapy, you should opt for transdermal rather than oral estrogen in order to minimize clotting risk.

If you have had a blood clot, even as a result of immobility or trauma, *and* you also have a family history of blood clots, you must avoid both oral and transdermal hormone therapy.

If you don't have any of the contraindications to hormone therapy, you can move to the next arrow on the flowchart shown in Figure 7.1, which shows you how to use your heart disease risk score to help make the decision about hormone therapy.

How to Use Coronary Heart Disease Risk Calculations to Guide Your Hormone-Therapy Decision

Accumulating data strongly suggest hormone therapy started soon after menopause, when arteries may still be healthy, has no adverse effect on CHD risk, while hormone therapy started many years after menopause, when arteries have advanced atherosclerosis, may increase risk. Heart attacks, if they are going to be precipitated by hormone therapy, tend to surface relatively quickly—often within the first year after a woman starts treatment. These findings give rise to the following guidelines:

• If your last menstrual period occurred 5 or fewer years ago and your arteries are relatively healthy, as indicated by a CHD risk score of less than 10 percent (low or very low risk), then starting or continuing oral or transdermal hormone therapy during this interval is not likely to increase your heart disease risk by any appreciable amount. (Indeed, as discussed in Chapter 4, it's possible that early initiation of hormone therapy may actually reduce your heart disease risk.) If your last menstrual period occurred 5 or fewer years ago and your CHD risk score is between 10 and 20 percent (moderate risk), you are not a candidate to start or continue oral therapy but you may still be a candidate for transdermal therapy. Transdermal estrogens may be preferable for those at moderate rather than low CHD risk because they avoid the undesirable first-pass liver effects (e.g., increased levels of triglyceride, blood clotting factors, and inflammation factors) of oral estrogens.

• If your last menstrual period occurred 6 to 10 years ago and your arteries are very healthy, as indicated by a CHD risk score of less than 5 percent (very low risk), then starting or continuing oral or transdermal hormone therapy during this interval is not likely to increase your heart disease risk by any appreciable amount. If your last menstrual period occurred 6 to 10 years ago and your CHD risk score is between 5 and 10 percent (low risk), you should not start oral hormone therapy but may be a candidate to start transdermal therapy, for the reasons mentioned in the previous bullet.

• If your last menstrual period occurred more than 10 years ago, you should not start hormone therapy for the first time, regardless of your CHD risk score. However, if you are more than 10 years past menopause and are currently taking hormone therapy or have taken it in the very recent past, you could consider remaining on—or resuming—such therapy if you require relief from moderate-to-severe menopausal symptoms that recur off treatment, provided that your CHD risk score is less than 5 percent (very low risk).

• If you have a personal history of or are at high risk of CHD, you should not take hormone therapy. If you suffer a heart attack or develop angina while taking hormone therapy, you should stop the hormones immediately.

Given what we know about the prevalence of heart disease risk factors in this country, more than 85 percent of women in the United States who are in their early 50s and past menopause will have a CHD risk score of less than 10 percent and will thus be eligible for hormone therapy provided that they have moderate-to-severe menopausal symptoms. Of course, CHD risk information needs to be considered alongside your risk of other diseases. If the guidelines suggest that you are an acceptable candidate on the basis of your CHD risk score and the number of years since your last menstrual period, move to the next arrow on the flowchart and continue to the next section.

How to Use Stroke Risk Calculations to Guide Your Hormone-Therapy Decision

Hormone therapy increases the risk of stroke. If your stroke risk score is less than 10 percent (low or very low risk), you may be a suitable candidate for hormone therapy. If your stroke risk score is 10 percent or more, you should avoid hormone therapy, regardless of how many years it's been since your last menstrual period. If you suffer a stroke while on hormone therapy, you should stop the hormones immediately.

Of course, factors other than risk of cardiovascular disease enter into the decision-making process, especially when deciding on how long to stay on hormone therapy. Keep on reading.

How to Use Breast Cancer Risk Calculations to Guide Your Hormone-Therapy Decision

Menopausal hormone therapy raises the risk of developing breast cancer, but the increase in risk is largely limited to women who take estrogen plus progestogen for at least five years or estrogen alone for more than seven years. Therefore, for most women, breast cancer concerns—unlike cardiovascular concerns—should not be high on the list of things to consider when deciding whether to take hormones for short-term relief of menopausal symptoms. The majority of women with an average or below-average risk of breast cancer (risk score of 25 points or less) can safely take estrogen plus progestogen for up to five years. Those with a slightly above average risk of breast cancer (risk score of 30 to 55 points) can safely take these hormones for two to three years, assuming that even a borderline increase in risk does not begin to emerge until four years of therapy, as was the case in the WHI trial. The majority of women with hysterectomy and a breast cancer risk score of 55 points or below can safely take estrogen alone for up to seven years. (The WHI estrogen-plus-progestin and estrogen-alone trials were stopped after 5.6 and 7.1 years, respectively, so there are no data from high-quality large-scale clinical trials on hormone therapy and breast cancer risk beyond those durations. Nevertheless, recent findings from the Nurses' Health Study suggest that estrogen alone can be taken for least 10 years without appreciably increasing breast cancer risk in women with hysterectomy.)

Breast cancer becomes more of a concern the longer a woman stays on hormone therapy. Because estrogen plus progestogen has been more strongly implicated than estrogen alone in long-term breast cancer risk, let's consider the two hormone preparations separately.

Estrogen plus Progestogen

• If your breast cancer risk is average or below average (risk score of 25 points or less) and you suffer from *intolerable* symptoms when you try to get off hormones after having taken them for five years, you could consider extending your estrogen-plus-progestogen use for another one to three years maximum—but only if your cardiovascular risk profile is still low enough (you'll need to revisit the heart disease and stroke guidelines outlined previously) *and* your osteoporosis risk is high enough (see the next section) to ensure that the overall risk-benefit balance of hormone use remains in your favor. At the very least, you should lower your dose and make a concerted effort to taper off the hormones at least once every 6 to 12 months.

• If your breast cancer risk score is slightly above average (risk score of 30 to 55 points), you should not even think about remaining on estrogen plus progestogen for more than three years.

Estrogen Alone

• If your breast cancer risk is below average (risk score of 15 points or less) and you have severe symptoms when you try to get off the hormone after having taken it for 7 years, you could consider remaining on estrogen for up to 10 years, provided that your cardiovascular risk profile is still acceptable. (Women who have had an early surgical menopause—removal of both ovaries prior to age 45—may be candidates for even longer-term use of estrogen alone. I return to this point shortly.)

• If your breast cancer risk is average (risk score of 20 to 25 points) and you have severe symptoms when you try to get off the hormone after having taken it for seven years, you could consider extending your estrogen use for another one to three years—but only if your cardiovascular risk is still low enough *and* your osteoporosis risk is high enough (see the next section) to ensure that the overall risk-benefit balance of hormone use remains acceptable. You should lower your dose and try to taper off the hormone at least once every 6 to 12 months.

- If your breast cancer risk score is slightly above average (risk score of 30 to 55 points), you should not take estrogen alone for more than seven years.

If you have had breast cancer, are known to carry a breast cancer susceptibility gene, or have a much-above-average risk of breast cancer (risk score of 60 points or more), I don't recommend that you take systemic hormone therapy for any length of time.

How to Use Osteoporotic Fracture Risk Calculations to Guide Your Hormone-Therapy Decision

Menopausal hormone therapy effectively slows aging-related bone loss and reduces the occurrence of osteoporotic fractures, but these bone benefits last only as long as you take the hormones. To get maximal protection, you'd have to take hormone therapy a very, very long time, because the average age at which women sustain hip fractures is close to 80—nearly three decades past menopause! Therefore, for most women, osteoporosis risk considerations are not all that important when deciding whether to take hormones for short-term relief of menopausal symptoms. And, as we've seen, long-term use is not advisable for most women, because of the increased breast cancer risk. However, when a woman at very low risk of breast cancer is contemplating extending her hormone use to keep persistent menopausal symptoms at bay, then osteoporosis considerations become more relevant. If a woman is at very high risk of osteoporotic hip fracture (risk score of 5 or more, if hip T-score is not known, or risk score of 8 or more, if hip T-score is known), the bone protection afforded by long-term estrogen use might just tip the argument in favor of her staying on hormone therapy. If she does, low-dose estrogen should be used.

Keep in mind that estrogen therapy is approved by the FDA for preventing osteoporosis but not for treating the condition once you already have it. If you have had a bone density scan that shows that you have osteoporosis, or if you have already suffered an osteoporotic fracture, then hormone therapy should not be the drug of choice for your bones; instead, you should consider a bisphosphonate or other alternative as described in Chapter 6.

Bottom Line

If you are younger, recently menopausal, without an overly high risk of adverse outcomes, and you have moderate-to-severe hot flashes or night sweats, the balance of benefits and risks of hormone therapy is sharply tilted in your favor. The benefits are likely to outweigh the risks if you choose to take menopause hormones to treat your symptoms in a prudent fashion—i.e., use the lowest effective dose for the shortest time necessary. On the other hand, if you are older, many years past menopause, at high risk of adverse outcomes, and don't have symptoms severe enough to disrupt your daily life, then you should shy away from hormone therapy; the potential risks outweigh the potential benefits.

Later I'll present several case studies to show you how these guidelines might work in the real world.

SPECIAL CONSIDERATIONS FOR WOMEN WITH EARLY MENOPAUSE

The guidelines for hormone-therapy decision making need to be slightly modified for women with early menopause.

Early Surgical Menopause

Premenopausal or perimenopausal women who have a hysterectomy to treat uncontrollable uterine bleeding, fibroids, or other noncancerous conditions sometimes elect to have both of their ovaries removed (bilateral oophorectomy) along with their uterus. Nine in ten women who have surgical menopause will experience severe hot flashes and night sweats as a result of the precipitous drop in estrogen that occurs upon removal of their ovaries, so many of them will be eligible for—and opt for—hormone therapy.

However, if you were younger than age 45 at the time of your bilateral oophorectomy, the requirement that you have bothersome hot flashes (although you most likely will) before being eligible for estrogen, and the upper desirable limit of seven years on the duration of estrogen use specified earlier, may not apply to you. Why do I say this? Few existing clinical trials have examined the benefits and risks of hormone therapy specifically among women with a surgically induced menopause at an early age. The participants in the WHI were all aged 50 and older, for example. But there is evidence from observational studies to suggest that there may be an increased risk of osteoporosis and possibly CHD that results directly from the dramatic loss of your body's own estrogen at a relatively early age. (As discussed in Chapter 1, although their hormonal output wanes in a natural menopause, the ovaries actually continue to produce some estrogen throughout a woman's life.) These increased risks are enough of a concern that I think it is quite reasonable to consider taking estrogen therapy until you reach the average age of menopause (age 51 in the United States), regardless of whether you are having hot flashes or how long you've already been on such therapy, provided you do so in close consultation with your healthcare provider. Indeed, many doctors will automatically start women on estrogen therapy immediately after an early oophorectomy to prevent the onset of severe menopausal symptoms and to preserve their bone and heart health.

Once you reach age 51, however, there is a much bigger chance that, if left to their own devices, your ovaries would have soon started ratcheting down their production of estrogen. That is, your menopause would be fast approaching, if it were not already here. Thus, the oophorectomy aside, you are very likely to experience the same balance of benefits and risks from hormone therapy as other menopausal women with your overall health profile. Therefore, within a few months or so after your 51st birthday, you should try to taper off estrogen therapy, mimicking a natural menopause (see the section "What's the Best Way to Stop?" for how to taper). If you don't start flashing intolerably, you should not take estrogen any longer. On the other hand, if you do start flashing, you could consider resuming the estrogen. Use all of the previously discussed guidelines to help you make that decision. When considering breast cancer risk, you can disregard the years of estrogen use before your 51st birthday, and start the clock at that point.

If you were aged 45 to 50 when you had your oophorectomy, you can use the flowchart and guidelines outlined earlier in this chapter to help you make the decision about whether to start estrogen therapy and how long to stay on it—but with one caveat: you may wish to move osteoporosis risk considerations somewhat higher on the priority list. If you have any of the major risk factors for osteoporosis (e.g., body weight less than 125 pounds, history of osteoporotic bone fracture in a first-degree relative, current smoker, lifelong low calcium intake), you should discuss with your doctor whether your risk of osteoporosis is high enough to warrant the use of estrogen therapy until age 51, even if you are not having intolerable hot flashes.

If you were aged 51 or older when you had your oophorectomy, you can—and should—use the flowchart and guidelines outlined in this chapter to help you make the decision about whether to start estrogen therapy and how long to stay on it. There's no need to make any modifications to the guidelines.

The story is different for women with oophorectomy performed to prevent (or treat) ovarian, uterine, or breast cancer. Women at high risk of breast cancer sometimes opt for a mastectomy (surgical removal of the breasts) to reduce their risk of the disease, and they sometimes have an "insurance" oophorectomy to minimize their exposure to ovarian estrogens, which could overstimulate any remaining breast tissue. If your ovaries have been removed for one of these reasons, you are not a good candidate for estrogen therapy, regardless of how old you were when the oophorectomy was performed—your risk of cancer is too high. However, if estrogen is of interest to you, these issues should be discussed with your own doctor.

Premature Natural Menopause

As is the case with early surgical menopause, few clinical trials have been conducted to assess the benefits and risks of hormone therapy in women with a premature natural menopause—that is, menopause before age 40. However, data from observational studies suggest that women with a premature natural menopause are at increased risk of developing osteoporosis and possibly CHD compared with other women, presumably because they spend so many more years without the protective effect of high, premenopausal levels of estrogen. Therefore, if you've had a natural menopause before age 40, it's reasonable to consider taking low-dose estrogen to age 45 or so to prevent bone loss and possibly preserve heart health, even if you aren't having hot flashes or other menopausal symptoms. Because you still have your uterus, you'll need to take a low-dose progestogen along with the estrogen to protect against endometrial cancer.

But, you may be wondering, isn't taking estrogen plus a progestogen for more than five years a very bad idea because of the unacceptable increase in breast cancer risk? For the vast majority of women, yes. But for the tiny fraction of women with a premature menopause, we simply don't know. Recall that breast cancer risk rises with the number of years between the onset and end of menstruation. It's possible that, among women in their mid- to late 40s and older, long-term use of estrogen plus progestogen increases the risk of breast cancer because it extends the number of years their bodies are exposed to high levels of these hormones beyond some threshold—that is, some particular duration of time. On the other hand, women who are very young when they go through natural menopause may have several more years in which they can safely take estrogen plus progestogen before they hit that threshold. But this is only a theory; more research is needed to clarify the issue.

Early Chemical- or Radiation-Induced Menopause

Chemotherapy or radiation therapy for cancer can cause a woman's periods to stop either temporarily or permanently. The older a woman is at the time of treatment, the greater the chance that menstruation will come to a permanent end. For example, a 45-year-old woman is about four times more likely to enter menopause following chemotherapy than is her 35-year-old counterpart. Chemical- and radiation-induced menopause—sometimes termed "medical menopause"—is poorly understood; it's unclear whether the ovaries lose the ability to manufacture any hormones at all or whether they are simply pushed ahead of schedule into producing the lower hormone levels typical of women who have experienced a natural menopause. We do know that, with medical menopause, the severity of hot flashes and other symptoms tends to fall somewhere between that associated with surgical menopause and that associated with natural menopause. It's reasonable to speculate that women with medical menopause have risks of osteoporosis and heart disease that lie between those of women with surgical menopause and those of women with natural menopause.

Assuming that she has not had breast, uterine, or ovarian cancer, can a woman with an early medical menopause (prior to age 45) take hormone therapy to protect her bones and heart? To a large extent, it depends on the type of cancer she has had. Other cancers besides gynecologic ones may be sensitive to estrogen, so it may not be a good idea to risk stimulating the growth of any stray cancer cells that may still be present. If you've had an early medical menopause—especially if you're also having menopausal symptoms—you should discuss with your oncologist or primary care doctor whether menopause hormones remain a viable option for you. With your oncologist's permission, I think it's reasonable to consider taking low-dose estrogen (plus progestogen, to protect your uterus) until at least age 45 if you do not have a history of a hormonally sensitive tumor.

STOPPING HORMONE THERAPY

As you have learned, hormone therapy should not be taken for an indefinite period of time.

How Do I Know When to Stop?

Hot flashes and night sweats improve or go away on their own within a few months to a few years of their onset in all but about 10 percent of women. Therefore, after you've been on hormone therapy for one to two years, you'll need to try stopping your hormone therapy on a periodic basis, perhaps every 6 to 12 months, to determine in a timely fashion whether your symptoms have improved to the point that you no longer need treatment.

Most women have no difficulty stopping hormone therapy. Observational studies find that 40 to 50 percent of women who start menopause hormones quit within one year, and 65 to 75 percent quit within two years, usually without the help of a healthcare provider.

Still, a substantial minority have trouble discontinuing their therapy because of the reemergence of symptoms. Hot flashes and night sweats that crop up after stopping hormone therapy are more common among women who started hormone therapy for treatment of such symptoms to begin with, but they are also occasionally reported by women who started therapy for other reasons, such as prevention of osteoporosis or CHD.

In women whose symptoms reemerge (or emerge for the first time) after stopping hormone therapy, there is no way to know ahead of time whether these symptoms will persist for a prolonged period of time or clear up within an acceptably short interval. Given this, you and your doctor will need to decide whether to restart hormone therapy or to try to tolerate symptoms until they improve or resolve. To make this decision in a sensible way, you should revisit the guidelines, which will help you systematically weigh all the pros and cons in light of how long it's been since your last menstrual period and how long you've taken hormones already.

What's the Best Way to Stop?

Should you stop hormones cold turkey or should you taper off gradually over several months? It's not clear which is the better approach. In one survey of women who had been taking hormone therapy for at least one year and tried to stop their hormones after hearing about the results of the WHI estrogen-plus-progestin trial, those who tapered off were slightly more successful in quitting than those who stopped abruptly, but the difference was not statistically significant.

At least 50 percent of women do not have severe symptoms when they stop their hormones abruptly, so you could try stopping cold turkey. If you have severe symptoms, you can restart your therapy and begin a slow taper over a three- to six-month period.

Tapering can be accomplished either by decreasing the daily dose of hormone therapy (dose taper), by decreasing the number of days per week that hormones are used (day taper), or some combination of the two. In a dose taper, you reduce your daily dose of hormone therapy in a stepwise fashion. For example, instead of your usual 0.625-milligram Premarin pill, drop to the 0.45-milligram pill for six to eight weeks, then to the 0.3-milligram pill for another six to eight weeks, and then stop the pills altogether. If you are using a matrix patch, which are designed to be worn from three days to one week (depending on the brand), you can trim away a portion of each patch with a scissors before applying it to get a smaller daily dose of hormones.

In a day taper, you gradually decrease the number of days per week that you take your usual dose of hormone therapy. For example, you continue to take your usual 0.625-milligram Premarin pill, but you skip the Saturday pill for two weeks or so. After that, you skip the Thursday as well as the Saturday pill for another two weeks; then you skip Tuesday, Thursday, and Saturday; and so forth, until you are completely off the pills. If you are using the patch, you apply it less often—instead of once every three days, you up the interval to once every six days, for example.

If you're using a pill, it might be easier to do a day rather than a dose taper, since it allows a smaller incremental reduction in weekly dose and doesn't require multiple new prescriptions. If you're wearing a patch, you might prefer to do a dose taper, because you can cut the patch with a scissors to reduce the dose in as small an increment as you like.

While tapering off estrogen, women also using a progestogen must make sure that they continue to take that hormone (albeit in lower doses) to offset the stimulatory effect of estrogen on the endometrium.

If you're having trouble tapering off hormone therapy, you could consider adding an SSRI antidepressant (Effexor, Paxil, or Prozac) for additional hot flash control while you taper; however, the effectiveness of this approach has not been evaluated in clinical trials.

Try not to taper in the summertime, if at all possible; because high temperatures can trigger hot flashes, it may be harder to tell if the heat wave you're feeling originated from within your body or from the outside.

Question 3: Am I at Ease with My Hormone-Therapy Decision?

As I said earlier, menopause is not an "estrogen-deficiency disease" requiring the intervention of medical science to achieve some optimal hormonal balance. If you don't want to take estrogen—or remain wary of it, even if you are an acceptable candidate by the objective medical criteria that I've outlined in this chapter—then, in my view, there is no compelling reason for you to do so, and no one should try to convince you otherwise. For example, if your hot flashes and night sweats would be replaced by constant panic attacks about the possibility of a slight increase in your risk of breast cancer, then hormone therapy is clearly not the right choice for you.

Keep in mind that menopause and hormone therapy are not synonymous. For many women, controlling menopausal symptoms and preventing diseases related to aging can best be accomplished by making healthy lifestyle choices, including abstaining from smoking, getting adequate physical activity, maintaining a healthy body weight (or, at the least, preventing further weight gain if you're overweight), eating a nutritious diet, and keeping stress levels in check. And for women with osteoporosis or at high risk of heart disease, there is an expanding array of non-hormonal medications that may offer a better balance of benefits and risks than hormone therapy over the longer term. But because clarifying the pluses and minuses of menopause hormones for women at different stages of the menopausal transition continues to be an area of active research, you (and your doctor) will need to stay tuned for the next—and as-yet-unwritten—chapter in this unfolding saga.

WORKING WITH YOUR HEALTHCARE PROVIDER

Making the initial hormone-therapy decision—and reevaluating the decision on a yearly basis—in an *informed* partnership with your doctor or other healthcare provider is vital. But you should be aware that most doctors tend to approach the issue of hormone therapy with beliefs and biases shaped by their own anecdotal experiences or the prevailing view of such therapy during their medical training. As we all do at one time or another, medical professionals may give undue emphasis to studies that lend support to their preconceived notions while discounting the studies that don't. Your healthcare provider may be predisposed toward or against the use of menopause hormones, so you want to be sure that you have the basic knowledge to discuss the pros and cons of your particular situation vis-à-vis this topic with him or her. I hope that this book has given you that knowledge and the tools to help you prepare for a meaningful discussion with your doctor about the hormone-therapy decision.

In the hustle-and-bustle atmosphere of a busy medical office, it's all too easy to get distracted, to forget to ask important questions, or to run out of time before you bring up all the issues that you want to discuss. Here are a few tips to help ensure a successful visit with your healthcare provider:

- If you have a lot of questions, consider making an appointment just to talk about hormone therapy. Explain the purpose of your visit when scheduling the appointment and again at the beginning of the appointment. For example, you might say, "I'm here because I may be going through menopause, and I want to talk about whether or not I should begin hormone therapy. I have three specific concerns that I'd like to discuss with you."

- Appointments usually fly by, so be efficient and assertive in your use of time. Know that you have the right to question your doctor's advice, diagnoses, and prescriptions. Save social chitchat for the last few minutes of your appointment, if there is time.

- Keep an up-to-date record of your perimenopausal and menopausal symptoms—a menopause journal—and review it before the visit to remind yourself of any items you want to discuss.

- Take the risk-factor questionnaires in this book with you to your appointment, and ask your doctor to help fill in any missing information.

- Prepare a written list of questions ahead of time, and bring the list to your appointment. To make sure you'll cover the most pressing issues, order these questions from most to least important. Some basic questions to ask:
  - Why should I take hormone therapy? Which type of hormone therapy do you recommend? (Remember, unless you've had an early surgical menopause or a premature natural menopause, hormone therapy should be taken *only* for relief of moderate-to-severe menopausal symptoms, not for bone or heart health.)
  - Why am I taking hormone therapy? Should I stop taking hormone therapy? What's the best way to stop?
  - Are there alternative ways to treat menopausal symptoms?
  - What are my risks for heart disease, stroke, deep-vein blood clots, breast cancer, and osteoporotic fracture?
  - What alternatives can help me prevent these illnesses?

- Practice your questions with a family member or friend to help prepare for the talk with your healthcare provider. This may also prove useful for clarifying which issues matter the most to you.

- To keep your anxiety in check, consider inviting a family member or friend to the appointment for support. Be sure this person is aware of your concerns ahead of time. If you don't trust yourself to remember the details of the conversation with your healthcare provider, ask your support person to take notes.

- Last but not least, be sure to let your doctor know of any personal preference you may have regarding hormone therapy. After all is said and done, the final decision is yours to make.

CASE STUDIES

Are these women candidates for menopausal hormone therapy? Here's how the guidelines presented in this book helped seven women make decisions about starting and stopping menopausal hormones.

Cheryl

Cheryl is 52 years old. When she was in her late 40s, her menstrual periods became so erratic that she gave up trying to predict their arrival. By comparison, her sporadic hot flashes were a minor inconvenience. Although her heavy periods occasionally wiped her out, she figured she'd just grin and bear it because she's never been a fan of medicines or medical interventions—"medical meddling," she says. Her patience was in part rewarded when her periods stopped 12 months ago. But around that time, she got the job promotion she'd been gunning for. As luck would have it, that's when her hot flashes and night sweats seemed to kick into high gear; none of the lifestyle changes she's tried—layering her clothes, keeping the air-conditioning cranked up, cutting back on coffee, and so forth—has helped. Cheryl is chronically sleep-deprived because of drenching night sweats that rouse her at least twice per night. Because of this, she feels unable to cope with her increased responsibilities at work and is thinking of resigning her new position. She wants rapid relief from her night sweats so she can handle her demanding job with more equanimity.

Is She a Candidate for Hormone Therapy?

Cheryl refers to the menopausal symptom questionnaire in Chapter 6 and rates her symptoms as adversely affecting her quality of life. So she meets this eligibility criterion for hormone therapy.

   The next step is an assessment of her health profile using the tools in Chapter 6. Cheryl is generally healthy and has no history of blood clots, doesn't smoke, isn't overweight (at 5 feet 4 inches and 140 pounds, her BMI is 24), and exercises regularly (or at least she did until she started her new job). At her last physical exam, her blood pressure was 136/84 mm Hg; her total cholesterol was 204 mg/dL; her HDL cholesterol was 56 mg/dL; and her triglycerides were 120 mg/dL. She has no family history of premature heart disease. Although her blood pressure and cholesterol are higher than ideal, her point totals on the CHD and stroke risk prediction tools are 12 and 4, respectively, indicating that she is at very low risk of cardiovascular disease over the next 10 years. (Because she's no longer exercising, she doesn't get credit for this health-promoting activity—that is, her score on the exercise question is 0, not −2.) Cheryl has no family history of breast cancer and is at average risk for this disease for a woman of her age. She's also at low or average risk of osteoporotic fracture.

Because Cheryl is in generally good health and has entered menopause only recently, the risks of short-term hormone therapy are much lower for her than they would be for an older woman well past menopause. I recommend that she start on a low dose of estrogen plus cyclical progestogen for three months to see if it helps with the night sweats and improves her sleep. Because her triglycerides are in a desirable range, I leave the choice of whether to use a pill or patch up to her. If she doesn't get adequate relief, we'll slowly bump up the dose, going no higher than the standard dose, in the months after that. If she's able to sleep through the night, she'll not only be able to concentrate at work, but she might also be motivated to resume her regular exercise routine, perhaps fitting in a brisk half-hour walk during her lunch break. And, in turn, these things should help lower her stress level.

Given her general aversion to medication, Cheryl's uncertain how long she will stay on the hormones. Looking a little further ahead, I tell Cheryl that we should revisit the hormone-therapy decision every six months or so. The chances are high that she'll be able to stop the hormones after two to three years without too much difficulty, which is when I would encourage most women in her situation to stop, even those who enthusiastically embrace "medical meddling." In any event, Cheryl should not take hormone therapy for more than five years, because the risk of breast cancer associated with combination hormones rises appreciably with long-term use.

Diane

Diane is 54 years old. Her last menstrual period occurred 18 months ago, and she's been experiencing mild-to-moderate hot flashes. She is in excellent health, is at low risk for heart disease and stroke, and wants to do everything she can to stay that way. An avid consumer of medical news, she's read about the latest research suggesting that hormone therapy may have heart benefits for women who are recently menopausal. She's wondering if she should take hormone therapy not only to cool her hot flashes but also to keep her heart healthy.

Is She a Candidate for Hormone Therapy?

When I question her, Diane, an energetic and outgoing real-estate agent, says that she is usually unfazed by her hot flashes, although they occasionally occur at inopportune times. For instance, a few weeks ago she had a somewhat embarrassing episode where, with house-hunting clients in her car, she had to pull over rather abruptly to take off her jacket and get some fresh air. I asked her how frequently this sort of thing happened, and she said "not often, maybe once a month, with a milder hot flash two or three times a week." She takes the symptom survey in Chapter 6 and scores low. Thus, to me, Diane doesn't meet the first of the eligibility criteria for hormone therapy—her menopausal symptoms simply aren't that severe. Even if hormone therapy could lower her risk of heart disease, that alone is not enough reason to take it because, like most medications, hormone therapy also has some risks. To control the occasional flash, I recommend that she use common-sense strategies, such as dressing in layers and avoiding spicy foods, coffee, and alcohol. We discuss that boosting her soy intake or trying black cohosh for a few months might also be helpful, and she finds that her symptoms become barely noticeable!

Evie

Evie is 50 years old. She had her first child at age 42 and during her pregnancy developed gestational diabetes, which, along with her obesity, placed her at elevated risk of type 2 diabetes. Indeed, five years after her daughter was born, she was diagnosed with this condition. The diabetes diagnosis spurred her to modify her diet and begin an exercise program, and she's lost 50 pounds, getting her BMI below 25, which helps her maintain her blood sugar at an acceptable, though not optimal, level without taking diabetes medications. Her cholesterol is elevated and her blood pressure is currently normal.

Evie's last menstrual period was nearly a year ago, and now she's having unbearable hot flashes on a frequent basis, often five or six per day. Because she's so much older than the mothers of her daughter's playmates, she's self-conscious about her age and at how flushed she sometimes becomes at neighborhood social gatherings. In fact, she's started to avoid many social situations because she's so discomfited by her burning face and ears. Lifestyle changes—although she drew the line at toting a hand-held electric fan around ("I'm too embarrassed to use it")—soy, and black cohosh haven't helped. Evie is quite eager to try hormone therapy.

Is She a Candidate for Hormone Therapy?

Unfortunately, hormone therapy is not a good option for her. Even though her diabetes is well controlled, Evie is at high risk of future cardiovascular disease. Diabetes, whether or not it's treated with medications, is considered a "heart-disease risk equivalent," meaning that cardiac risk is approximately as great as for a person with a prior diagnosis of heart disease (see Chapter 6). If she were to take menopause hormones, even for a short time, she would face an unacceptably large increase in her risk of heart attack and stroke. Because lifestyle changes haven't provided relief, I suggest that she try an SSRI antidepressant to cool her hot flashes. Clinical trials show that several work; venlafaxine (Effexor) appears to be the most effective. The medication may have some side effects, including dry mouth, appetite changes, and nausea, but these typically fade within a few weeks. I tell Evie that clinical experience with patients who have taken SSRIs for many years to treat depression suggests that these drugs are reasonably safe for long-term use but that she probably won't need the medication for more than a few years because menopausal symptoms tend to wane over time. In the unlikely event that her symptoms persist for longer than that, she'll be able to continue taking the Effexor.

Fern

Fern is 53 years old. Her last menstrual period was two years ago, and, ever since, she's been suffering from intolerable hot flashes and night sweats that haven't abated with lifestyle changes and various nonhormonal prescription medicines. Because her 74-year-old aunt was diagnosed with breast cancer a decade ago, Fern was initially reluctant to consider hormone therapy, but she's now wondering if menopause hormones are a possibility for her.

Is She a Candidate for Hormone Therapy?

A check of Fern's cardiovascular risk factor profile shows she's at low risk of heart disease and stroke. At 5 feet 6 inches and 165 pounds, Fern is slightly overweight; she's also sedentary, rarely drinks alcohol, doesn't take multivitamins, is not Ashkenazi Jewish, got her first period at age 13, has never given birth to a child, has never taken birth control pills, and hasn't had a breast biopsy because her past mammograms have not suggested any reason for concern. These factors, in combination with her aunt's history of breast cancer, give her a breast cancer risk score of 35 points (see Chapter 6). This places her at slightly elevated risk of breast cancer compared with a typical woman of her age.

Still, I feel comfortable in prescribing a strictly *short-term* course of low-dose estrogen plus cyclic natural progesterone to treat Fern's severe menopausal symptoms. But I warn her that I do not recommend that she stay on hormone therapy for more than three years to avoid raising her breast cancer risk further. I also tell her to remain vigilant about having her yearly mammogram and breast exams performed by her healthcare provider, as well as doing self-exams.

Gabrielle

Gabrielle is 42 years old. She recently had a hysterectomy to treat uncontrollable uterine bleeding, and her ovaries were removed along with her uterus. Shortly after the operation, Gabrielle began having severe hot flashes and night sweats. She's at low risk of heart disease and stroke, at average risk of breast cancer, and, other than the fact that she's small-boned and slender, not at particularly high risk of fracture by the osteoporotic fracture risk calculator (Chapter 6). However, because of her early surgical menopause, she'll spend nearly 10 years more than the average woman without the protective effect of her body's own estrogen, which will appreciably raise her risk of fragile bones by the time she's 60 or so.

Is She a Candidate for Hormone Therapy?

To relieve her hot flashes and protect against osteoporosis, I recommend that Gabrielle take low-dose estrogen. Because she no longer has her uterus, she has no need to take a progestogen to protect the uterine lining. Provided her health profile stays largely the same, she can stay on estrogen without worry until she's age 51, the average age of natural menopause (see Chapter 6 for discussion). At that point, she should taper off the hormone gradually to mimic a natural menopause, which may prevent the recurrence of hot flashes. If moderate-to-severe hot flashes do recur, she will need to decide whether to resume estrogen therapy. If she does resume therapy, Gabrielle can reset the estrogen-therapy clock to zero years to decide how long to remain on the hormone and can use the flowchart to guide decision making. In any event, Gabrielle should also begin an exercise program focused on weight-bearing activity to maintain her bone strength and make sure she has adequate calcium and vitamin D in her diet or through supplements.

Heather

Heather is age 58. She had a natural menopause at age 52 with hot flashes and night sweats severe enough to disrupt her sleep and peace of mind and has been taking estrogen plus progestogen to control these symptoms for five years. She's tried to taper off hormone therapy twice in the last year, but her symptoms always seem to reassert themselves with a terrible vengeance, even after she's been off hormones for several months.

Should She Stay on Hormone Therapy?

Heather scores high on the symptom survey (Chapter 6). She's at very low risk of heart disease and stroke, so from that perspective, it would be reasonable for her to continue her hormone therapy for a while longer. But she's also at slightly above-average risk of breast cancer, as her mother had the disease. Long-term use of estrogen-plus-progestogen therapy significantly boosts breast cancer risk, so it's not advisable for most women—and definitely not for someone with a higher-than-usual risk to begin with. I suggest that Heather taper off the hormones again, but this time I write a prescription for the antidepressant Effexor and tell her to start it a month before starting the hormone taper and to stay on it for at least six months after coming completely off the hormones to give her body sufficient time to adjust to its lower estrogen level. Unfortunately, Heather does not tolerate Effexor—or Paxil, the other SSRI antidepressant I start her on—very well; these drugs make her quite drowsy. So I try her on gabapentin (Neurontin), which cools her hot flashes sufficiently— and without side effects—to allow her to discontinue her hormone therapy.

Isobel

Isobel is age 62. She had a surgical menopause (hysterectomy with oophorectomy) at age 54 and has been taking estrogen alone to control her hot flashes for seven years. She tries to taper but continues to have severe symptoms, even after three months off estrogen. She is at average risk of heart disease and at average risk of breast cancer. Isobel is small-boned, and Isobel's mother sustained a hip fracture when she was age 65.

Should She Stay on Hormone Therapy?

Taking estrogen alone is less likely to increase breast cancer risk than taking estrogen plus progestogen, but estrogen alone may nevertheless increase such risk with longer-term use. Although Isobel's breast cancer risk may rise with longer-term use of estrogen, her osteoporosis risk may drop. She needs to weigh the two factors. In her case, osteoporosis concerns might outweigh the increased breast cancer risk, and she could continue taking estrogen for two to three more years to control her hot flashes if she found her menopausal symptoms to be absolutely intolerable, using as low a dose as possible. On the other hand, there are other proven strategies to prevent osteoporosis, including making sure she gets sufficient weight-bearing exercise, calcium, and vitamin D, and taking a bisphosphonate or other bone-protecting medication if her bone density T-scores are low enough to warrant such use. I encourage Isobel to try to discontinue the estrogen for at least six months but will revisit the decision with her at that time if her hot flashes are severe and impair her quality of life.

REFERENCES

◉

CHAPTER 1

1. Weiss, G., J. H. Skurnick, L. T. Goldsmith, et al. "Menopause and Hypothalamic-Pituitary Sensitivity to Estrogen." *JAMA* 292 (2004): 2991–96.
2. Gold, E. B., J. Bromberger, S. Crawford, et al. "Factors Associated with Age at Natural Menopause in a Multiethnic Sample of Midlife Women." *American Journal of Epidemiology* 153 (2001): 865–74.

CHAPTER 2

1. NIH State-of-the-Science Panel. "National Institutes of Health State-of-the-Science Conference Statement: Management of Menopause-Related Symptoms." *Annals of Internal Medicine* 142 (2005): 1003–13.
2. Gold, E. B., G. Block, S. Crawford, et al. "Lifestyle and Demographic Factors in Relation to Vasomotor Symptoms: Baseline Results from the Study of Women's Health Across the Nation." *American Journal of Epidemiology* 159 (2004): 1189–99.
3. Freedman, R. R. "Pathophysiology and Treatment of Menopausal Hot Flashes." *Seminars in Reproductive Medicine* 23 (2005): 117-25.
4. Krebs, E. E., K. E. Ensrud, R. MacDonald, and T. J. Wilt. "Phytoestrogens for Treatment of Menopausal Symptoms: A Systematic Review." *Obstetrics and Gynecology* 104 (2004): 824–36.
5. Osmers, R., M. Friede, E. Liske, et al. "Efficacy and Safety of Isopropanolic Black Cohosh Extract for Climacteric Symptoms." *Obstetrics and Gynecology* 105 (2005): 1074–83.

6. Frei-Kleiner, S., W. Schaffner, V. W. Rahlfs, et al. "Cimicifuga Racemosa Dried Ethanolic Extract in Menopausal Disorders: A Double-Blind Placebo-Controlled Clinical Trial." *Maturitas* 51 (2005): 397–404.

7. Lee, I-M., N. R. Cook, J. M. Gaziano, et al. "Vitamin E in the Primary Prevention of Cardiovascular Disease and Cancer: The Women's Health Study: A Randomized Controlled Trial." *JAMA* 294 (2005): 56–65.

8. Utian, W. H., D. Shoupe, G. Bachmann, et al. "Relief of Vasomotor Symptoms and Vaginal Atrophy with Lower Doses of Conjugated Equine Estrogens and Medroxyprogesterone Acetate." *Fertility and Sterility* 75 (2001): 1065–79.

9. American College of Obstetricians and Gynecologists Hormone Therapy Task Force. "Vasomotor Symptoms." *Obstetrics and Gynecology* 104 (2004): 106S–117S.

10. Pandya, K. J., J. Roscoe, E. Pajon, et al. "A Preliminary Report of a Double-Blind Placebo Controlled Trial of Gabapentin for Control of Hot Flashes in Women with Breast Cancer: A University of Rochester Cancer Center CCOP study [abstract]." *Proceedings: American Society of Clinical Oncology* 23 (2004): 8015.

11. Pandya, K. J., R. F. Raubertas, P. J. Flynn, et al. "Oral Clonidine in Postmenopausal Patients with Breast Cancer Experiencing Tamoxifen-Induced Hot Flashes: A University of Rochester Cancer Center Community Clinical Oncology Program Study." *Annals of Internal Medicine* 132 (2000): 788–93.

12. Parker, W. H., M. S. Broder, Z. Liu, et al. "Ovarian Conservation at the Time of Hysterectomy for Benign Disease." *Obstetrics and Gynecology* 106 (2005): 219–26.

13. Kravitz, H. M., I. Janssen, N. Santoro, et al. "Relationship of Day-to-Day Reproductive Hormone Levels to Sleep in Midlife Women." *Archives of Internal Medicine* 165 (2005): 2370–76.

14. Kravitz, H. M., P. A. Ganz, J. Bromberger, et al. "Sleep Difficulty in Women at Midlife: A Community Survey of Sleep and the Menopausal Transition." *Menopause* 10 (2003): 19–28.

15. Ayas, N. T., D. P. White, J. E. Manson, et al. "A Prospective Study of Sleep Duration and Coronary Heart Disease in Women." *Archives of Internal Medicine* 163 (2003): 205–9.

16. Hlatky, M. A., D. Boothroyd, E. Vittinghoff, et al. "Quality-of-Life and Depressive Symptoms in Postmenopausal Women After Receiving Hormone Therapy: Results from the Heart and Estrogen/Progestin Replacement Study (HERS) Trial." *JAMA* 287 (2002): 591–97.

17. Hays, J., J. K. Ockene, R. L. Brunner, et al. "Effects of Estrogen Plus Progestin on Health-Related Quality of Life." *New England Journal of Medicine* 348 (2003): 1839–54.

18. Brunner, R. L., M. Gass, A. Aragaki, et al. "Effects of Conjugated Equine Estrogen on Health-Related Quality of Life in Postmenopausal Women with Hysterectomy: Results from the Women's Health Initiative Randomized Clinical Trial." *Archives of Internal Medicine* 165 (2005): 1976–86.

19. Santoro, N., J. Torrens, S. Crawford, et al. "Correlates of Circulating Androgens in Mid-Life Women: The Study of Women's Health Across the Nation." *Journal of Clinical Endocrinology and Metabolism* 90 (2005): 4836–45.

20. Davis, S. R., S. L. Davison, S. Donath, and R. J. Bell. "Circulating Androgen Levels and Self-Reported Sexual Function in Women." *JAMA* 294 (2005): 91–96.

21. Sternfeld, B., H. Wang, C. P. Quesenberry, Jr., et al. "Physical Activity and Changes in Weight and Waist Circumference in Midlife Women: Findings from the Study of Women's Health Across the Nation." *American Journal of Epidemiology* 160 (2004): 912–22.

22. Kuller, L. H., L. R. Simkin-Silverman, R. R. Wing, et al. "Women's Healthy Lifestyle Project: A Randomized Clinical Trial: Results at 54 Months." *Circulation* 103 (2001): 32–37.

23. Norman, R. J., I. H. Flight, and M. C. Rees. "Oestrogen and Progestogen Hormone Replacement Therapy for Peri-Menopausal and Post-Menopausal Women: Weight and Body Fat Distribution." Cochrane Database Systemic Reviews 2000: CD001018.

24. Espeland, M. A., M. L. Stefanick, D. Kritz-Silverstein, et al. "Effect of Postmenopausal Hormone Therapy on Body Weight and Waist and Hip Girths." *Journal of Clinical Endocrinology and Metabolism* 82 (1997): 1549–56.

25. Manson, J. E., J. Hsia, K. C. Johnson, et al. "Estrogen Plus Progestin and the Risk of Coronary Heart Disease." *New England Journal of Medicine* 349 (2003): 523–34.

26. Hsia, J., R. D. Langer, J. E. Manson, et al. "Conjugated Equine Estrogens and the Risk of Coronary Heart Disease: The Women's Health Initiative." *Archives of Internal Medicine* 166 (2006): 357–65.

27. Brown, J. S., E. Vittinghoff, A. M. Kanaya, et al. "Urinary Tract Infections in Postmenopausal Women: Effect of Hormone Therapy and Risk Factors." *Obstetrics and Gynecology* 98 (2001): 1045–52.

28. Grodstein, F., K. Lifford, N. M. Resnick, and G. C. Curhan. "Postmenopausal Hormone Therapy and Risk of Developing Urinary Incontinence." *Obstetrics and Gynecology* 103 (2004): 254–60.

29. Hendrix, S. L., B. B. Cochrane, I. E. Nygaard, et al. "Effects of Estrogen with and Without Progestin on Urinary Incontinence." *JAMA* 293 (2005): 935–48.

30. Grady, D., J. S. Brown, E. Vittinghoff, et al. "Postmenopausal Hormones and Incontinence: The Heart and Estrogen/Progestin Replacement Study." *Obstetrics and Gynecology* 97 (2001): 116–20.

31. Steinauer, J. E., L. E. Waetjen, E. Vittinghoff, et al. "Postmenopausal Hormone Therapy: Does It Cause Incontinence?" *Obstetrics and Gynecology* 106 (2005): 940–45.

32. Waetjen, L. E., J. S. Brown, E. Vittinghoff, et al. "The Effect of Ultralow-Dose Transdermal Estradiol on Urinary Incontinence in Postmenopausal Women." *Obstetrics and Gynecology* 106 (2005): 946–52.

33. American College of Obstetricians and Gynecologists Hormone Therapy Task Force. "Skin." *Obstetrics and Gynecology* 104 (2004): 92S–96S.

34. Dunn, L. B., M. Damesyn, A. A. Moore, et al. "Does Estrogen Prevent Skin Aging? Results from the First National Health and Nutrition Examination Survey (NHANES I)." *Archives of Dermatology* 133 (1997): 339–42.

CHAPTER 3

1. Hersh, A. L., M. L. Stefanick, and R. S. Stafford. "National Use of Postmenopausal Hormone Therapy: Annual Trends and Response to Recent Evidence." *JAMA* 291 (2004): 47–53.

2. Grodstein, F., J. E. Manson, G. A. Colditz, et al. "A Prospective, Observational Study of Postmenopausal Hormone Therapy and Primary Prevention of Cardiovascular Disease." *Annals of Internal Medicine* 133 (2000): 933–41.

3. Writing Group for the PEPI Trial. "Effects of Estrogen or Estrogen/Progestin Regimens on Heart Disease Risk Factors in Postmenopausal Women. The Postmenopausal Estrogen/Progestin Interventions (PEPI) Trial." *JAMA* 273 (1995): 199–208.

4. Hulley, S., D. Grady, T. Bush, et al. "Randomized Trial of Estrogen Plus Progestin for Secondary Prevention of Coronary Heart Disease in Postmenopausal

Women. Heart and Estrogen/Progestin Replacement Study (HERS) Research Group." *JAMA* 280 (1998): 605–13.

5. Grady, D., D. Herrington, V Bittner, et al. "Cardiovascular Disease Outcomes During 6.8 Years of Hormone Therapy: Heart and Estrogen/progestin Replacement Study Follow-Up (HERS II)." *JAMA* 288 (2002): 49–57.

6. Writing Group for the Women's Health Initiative Investigators. "Risks and Benefits of Estrogen Plus Progestin in Healthy Postmenopausal Women: Principal Results from the Women's Health Initiative Randomized Controlled Trial." *JAMA* 288 (2002): 321–33.

7. Women's Health Initiative Steering Committee. "Effects of Conjugated Equine Estrogen in Postmenopausal Women with Hysterectomy: The Women's Health Initiative Randomized Controlled Trial." *JAMA* 291 (2004): 1701–12.

Chapter 4

1. Manson, J. E., J. Hsia, K. C. Johnson, et al. "Estrogen Plus Progestin and the Risk of Coronary Heart Disease." *New England Journal of Medicine* 349 (2003): 523–34.

2. Hsia, J., R. D. Langer, J. E. Manson, et al. "Conjugated Equine Estrogens and the Risk of Coronary Heart Disease: The Women's Health Initiative." *Archives of Internal Medicine* 166 (2006): 357–65.

3. Hulley, S., D. Grady, T. Bush, et al. "Randomized Trial of Estrogen Plus Progestin for Secondary Prevention of Coronary Heart Disease in Postmenopausal Women. Heart and Estrogen/Progestin Replacement Study (HERS) Research Group." *JAMA* 280 (1998): 605–13.

4. Grady, D., D. Herrington, V. Bittner, et al. "Cardiovascular Disease Outcomes During 6.8 Years of Hormone Therapy: Heart and Estrogen/Progestin Replacement Study Follow-Up (HERS II)." *JAMA* 288 (2002): 49–57.

5. Rodriguez, C., E. E. Calle, A. V. Patel, et al. "Effect of Body Mass on the Association Between Estrogen Replacement Therapy and Mortality Among Elderly U.S. Women." *American Journal of Epidemiology* 153 (2001): 145–52.

6. Grodstein, F., J. E. Manson, and M. J. Stampfer. "Hormone Therapy and Coronary Heart Disease: The Role of Time Since Menopause and Age at Hormone Initiation." *Journal of Women's Health* 15 (2006): 35–44.

7. Salpeter, S. R., J. M. E. Walsh, E. Greyber, E. E. Salpeter. "Coronary Heart Disease Events Associated with Hormone Therapy in Younger and Older Women: A Meta-Analysis." *Journal of General Internal Medicine* 21 (2006): 363–66.

8. Williams, R. S., D. Christie, and C. Sistrom. "Assessment of the Understanding of the Risks and Benefits of Hormone Replacement Therapy (HRT) in Primary Care Physicians." *American Journal of Obstetrics and Gynecology* 193 (2005): 551–56.

9. Mikkola, T. S., and T. B. Clarkson. "Estrogen Replacement Therapy, Atherosclerosis, and Vascular Function." *Cardiovascular Research* 53 (2002): 605–19.

10. Hodis, H. N., W. J. Mack, R. A. Lobo, et al. "Estrogen in the Prevention of Atherosclerosis. A Randomized, Double-Blind, Placebo-Controlled Trial." *Annals of Internal Medicine* 135 (2001): 939–53.

11. Grodstein, F., J. E. Manson, and M. J. Stampfer. "Postmenopausal Hormone Use and Secondary Prevention of Coronary Events in the Nurses' Health Study: A Prospective, Observational Study." *Annals of Internal Medicine* 135 (2001): 1–8.

12. Nelson, H. D. "Assessing Benefits and Harms of Hormone Replacement Therapy: Clinical Applications." *JAMA* 288 (2002): 882-84.

13. Grodstein, F., J. E. Manson, G. A. Colditz, et al. "A Prospective, Observational Study of Postmenopausal Hormone Therapy and Primary Prevention of Cardiovascular Disease." *Annals of Internal Medicine* 133 (2000): 933–41.

14. Paganini-Hill, A. "Hormone Replacement Therapy and Stroke: Risk, Protection or No Effect?" *Maturitas* 38 (2001): 243–61.

15. Wassertheil-Smoller, S., S. L. Hendrix, M. Limacher, et al. "Effect of Estrogen Plus Progestin on Stroke in Postmenopausal Women: The Women's Health Initiative: A Randomized Trial." *JAMA* 289 (2003): 2673–84.

16. Women's Health Initiative Steering Committee. "Effects of Conjugated Equine Estrogen in Postmenopausal Women with Hysterectomy: The Women's Health Initiative Randomized Controlled Trial." *JAMA* 291 (2004): 1701–12.

17. Viscoli, C. M., L. M. Brass, W. N. Kernan, et al. "A Clinical Trial of Estrogen-Replacement Therapy After Ischemic Stroke." *New England Journal of Medicine* 345 (2001): 1243–49.

18. Miller, J., B. K. Chan, and H. D. Nelson. "Postmenopausal Estrogen Replacement and Risk for Venous Thromboembolism: A Systematic Review and Meta-Analysis for the U.S. Preventive Services Task Force." *Annals of Internal Medicine* 136 (2002): 680–90.

19. Scarabin, P. Y., E. Oger, and G. Plu-Bureau. "Differential Association of Oral and Transdermal Oestrogen-Replacement Therapy with Venous Thromboembolism Risk." *Lancet* 362 (2003): 428–32.

20. Smith, N.L., S. R. Heckbert, R. N. Lemaitre, et al. "Esterified Estrogens and Conjugated Equine Estrogens and the Risk of Venous Thrombosis." *JAMA* 292 (2004): 1581–87.

21. Barrett-Connor, E., L. E. Wehren, E. S. Siris, et al. "Recency and Duration of Postmenopausal Hormone Therapy: Effects on Bone Mineral Density and Fracture Risk in the National Osteoporosis Risk Assessment (NORA) Study." *Menopause* 10 (2003): 412–19.

22. Banks, E., V. Beral, G. Reeves, et al. "Fracture Incidence in Relation to the Pattern of Use of Hormone Therapy in Postmenopausal Women." *JAMA* 291 (2004): 2212–20.

23. Cauley, J. A., J. Robbins, Z. Chen, et al. "Effects of Estrogen Plus Progestin on Risk of Fracture and Bone Mineral Density: The Women's Health Initiative Randomized Trial." *JAMA* 290 (2003): 1729–38.

24. Prestwood, K. M., A. M. Kenny, A. Kleppinger, and M. Kulldorff. "Ultralow-Dose Micronized 17Beta-Estradiol and Bone Density and Bone Metabolism in Older Women: A Randomized Controlled Trial." *JAMA* 290 (2003): 1042–48.

25. Ettinger, B., K. E. Ensrud, R. Wallace, et al. "Effects of Ultralow-Dose Transdermal Estradiol on Bone Mineral Density: A Randomized Clinical Trial." *Obstetrics and Gynecology* 104 (2004): 443–51.

26. Beatson, G. T. "On the Treatment of Inoperable Cases of Carcinoma of the Mamma: Suggestions for a New Method of Treatment with Illustrative Cases." *Lancet* 2 (1896): 104–7.

27. Colditz, G. A., K. A. Atwood, K. Emmons, et al. "Harvard Report on Cancer Prevention Volume 4: Harvard Cancer Risk Index." *Cancer Causes Control* 11 (2000): 477–88.

28. Endogenous Hormones and Breast Cancer Collaborative Group. "Endogenous Sex Hormones and Breast Cancer in Postmenopausal Women: Reanalysis of Nine Prospective Studies." *Journal of the National Cancer Institute* 94 (2002): 606–16.

29. Collaborative Group on Hormonal Factors in Breast Cancer. "Breast Cancer and Hormone Replacement Therapy: Collaborative Reanalysis of Data from 51 Epidemiological Studies of 52,705 Women with Breast Cancer and 108,411 Women Without Breast Cancer." *Lancet* 350 (1997): 1047–59.

30. Porch, J. V., I-M. Lee, N. R. Cook, et al. "Estrogen-Progestin Replacement Therapy and Breast Cancer Risk: The Women's Health Study (United States)." *Cancer Causes Control* 13 (2002): 847–54.

31. Chen, W. Y., J. E. Manson, S. E. Hankinson, et al. "Unopposed Estrogen Therapy and the Risk of Invasive Breast Cancer." *Archives of Internal Medicine* 166 (2006): 1027–32.

32. Million Women Study Collaborators. "Breast Cancer and Hormone-Replacement Therapy in the Million Women Study." *Lancet* 362 (2003): 419–27.

33. Colditz, G. A., S. E. Hankinson, D. J. Hunter, et al. "The Use of Estrogens and Progestins and the Risk of Breast Cancer in Postmenopausal Women." *New England Journal of Medicine* 332 (1995): 1589–93.

34. Greendale, G. A., B. A. Reboussin, A. Sie, et al. "Effects of Estrogen and Estrogen-Progestin on Mammographic Parenchymal Density." *Annals of Internal Medicine* 130 (1999): 262–69.

35. McTiernan, A., C. F. Martin, J. D. Peck, et al. "Estrogen-Plus-Progestin Use and Mammographic Density in Postmenopausal Women: Women's Health Initiative Randomized Trial." *Journal of the National Cancer Institute* 97 (2005): 1366–76.

36. Preston-Martin, S., M. C. Pike, R. K. Ross, et al. "Increased Cell Division as a Cause of Human Cancer." *Cancer Research* 50 (1990): 7415–21.

37. Hulley, S., C. Furberg, E. Barrett-Connor, et al. "Noncardiovascular Disease Outcomes During 6.8 Years of Hormone Therapy: Heart and Estrogen/Progestin Replacement Study Follow-Up (HERS II)." *JAMA* 288 (2002): 58–66.

38. Chlebowski, R. T., S. L. Hendrix, R. D. Langer, et al. "Influence of Estrogen Plus Progestin on Breast Cancer and Mammography in Healthy Postmenopausal Women: The Women's Health Initiative Randomized Trial." *JAMA* 289 (2003): 3243–53.

39. Fournier, A., F. Berrino, E. Riboli, et al. "Breast Cancer Risk in Relation to Different Types of Hormone Replacement Therapy in the E3N-EPIC Cohort." *International Journal of Cancer* 114 (2005): 448–54.

40. Holmberg, L., and H. Anderson. "HABITS (Hormonal Replacement Therapy After Breast Cancer—Is It Safe?), a Randomised Comparison: Trial Stopped." *Lancet* 363 (2004): 453–55.

41. Grady, D., T. Gebretsadik, K. Kerlikowske, et al. "Hormone Replacement Therapy and Endometrial Cancer Risk: A Meta-Analysis." *Obstetrics and Gynecology* 85 (1995): 304–13.

42. Writing Group for the PEPI Trial. "Effects of Estrogen or Estrogen/Progestin Regimens on Heart Disease Risk Factors in Postmenopausal Women. The Postmenopausal Estrogen/Progestin Interventions (PEPI) Trial." *JAMA* 273 (1995): 199–208.

43. Writing Group for the Women's Health Initiative Investigators. "Risks and Benefits of Estrogen Plus Progestin in Healthy Postmenopausal Women: Principal Results from the Women's Health Initiative Randomized Controlled Trial." *JAMA* 288 (2002): 321–33.

44. Anderson, G. L., H. L. Judd, A. M. Kaunitz, et al. "Effects of Estrogen Plus Progestin on Gynecologic Cancers and Associated Diagnostic Procedures: The Women's Health Initiative Randomized Trial." *JAMA* 290 (2003): 1739–48.

45. Pickar, J. H., I. T. Yeh, J. E. Wheeler, et al. "Endometrial Effects of Lower Doses of Conjugated Equine Estrogens and Medroxyprogesterone Acetate: Two-Year Substudy Results." *Fertility and Sterility* 80 (2003): 1234–40.

46. Johnson, S. R., B. Ettinger, J. L. Macer, et al. "Uterine and Vaginal Effects of Unopposed Ultralow-Dose Transdermal Estradiol." *Obstetrics and Gynecology* 105 (2005): 779–87.

47. Grodstein, F., M. E. Martinez, E. A. Platz, et al. "Postmenopausal Hormone Use and Risk for Colorectal Cancer and Adenoma." *Annals of Internal Medicine* 128 (1998): 705–12.

48. Chlebowski, R. T., J. Wactawski-Wende, C. Ritenbaugh, et al. "Estrogen Plus Progestin and Colorectal Cancer in Postmenopausal Women." *New England Journal of Medicine* 350 (2004): 991–1004.

49. Lacey, J. V., Jr., P. J. Mink, J. H. Lubin, et al. "Menopausal Hormone Replacement Therapy and Risk of Ovarian Cancer." *JAMA* 288 (2002): 334–41.

50. Rodriguez, C., A. V. Patel, E. E. Calle, et al. "Estrogen Replacement Therapy and Ovarian Cancer Mortality in a Large Prospective Study of U.S. Women." *JAMA* 285 (2001): 1460–65.

51. Grodstein, F., G. A. Colditz, and M. J. Stampfer. "Postmenopausal Hormone Use and Cholecystectomy in a Large Prospective Study." *Obstetrics and Gynecology* 83 (1994): 5–11.

52. Cirillo, D. J., R. B. Wallace, R. J. Rodabough, et al. "Effect of Estrogen Therapy on Gallbladder Disease." *JAMA* 293 (2005): 330–39.

53. Simon, J. A., D. B. Hunninghake, S. K. Agarwal, et al. "Effect of Estrogen Plus Progestin on Risk for Biliary Tract Surgery in Postmenopausal Women with Coronary Artery Disease. The Heart and Estrogen/Progestin Replacement Study." *Annals of Internal Medicine* 135 (2001): 493–501.

54. Hampson, E. "Estrogen-Related Variations in Human Spatial and Articulatory-Motor Skills." *Psychoneuroendocrinology* 15 (1990): 97–111.

55. Barrett-Connor, E., and D. Goodman-Gruen. "Cognitive Function and Endogenous Sex Hormones in Older Women." *Journal of the American Geriatrics Society* 47 (1999): 1289–93.

56. Yaffe, K., L. Y. Lui, D. Grady, et al. "Cognitive Decline in Women in Relation to Non-Protein-Bound Oestradiol Concentrations." *Lancet* 356 (2000): 708–12.

57. Geerlings, M. I., L. J. Launer, F. H. de Jong, et al. "Endogenous Estradiol and Risk of Dementia in Women and Men: The Rotterdam Study." *Annals of Neurology* 53 (2003): 607–15.

58. Lebrun, C. E., Y. T. van der Schouw, F. H. de Jong, et al. "Endogenous Oestrogens Are Related to Cognition in Healthy Elderly Women." *Clinical Endocrinology* (Oxford) 63 (2005): 50–55.

59. McEwen, B. "Estrogen Actions Throughout the Brain." *Recent Progress in Hormone Research* 57 (2002): 357–84.

60. Maki, P. M., and S. M. Resnick. "Longitudinal Effects of Estrogen Replacement Therapy on PET Cerebral Blood Flow and Cognition." *Neurobiology of Aging* 21 (2000): 373–83.

61. LeBlanc, E. S., J. Janowsky, B. K. Chan, and H. D. Nelson. "Hormone Replacement Therapy and Cognition: Systematic Review and Meta-Analysis." *JAMA* 285 (2001): 1489–99.

62. Nelson, H. D., L. L. Humphrey, P. Nygren, et al. "Postmenopausal Hormone Replacement Therapy: Scientific Review." *JAMA* 288 (2002): 872–81.

63. Zandi, P. P., M. C. Carlson, B. L. Plassman, et al. "Hormone Replacement Therapy and Incidence of Alzheimer Disease in Older Women: The Cache County Study." *JAMA* 288 (2002): 2123–29.

64. Matthews, K., J. Cauley, K. Yaffe, and J. M. Zmuda. "Estrogen Replacement Therapy and Cognitive Decline in Older Community Women." *Journal of the American Geriatrics Society* 47 (1999): 518–23.

65. Sherwin, B. B. "Surgical Menopause, Estrogen, and Cognitive Function in Women: What Do the Findings Tell Us?" *Annals of the New York Academy of Science* 1052 (2005): 3–10.

66. Henderson, V. W., A. Paganini-Hill, B. L. Miller, et al. "Estrogen for Alzheimer's Disease in Women: Randomized, Double-Blind, Placebo-Controlled Trial." *Neurology* 54 (2000): 295–301.

67. Mulnard, R. A., C. W. Cotman, C. Kawas, et al. "Estrogen Replacement Therapy for Treatment of Mild to Moderate Alzheimer Disease: A Randomized Controlled Trial." *JAMA* 283 (2000): 1007–15.

68. Wang, P. N., S. Q. Liao, R. S. Liu, et al. "Effects of Estrogen on Cognition, Mood, and Cerebral Blood Flow in AD: A Controlled Study." *Neurology* 54 (2000): 2061–66.

69. Grady, D., K. Yaffe, M. Kristof, et al. "Effect of Postmenopausal Hormone Therapy on Cognitive Function: The Heart and Estrogen/Progestin Replacement Study." *American Journal of Medicine* 113 (2002): 543–48.

70. Shumaker, S. A., C. Legault, L. Kuller, et al. "Conjugated Equine Estrogens and Incidence of Probable Dementia and Mild Cognitive Impairment in Postmenopausal Women: Women's Health Initiative Memory Study." *JAMA* 291 (2004): 2947–58.

71. Shumaker, S. A., C. Legault, L. Thal, et al. "Estrogen Plus Progestin and the Incidence of Dementia and Mild Cognitive Impairment in Postmenopausal Women: The Women's Health Initiative Memory Study: A Randomized Controlled Trial." *JAMA* 289 (2003): 2651–62.

72. Manson, J. E., E. B. Rimm, G. A. Colditz, et al. "A Prospective Study of Postmenopausal Estrogen Therapy and Subsequent Incidence of Non-Insulin-Dependent Diabetes Mellitus." *Annals of Epidemiology* 2 (1992): 665–73.

73. Margolis, K. L., D. E. Bonds, R. J. Rodabough, et al. "Effect of Oestrogen Plus Progestin on the Incidence of Diabetes in Postmenopausal Women: Results from the Women's Health Initiative Hormone Trial." *Diabetologia* 47 (2004): 1175–87.

74. Kanaya, A. M., D. Herrington, E. Vittinghoff, et al. "Glycemic Effects of Postmenopausal Hormone Therapy: The Heart and Estrogen/Progestin Replacement Study. A Randomized, Double-Blind, Placebo-Controlled Trial." *Annals of Internal Medicine* 138 (2003): 1–9.

75. Bonds, D. E., N. Lasser, L. Qi, et al. "The Effect of Conjugated Equine Oestrogen on Diabetes Incidence: The Women's Health Initiative Randomised Trial." *Diabetologia* 49 (2006): 459–68.

76. Sanchez-Guerrero, J., M. H. Liang, E. W. Karlson, et al. "Postmenopausal Estrogen Therapy and the Risk for Developing Systemic Lupus Erythematosus." *Annals of Internal Medicine* 122 (1995): 430–33.

77. Meier, C. R., M. C. Sturkenboom, A. S. Cohen, and H. Jick. "Postmenopausal Estrogen Replacement Therapy and the Risk of Developing Systemic Lupus

Erythematosus or Discoid Lupus." *Journal of Rheumatology* 25 (1998): 1515–19.

78. Karlson, E. W., L. A. Mandl, S. E. Hankinson, and F. Grodstein. "Do Breast-Feeding and Other Reproductive Factors Influence Future Risk of Rheumatoid Arthritis? Results from the Nurses' Health Study." *Arthritis and Rheumatism* 50 (2004): 3458–67.

79. Buyon, J. P., M. A. Petri, M. Y. Kim, et al. "The Effect of Combined Estrogen and Progesterone Hormone Replacement Therapy on Disease Activity in Systemic Lupus Erythematosus: A Randomized Trial." *Annals of Internal Medicine* 142 (2005): 953–62.

80. Barr, R. G., C. C. Wentowski, F. Grodstein, et al. "Prospective Study of Postmenopausal Hormone Use and Newly Diagnosed Asthma and Chronic Obstructive Pulmonary Disease." *Archives of Internal Medicine* 164 (2004): 379–86.

81. Carlson, C. L., M. Cushman, P. L. Enright, et al. "Hormone Replacement Therapy Is Associated with Higher FEV1 in Elderly Women." *American Journal of Respiratory and Critical Care Medicine* 163 (2001): 423–28.

82. Nevitt, M. C., D. T. Felson, E. N. Williams, and D. Grady. "The Effect of Estrogen Plus Progestin on Knee Symptoms and Related Disability in Postmenopausal Women: The Heart and Estrogen/Progestin Replacement Study, a Randomized, Double-Blind, Placebo-Controlled Trial." *Arthritis and Rheumatism* 44 (2001): 811–18.

83. Barnabei, V. M., B. B. Cochrane, A. K. Aragaki, et al. "Menopausal Symptoms and Treatment-Related Effects of Estrogen and Progestin in the Women's Health Initiative." *Obstetrics and Gynecology* 105 (2005): 1063–73.

84. Hlatky, M. A., D. Boothroyd, E. Vittinghoff, et al. "Quality-of-Life and Depressive Symptoms in Postmenopausal Women After Receiving Hormone Therapy: Results from the Heart and Estrogen/Progestin Replacement Study (HERS) Trial." *JAMA* 287 (2002): 591–97.

85. Greendale, G. A., B. A. Reboussin, P. Hogan, et al. "Symptom Relief and Side Effects of Postmenopausal Hormones: Results from the Postmenopausal Estrogen/Progestin Interventions Trial." *Obstetrics and Gynecology* 92 (1998): 982–88.

86. Hays, J., J. K. Ockene, R. L. Brunner, et al. "Effects of Estrogen Plus Progestin on Health-Related Quality of Life." *New England Journal of Medicine* 348 (2003): 1839–54.

87. Brunner, R. L., M. Gass, A. Aragaki, et al. "Effects of Conjugated Equine Estrogen on Health-Related Quality of Life in Postmenopausal Women with Hysterectomy: Results from the Women's Health Initiative Randomized Clinical Trial." *Archives of Internal Medicine* 165 (2005): 1976–86.

CHAPTER 5

1. Utian, W. H., D. Shoupe, G. Bachmann, et al. "Relief of Vasomotor Symptoms and Vaginal Atrophy with Lower Doses of Conjugated Equine Estrogens and Medroxyprogesterone Acetate." *Fertility and Sterility* 75 (2001): 1065–79.

2. Fournier, A., F. Berrino, E. Riboli, et al. "Breast Cancer Risk in Relation to Different Types of Hormone Replacement Therapy in the E3N-EPIC Cohort." *International Journal of Cancer* 114 (2005): 448–54.

3. Lobo, R. A., R. C. Rosen, H. M. Yang, et al. "Comparative Effects of Oral Esterified Estrogens with and Without Methyltestosterone on Endocrine Profiles and Dimensions of Sexual Function in Postmenopausal Women with Hypoactive Sexual Desire." *Fertility and Sterility* 79 (2003): 1341–52.

4. Shifren, J. L., G. D. Braunstein, J. A. Simon, et al. "Transdermal Testosterone Treatment in Women with Impaired Sexual Function After Oophorectomy." *New England Journal of Medicine* 343 (2000): 682–88.

5. Braunstein, G. D., D. A. Sundwall, M. Katz, et al. "Safety and Efficacy of a Testosterone Patch for the Treatment of Hypoactive Sexual Desire Disorder in Surgically Menopausal Women: A Randomized, Placebo-Controlled Trial." *Archives of Internal Medicine* 165 (2005): 1582–89.

6. Buster, J. E., S. A. Kingsberg, O. Aguirre, et al. "Testosterone Patch for Low Sexual Desire in Surgically Menopausal Women: A Randomized Trial." *Obstetrics and Gynecology* 105 (2005): 944–52.

7. Arlt, W., F. Callies, J. C. van Vlijmen, et al. "Dehydroepiandrosterone Replacement in Women with Adrenal Insufficiency." *New England Journal of Medicine* 341 (1999): 1013–20.

8. Lovas, K., G. Gebre-Medhin, T. S. Trovik, et al. "Replacement of Dehydroepiandrosterone in Adrenal Failure: No Benefit for Subjective Health Status and Sexuality in a 9-Month, Randomized, Parallel Group Clinical Trial." *Journal of Clinical Endocrinology and Metabolism* 88 (2003): 1112–18.

CHAPTER 6

1. Ford, E. S., W. H. Giles, and A. H. Mokdad. "Increasing Prevalence of the Metabolic Syndrome Among U.S. Adults." *Diabetes Care* 27 (2004): 2444–49.

2. Wilson, P. W., R. B. D'Agostino, D. Levy, et al. "Prediction of Coronary Heart Disease Using Risk Factor Categories." *Circulation* 97 (1998): 1837–47.

3. Expert Panel on Detection, Evaluation, and Treatment of High Blood Cholesterol in Adults. "Executive Summary of the Third Report of the National Cholesterol Education Program (NCEP) Expert Panel on Detection, Evaluation, and Treatment of High Blood Cholesterol in Adults (Adult Treatment Panel III)." *JAMA* 285 (2001): 2486–97.

4. Kris-Etherton, P. M., W. S. Harris, and L. J. Appel. "Fish Consumption, Fish Oil, Omega-3 Fatty Acids, and Cardiovascular Disease." *Circulation* 106 (2002): 2747–57.

5. Centers for Disease Control and Prevention. "Trends in Intake of Energy and Macronutrients—United States, 1971–2000." *Morbidity and Mortality Weekly Report (MMWR)* 53 (2004): 80–82.

6. Schoenborn, C. A., and P. Barnes. "Leisure-Time Physical Activity Among Adults, U.S. 1997–98." Advance Data from Vital and Health Statistics, no. 325. Hyattsville MD: National Center for Health Statistics, 2002.

7. Calle, E. E., and R. Kaaks. "Overweight, Obesity and Cancer: Epidemiological Evidence and Proposed Mechanisms." *Nature Reviews Cancer* 4 (2004): 579–91.

8. Rosengren, A., S. Hawken, S. Ounpuu, et al. "Association of Psychosocial Risk Factors with Risk of Acute Myocardial Infarction in 11,119 Cases and 13,648 Controls from 52 Countries (the INTERHEART Study): Case-Control Study." *Lancet* 364 (2004): 953–62.

9. Narayan, K. M., J. P. Boyle, T. J. Thompson, et al. "Lifetime Risk for Diabetes Mellitus in the United States." *JAMA* 290 (2003): 1884–90.

10. Ridker, P. M., N. R. Cook, I-M. Lee, et al. "A Randomized Trial of Low-Dose Aspirin in the Primary Prevention of Cardiovascular Disease in Women." *New England Journal of Medicine* 352 (2005): 1293–304.

11. Lee, I-M., N. R. Cook, J. M. Gaziano, et al. "Vitamin E in the Primary Prevention of Cardiovascular Disease and Cancer: The Women's Health Study: A Randomized Controlled Trial." *JAMA* 294 (2005): 56–65.

12. Bassuk, S. S., C. M. Albert, N. R. Cook, et al. "The Women's Antioxidant Cardiovascular Study: Design and Baseline Characteristics of Participants." *Journal of Women's Health* 13 (2004): 99–117.

13. D'Agostino, R. B., P. A. Wolf, A. J. Belanger, and W. B. Kannel. "Stroke Risk Profile: Adjustment for Antihypertensive Medication. The Framingham Study." *Stroke* 25 (1994): 40–43.

14. Baigent, C., A. Keech, P. M. Kearney, et al. "Efficacy and Safety of Cholesterol-Lowering Treatment: Prospective Meta-Analysis of Data from 90,056 Participants in 14 Randomised Trials of Statins." *Lancet* 366 (2005): 1267–78.

15. Zhang, S., D. J. Hunter, S. E. Hankinson, et al. "A Prospective Study of Folate Intake and the Risk of Breast Cancer." *JAMA* 281 (1999): 1632–37.

16. Smith-Warner, S. A., D. Spiegelman, S. S. Yaun, et al. "Intake of Fruits and Vegetables and Risk of Breast Cancer: A Pooled Analysis of Cohort Studies." *JAMA* 285 (2001): 769–76.

17. Boyd, N. F., J. Stone, K. N. Vogt, et al. "Dietary Fat and Breast Cancer Risk Revisited: A Meta-Analysis of the Published Literature." *British Journal of Cancer* 89 (2003): 1672–85.

18. MacLean, C. H., S. J. Newberry, W. A. Mojica, et al. "Effects of Omega-3 Fatty Acids on Cancer Risk: A Systematic Review." *JAMA* 295 (2006): 403–15.

19. Sacks, F. M., A. Lichtenstein, L. Van Horn, W. Harris, P. Kris-Etherton, and M. Winston. "Soy Protein, Isoflavones, and Cardiovascular Health. An American Heart Association Science Advisory for Professionals from the Nutrition Committee." *Circulation* 113 (2006): 1034–44.

20. Prentice, R. L., B. Caan, R. T. Chlebowski, et al. "Low-Fat Dietary Pattern and Risk of Invasive Breast Cancer: The Women's Health Initiative Randomized Controlled Dietary Modification Trial." *JAMA* 295 (2006): 629–42.

21. Howard, B. V., L. Van Horn, J. Hsia, et al. "Low-Fat Dietary Pattern and Risk of Cardiovascular Disease: The Women's Health Initiative Randomized Controlled Dietary Modification Trial." *JAMA* 295 (2006): 655–66.

22. Colditz, G. A., and C. J. Stein. *Handbook of Cancer Risk Assessment and Prevention.* Sudbury MA: Jones and Bartlett Publishers, 2004.

23. Siris, E. S., P. D. Miller, E. Barrett-Connor, et al. "Identification and Fracture Outcomes of Undiagnosed Low Bone Mineral Density in Postmenopausal Women: Results from the National Osteoporosis Risk Assessment." *JAMA* 286 (2001): 2815–22.

24. Black, D. M., M. Steinbuch, L. Palermo, et al. "An Assessment Tool for Pre-
    dicting Fracture Risk in Postmenopausal Women." *Osteoporosis International*
    12 (2001): 519–28.
25. Jackson, R. D., A. Z. LaCroix, M. Gass, et al. "Calcium Plus Vitamin D Sup-
    plementation and the Risk of Fractures." *New England Journal of Medicine* 354
    (2006): 669–83.

INDEX

⊙